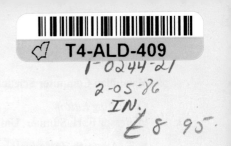

Information Theory for Information Technologists

Macmillan Computer Science Series

Consulting Editor
Professor F. H. Sumner, University of Manchester

S. T. Allworth, *Introduction to Real-time Software Design*
Ian O. Angell, *A Practical Introduction to Computer Graphics*
G. M. Birtwistle, *Discrete Event Modelling on Simula*
T. B. Boffey, *Graph Theory in Operations Research*
Richard Bornat, *Understanding and Writing Compilers*
J. K. Buckle, *The ICL 2900 Series*
J. K. Buckle, *Software Configuration Management*
J. C. Cluley, *Interfacing to Microprocessors*
Robert Cole, *Computer Communications*
Derek Coleman, *A Structured Programming Approach to Data**
Andrew J. T. Colin, *Fundamentals of Computer Science*
Andrew J. T. Colin, *Programming and Problem-solving in Algol 68**
S. M. Deen, *Fundamentals of Data Base Systems**
P. M. Dew and K. R. James, *Introduction to Numerical Computation in Pascal*
K. C. E. Gee, *Introduction to Local Area Computer Networks*
J. B. Gosling, *Design of Arithmetic Units for Digital Computers*
David Hopkin and Barbara Moss, *Automata**
Roger Hutty, *Fortran for Students*
Roger Hutty, *Z80 Assembly Language Programming for Students*
Roland N. Ibbett, *The Architecture of High Performance Computers*
H. Kopetz, *Software Reliability*
E. V. Krishnamurthy, *Introductory Theory of Computer Science*
Graham Lee, *From Hardware to Software: an introduction to computers*
A. M. Lister, *Fundamentals of Operating Systems, second edition**
G. P. McKeown and V. J. Rayward-Smith, *Mathematics for Computing*
Brian Meek, *Fortran, PL/1 and the Algols*
Derrick Morris, *An Introduction to System Programming – Based on the PDP11*
Derrick Morris and Roland N. Ibbett, *The MU5 Computer System*
John Race, *Case Studies in Systems Analysis*
L. E. Scales, *Introduction to Non-Linear Optimization*
Colin J. Theaker and Graham R. Brookes, *A Practical Course on Operating Systems*
M. J. Usher, *Information Theory for Information Technologists*
B. S. Walker, *Understanding Microprocessors*
Peter J. L. Wallis, *Portable Programming*
I. R. Wilson and A. M. Addyman, *A Practical Introduction to Pascal – with BS 6192, second edition*

*The titles marked with an asterisk were prepared during the Consulting Editorship of Professor J. S. Rohl, University of Western Australia.

Information Theory for Information Technologists

M. J. Usher

Department of Cybernetics
University of Reading

MACMILLAN

First published 1984 by
Higher and Further Education Division
MACMILLAN PUBLISHERS LTD
London and Basingstoke
Companies and representatives
throughout the world

Typeset in 10/12 Press Roman by
RDL Artset Ltd, Sutton, Surrey

Printed in Hong Kong

British Library Cataloguing in Publication Data

Usher, J.
    Information theory for information
    technologists.–(Macmillan computer
    science series)
    1. Information theory
    I. Title
    001.53'9   Q360

ISBN 0-333-36702-2
ISBN 0-333-36703-0 Pbk

Contents

Preface

Information Technology may be defined as the acquisition, storage, processing, communication and display of information. As a technology it is unique in that it refers to an abstract concept -- information; all previous technologies have been linked to specific physical concepts. Information Technology is thus independent of the physical technologies used to implement it, and its principles will therefore continue unchanged despite the considerable technological developments expected in the next few years.

Information Theory, the science of quantification, coding and communication of information, is the basis of Information Technology. It is a precise, quantitative theory developed largely during and after the Second World War. Some of its theorems were at first considered impractical but recent technological developments have changed this and strongly underlined the importance of fundamental theory as a basis for technology.

The aim of this book is to present the fundamentals of Information Theory in a manner suitable for persons working in or interested in the field of Information Technology. Quantity of information is first defined, and the concepts of entropy and redundancy introduced, with application to the English language. Information in noisy channels is then considered, and various interpretations of information transfer presented: this leads on to the requirement of coding information before transmission, either in noiseless or noisy channels, and to Shannon's fundamental theorem.

In order to consider more general signals than purely digital or discrete signals, a review of signal and noise theory is required, including probability distributions, electrical noise, the Fourier Theory of signals and sampling theory. This paves the way for a study of the information capacity of a general channel and the ideal communication theorem. Finally a review of communication systems is presented in the light of Information Theory, together with examples of the applications of Information Theory to recent developments such as speech processing and recognition, sound generation, music synthesis and character recognition.

The book is based largely on a second-year course of about 30 lectures given to Cybernetics honours degree students. The approach adopted is one of intuitive understanding rather than rigorous formal theory. It is suitable for both specialist courses in Information Technology and for the new one-year conversion courses; arts-based graduates on these courses are advised to omit chapters 8 and 9 on first reading. Many of the worked examples and exercises are based on Reading University examination questions set by the author, who is pleased

to acknowledge the University's permission to publish them. His only regret is
that he has seriously depleted his stock of such questions for future years. Early
retirement looms large indeed.

Reading, 1984   M.J. USHER

Acknowledgements

The author wishes to thank Professor P. B. Fellgett, Head of the Department of Cybernetics at Reading, for his suggestions and encouragement during the development of the lecture course, and Mr B.S. Walker, of the same department who persuaded him to write it as a book. He also acknowledges the assistance of the many Cybernetics students, whose subtle hints have considerably influenced the final content; they fell asleep.

1 Information and its Quantification

1.1 Introduction

Information Theory is concerned with the quantification, coding and transmission of information. Some of the basic ideas were formulated by Nyquist (1924) and by Hartley (1928), but the subject received a considerable boost during and shortly after the Second World War, largely due to Shannon, who is regarded as the founder of the modern theory (see Shannon and Weaver, 1949). Some of Shannon's work was at first considered rather academic and impractical, but the technological developments of the last few years have changed this. Technology has caught up with Information Theory and the newly coined Information Technology is having great effects on our society. It may even make the writer redundant.

In order to understand the various sections of Information Theory and to appreciate its overall unity we will consider the general communication system shown in figure 1.1.

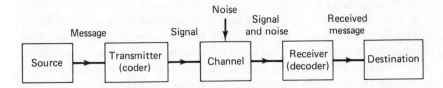

Figure 1.1 A general communication channel

This could represent a radio communication system in which music is being broadcast. The source would be a disc but the music produced would have to be changed into suitable electrical signals (that is, 'coded') before it could be transmitted over the radio channel. Some noise, electrical interference etc. would be added in transmission, and more at the receiver. The receiver has to 'decode' the electrical signals and produce the music via a loudspeaker in order to be heard by the listener (the destination). Alternatively the figure could represent a lecturer talking to his students; the source would be in his mind (or in his notes if he had not prepared the lecture), the coder would be the process of changing thoughts into sound waves and the noise would be the students chattering or shuffling their feet etc. The received message would in general differ somewhat from the transmitted message.

1

The essential parts of the information transmission process can thus be appreciated. We need to be able to analyse sources of information, to determine in particular the amount of information and its form. In general the information will not be in a suitable form for direct transmission in the channel, and various methods of coding it must be studied both in the sense of actual binary codes and of modulating some carrier signal. We will have to consider communication channels and their properties; in addition, since the information is usually transmitted in the form of an electrical signal, the study of signals and noise is very important. The decoding process may be similar to that in encoding, though different aspects are involved since we may be trying to determine the transmitted message from a seriously distorted signal. Overall, we may be interested in the accuracy of transmission, the speed of transmission and, of course, the amount of information transmitted.

1.2 Quantity of Information

Information has both qualitative and quantitative aspects. Two television programmes, say *Panorama* and *Doctor Who*, may have the same quantity of information in a mathematical sense, but are usually considered to have very different qualitative values. Actually *Doctor Who* probably has a greater quantity of information, being somewhat more spectacular, though the form of picture providing most information would be a totally random one (perhaps even more sleep-inducing than *Panorama*).

Information Theory is concerned only with quantitative values, of course, and the first step in the subject is to define what we mean by quantity of information. A dictionary definition of information is 'Knowledge; intelligence given', which is not particularly helpful since the same dictionary defines both knowledge and intelligence in terms of information. However, in order to fix our ideas we will imagine that one person is speaking to another by telephone, imparting information, knowledge or intelligence. If the speaker says 'the sun has risen today' or 'your name is Mr Brown', the listener may be somewhat uninterested (unless his name is Mr White). However, if he says 'I am pleased to tell you that you have just won the pools' the listener's reaction will be very different. The amount of information conveyed in an event (a statement in this case) depends on the probability of the event. If someone is told something he already knows, so that the probability before being told it was already unity, the probability remains at unity after being told it. On the other hand, if one is told something that was relatively improbable, the probability changes from a small value before being told to unity afterwards. Similarly, if the speaker reads out letters of the alphabet, each letter is worth more information than if he reads out numerals (between 0 and 9) and considerably more than if he reads out a string of 0s and 1s.

A satisfactory definition of quantity of information must thus involve the probability of the event. Moreover, since longer messages convey proportionally more information than shorter ones, we must also ensure that our definition incorporates this. Another factor of importance is the reliability of the information; if we were unsure of the motives of the speaker in the examples above then even after the event the probability may be less than unity. However, in this chapter we will ignore this possibility, and our speaker will always tell the truth.

We will consider a specific example in which the speaker is telling the listener the position of a piece on a chessboard. We will assume that a numbering system has been agreed in advance, as in figure 1.2.

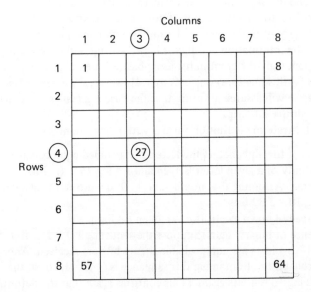

Figure 1.2   Chessboard

The speaker could give the position in two ways. He could simply state the number of the square, or he could separately give the column and the row. In the first case the probability before the event is 1/64 and afterwards unity. In the second case, when being told the row, the probability is 1/8 before and unity (for the row) afterwards; similarly it changes from 1/8 to unity for the columns. Clearly both methods must impart the same information; the sum of the information regarding the row and that regarding the column must give that regarding the actual square. We can see that the information is summed while the probabilities are multiplied ($1/8 \times 1/8 = 1/64$) and this immediately points to a definition involving a logarithm of the probability

$$\text{Quantity of information } I = -\log p$$

(a minus sign is chosen to make I positive, since $p < 1$). We can see immediately that this satisfies the above requirements.

(i) Number of square $I = -\log \frac{1}{64} = \log 64$

(ii) (a) Row $I_a = -\log \frac{1}{8} = \log 8$

    (b) Column $I_b = -\log \frac{1}{8} = \log 8$

Taking logs to base 2 for convenience, $\log_2 64 = 6$ and $\log_2 8 = 3$, so we have, as required

$$I = I_a + I_b$$

The definition thus satisfies our intuitive requirements; it depends on probability and messages add in the correct manner.

If we take logs to base 2 the unit of information is known as the *bit* (*binary digit*). In a binary system producing 0s and 1s with equal probability, $p(0) = p(1) = \frac{1}{2}$, so the information per digit is $\log_2 2 = 1$ bit. Other bases may be used, with correspondingly different units; using base e for example, one gets *nats* and using base 3 (with some care) one gets *trits*. However, since base 2 is almost always used, we will assume in future that the base is 2 (unless specified otherwise) and omit the subscript.

We will illustrate the definition further with a few examples.

(i)   Letters of the alphabet. If the letters are assumed equiprobable, then the probability of a given letter is $1/26$ and $I = \log 26 = 4.7$ bits.

(ii)   Numerals. Assuming that numbers from 0 to 9 are equiprobable, $I = \log 10 = 3.32$ bits.

(iii) An already-known event. If $p = 1$, then $I = \log 1 = 0$.

(iv) Sequence of binary digits. Suppose the sequence 1 0 1 1 of four digits is sent. If 0s and 1s are equiprobable then 4 bits are received. Alternatively, the probability of obtaining this sequence is $(\frac{1}{2})^4 = 1/16$, so the information is $\log 16 = 4$ bits again. (This confirms again that the definition gives the correct result regarding the length of the message.)

1.3 Average Information: Entropy

In practice we are often more interested in the average information conveyed in some process than in the specific information in each event. For example, a source may produce a set of events of probability $p_1, p_2, p_3 \ldots p_i \ldots p_n$. In a long sequence of n events, event 1 will occur $n \times p_1$ times, contributing $n \times -\log p_1$ bits. The average information over all the events is called the *entropy H*, and is given by

$$H = - \sum_{i=1}^{n} p_i \log p_i \text{ bits}$$

In the case of letters of the alphabet, the probabilities are not really all the same (as assumed above). The entropy is given by

$$H = -(p(A) \log p(A) + p(B) \log p(B) + \ldots + p(Z) \log p(Z))$$

$$\approx 4.1 \text{ bits (using standard values for } p(A), p(B) \text{ etc.)}$$

The units are often given as bits/letter or bits/symbol to stress the average nature of the measure.

The term 'entropy' was deliberately chosen for the name of the measure of average information, because of its similarity to entropy in thermodynamics. In thermodynamics, entropy is a measure of the degree of disorder of a system, and disorder is clearly related to information. The paradox of Maxwell's demon, who separates hot and cold molecules and thereby contravenes the second law of thermodynamics, can be solved (somewhat philosophically) by assuming that the demon requires 'information' in order to effect the separation.

EXAMPLE 1.1

A binary source produces a stream of 0s and 1s with probabilities $p(0) = 1/8$ and $p(1) = 7/8$ respectively. Find the entropy.

$$H = -\sum_i p_i \log p_i = -(\tfrac{1}{8} \log \tfrac{1}{8} + \tfrac{7}{8} \log \tfrac{7}{8}) = 0.55 \text{ bits}$$

It is very important to realise that a *binary digit* is not the same as a *bit* of information. A stream of binary digits can carry a *maximum of one bit per digit*, which occurs when the 0s and 1s are equally probable. The term *binit* is sometimes used to mean binary digit, stressing its difference from the bit. A plot of H versus $p(0)$, as $p(0)$ varies from 0 to 1, is shown in figure 1.3.

The entropy is unity only for $p(0) = p(1) = \tfrac{1}{2}$, falling to zero for $p(0) = 1$ or $p(0) = 0$. This is because a continuous stream of digits of the same type (all 1s

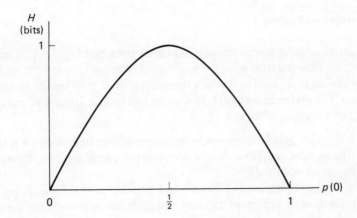

Figure 1.3 Variation of average information with probability for a binary source

or all 0s) does not convey any information. In a similar way, the entropy of a set of events is a maximum when they are equiprobable, as in the cases considered above for letters of the alphabet.

1.4 Redundancy

Redundancy is an important concept in Information Theory, particularly in connection with language. It is the presence of more symbols in a message than is strictly necessary. For example, in a binary system of two symbols A and B, we could code A as 0 0 0 and B as 1 1 1 (instead of A = 0, B = 1). This gives some protection against errors, since one binary error in three digits could be tolerated (assuming a majority is used for decision at the receiver).

$$\text{Redundancy} = \frac{\text{maximum entropy} - \text{actual entropy}}{\text{maximum entropy}}$$

In the above example, $R = (3 - 1)/3 = 2/3$, since three digits could carry three bits, but actually carry only one. Spoken languages usually have high redundancy, permitting them to be understood in the presence of noise or errors. For example, if one received the message

CAMINK HINE TINOGHT

or

SAX IR BIST*

most people would easily understand what was intended. English has a redundancy of about 80 per cent, and this will be considered in some detail in the next chapter.

1.5 Exercises on Chapter 1

These exercises can be done without a calculator, given that $\log_2 3 = 1.58$ and $\log_2 5 = 2.32$. However, it is generally much quicker to use one, and the reader is strongly advised to do so. The formula for entropy lends itself readily to such evaluation. The preferred method is to work in logs to base 10, and to multiply by 3.322 (= $1/\log_{10} 2$) at the end.

1.5.1. What is the gain in information on being told that when a dice was thrown (i) a six occurred, (ii) a six or a one occurred, (iii) a one, two, three, four, five or six occurred?

1.5.2. A picture is composed of 20 rows and 20 columns of dots, each dot having three possible degrees of darkness. Calculate the information in the picture:

---

*For anyone lucky enough to be unfamiliar with the game of cricket, the phrase 'six or bust' is derived from it.

(i) assuming that the shades are equally probable,

(ii) assuming that the probabilities are 1/8, 1/4, 5/8.

Note: You may assume that it is agreed in advance how the dots will be arranged (as is usually the case in transmitting pictures).

1.5.3. A source produces two symbols A and B with probabilities 1/4 and 3/4 respectively. Find the average information received per second:

(i) assuming that A and B each takes 1 s,

(ii) assuming that A takes 1 s and B takes 2 s.

2 Information in Language

2.1 Basic Probability Theory

We have already seen from chapter 1 that the idea of probability is absolutely basic in Information Theory. It is necessary to develop some of the important rules and results of probability theory before we can attempt to analyse the information content of a language such as English. In the mathematical sections of this book a fairly intuitive approach will be adopted, based on an understanding of the processes involved, rather than a strictly rigorous mathematical presentation. Mathematics will be viewed as a tool for the efficient representation and analysis of ideas, rather than a study for its own sake. We will avoid formal proofs except where such proofs are instructive or add to our understanding of the subject.

When we think of the probability of occurrence of an event, such as say the letter 'A' in English text, we mean the relative number of occurrences of 'A' in a long sample of text, that is

$$p(A) = \frac{\text{number of occurrences of A}}{\text{total number of letters in the sample of text}}$$

Strictly $p(A)$ is the limit of this ratio as the number of letters in the sample is made indefinitely large. In general, the probability of occurrence of any letter will be given by

$$p(i) = \lim_{N \to \infty} \frac{n_i}{N}$$

where n_i is the number of occurrences in a text of N letters. Clearly, the sum of the probabilities of all possible letters must be unity; that is

$$\sum_{i=A}^{i=Z} p(i) = 1$$

General laws

There are two important rules of probability, the sum rule and the product rule. The sum rule applies to events that are mutually exclusive — that is, to events that cannot happen at the same time. A single throw of a dice must result in a number from one to six, so the events (one, six etc.) are mutually exclusive. The sum rule simply says that the probability of occurrence of one of a selected set of events is the sum of the probabilities of those events. For example, the probability of throwing a two or a three in one throw of a dice is $1/6 + 1/6 = 1/3$, since the probability of any number is 1/6. Similarly the probability of throwing one, two, three, four, five or six is clearly $1/6 + 1/6 + 1/6 + 1/6 + 1/6 + 1/6 = 1$. Formally

$$p(\text{A or B or C or} \ldots) = p(\text{A}) + p(\text{B}) + p(\text{C}) + \ldots$$

The product rule applies to independent events that occur simultaneously, and states that the probability of a set of such events is given by the product of the individual probabilities. For example, if two dice are thrown together, the probability of each being a six is $1/6 \times 1/6 = 1/36$. Formally

$$p(\text{A and B and C and} \ldots) = p(\text{A}) \times p(\text{B}) \times p(\text{C}) \ldots$$

Conditional probability

Unfortunately many events in the real world are not completely independent, but depend on other events. In a sequence of letters of the alphabet the probability of say a U after a Q is very high whereas that of a Q after a U is quite low. Such events are known as conditionally or partially dependent events, and the probabilities that describe them as conditional probabilities.

For two conditionally dependent events A and B, the probability of A and B occurring together is given by

$$p(\text{A and B}) = p(\text{A}) \times p(\text{B/A}) = p(\text{B}) \times p(\text{A/B})$$

where $p(\text{A/B})$ means the probability of A *given* that B has already occurred. The product rule is really a special case of this relation, since if A and B were independent then $p(\text{B/A}) \rightarrow p(\text{B})$ and $p(\text{A and B}) \rightarrow p(\text{A}) \times p(\text{B})$. Conversely, if A and B were totally dependent then $p(\text{B/A}) \rightarrow 1$ and $p(\text{A and B}) \rightarrow p(\text{A})$.

EXAMPLE 2.1

Suppose that the probability of the weather being cold is 0.3, that of it being cloudy is 0.4 and that of it being both cold and cloudy at the same time is 0.2. What is the probability, given that a day is cloudy, of it being cold?

$$p(\text{cold and cloudy}) = p(\text{cloudy}) \times p(\text{cold/cloudy})$$

Therefore

$$p(\text{cold/cloudy}) = 0.2/0.4 = \tfrac{1}{2}$$

(We can also evaluate $p(\text{cloudy/cold}) = 2/3$.)

Application to sequences of letters

When applying these ideas to sequences of letters the same formulae can be used, except that the order of letters is now important. The various letters in a sequence may be conditionally dependent, but the probability of a sequence, say, A, B is not necessarily the same as that of B, A; that is

$$p(A, B) = p(A) \times p(B/A)$$

$$p(B, A) = p(B) \times p(A/B)$$

but $p(A, B)$ may not be equal to $p(B, A)$, unlike the case of *simultaneous* events considered above. $p(A)$ and $p(B)$ will be referred to as 'single' probabilities, $p(A, B)$ and $p(B, A)$ as 'joint' probabilities, and $p(A/B)$ and $p(B/A)$ as conditional probabilities.

The various relationships that exist in such a sequence are conveniently illustrated by an example.

EXAMPLE 2.2

A simple language consists of only two symbols A and B. Find the single, joint and conditional probabilities of A and B, assuming that the values found from the limited sequence below are typical of a very long sequence

A A B B B A A A A B B A A A B B B A A A ¦ A

(it is necessary to know the 21st letter in order to have 20 pairs of symbols).

$p(A)$ $= \frac{12}{20}$, $p(B)$ $= \frac{8}{20}$ by simply counting A's and B's.

$p(A,A) = \frac{9}{20}$, $p(B,B) = \frac{5}{20}$, $p(A,B) = \frac{3}{20}$, $p(B,A) = \frac{3}{20}$ by counting pairs.

$p(A/B) = \frac{3}{8}$, $p(B/B) = \frac{5}{8}$ by counting the number of times an A or B comes after a B.

$p(A/A) = \frac{9}{12}$, $p(B/A) = \frac{3}{12}$ by counting A's or B's after an A.

It can be seen that $p(A, B) = p(A) \times p(B/A)$, etc.; indeed, we could have evaluated the conditional probabilities this way instead of counting.

It is important to note that the sum of the single probabilities $p(A), p(B)$ is unity, as is that of the joint probabilities $p(A, A), p(A, B)$, etc. Also, the two groups of conditional probabilities ($p(A/B), p(B/B)$ and $p(A/A), p(B/A)$) both sum to unity. These relations are summarised below, i representing the first symbol in a pair and j the second.

(i) $\sum_i p(i) = \sum_j p(j) = 1$ for example, $p(A) + p(B) = 1$

(ii) $\sum_i \sum_j p(i, j) = 1$ for example,
$p(A, A) + p(A, B) + p(B, A) + p(B, B) = 1$

(iii) $\sum_j p(j/i) = 1$ for example, $p(A/A) + p(B/A) = 1$

The single probabilities can be obtained from the joint probabilities from

(iv) $p(i) = \sum_j p(i, j)$ or $p(j) = \sum_i p(i, j)$

That is, by summing the joint probabilities over the first or second symbols; for example

$$p(A) = p(A, B) + p(A, A) \quad \text{(summed over second symbols)}$$

or

$$p(B) = p(A, B) + p(B, B) \quad \text{(summed over first symbols)}$$

Since $p(A)$ is also given by $p(B, A) + p(A, A)$ (summed over first symbols) it follows that $p(A, B) = p(B, A)$ in this case. This is true only for *binary* sequences and is clearly untrue for the alphabet ($p(Q, U) \neq p(U, Q)$ etc.).

2.2 Conditional Entropy

In a sequence of letters in a language such as English, the probabilities of given letters are strongly governed by those of the preceding letter or letters. This is known as intersymbol influence; in English it may stretch over many letters, words or even whole sentences. It is interesting to note that the effect is the equivalent of the bandwidth of a communication channel, which governs the rate at which the signal may change.

Consider a sequence of letters in which intersymbol influence extends only over pairs of adjacent letters. For two such letters i and j, the information obtained when j is received is $-\log p(j/i)$; that is, minus the logarithm of the probability of receiving j, *given* that i has been received. In order to find the average information over all letters we simply have to average over all possible pairs of letters i, j. The result is known as the conditional entropy $H(j/i)$ of the sequence, and represents the information per letter in such a sequence

$$H(j/i) = - \sum_i \sum_j p(i, j) \log p(j/i)$$

EXAMPLE 2.3

Evaluate the conditional entropy for the sequence in example 2.2 above, and hence deduce the redundancy of the language.

There are four pairs of symbols AA, BB, AB and BA. Thus

$$H(j/i) = - [p(A, A) \log p(A/A) + p(B, B) \log p(B/B)$$
$$+ p(A, B) \log p(B/A) + p(B, A) \log p(A/B)]$$
$$= \tfrac{9}{20} \log \tfrac{9}{12} + \tfrac{5}{20} \log \tfrac{5}{8} + \tfrac{3}{20} \log \tfrac{3}{12} + \tfrac{3}{20} \log \tfrac{3}{8}$$
$$= 0.868 \text{ bits/symbol}$$

If no intersymbol influence had been present the information would have been given by

$$H(i) = - \sum_i p(i) \log p(i)$$

That is

$$H(i) = - (p(A) \log p(A) + p(B) \log p(B))$$

$$= - (0.8 \log 0.8 + 0.2 \log 0.2)$$

$$= 0.971 \text{ bits/symbol}$$

The redundancy is given by

$$R = \frac{\text{maximum entropy} - \text{actual entropy}}{\text{maximum entropy}}$$

The maximum entropy would occur for independent and equiprobable symbols and is clearly 1 bit per symbol. Thus

$$R = \frac{1 - 0.868}{1} = 13 \text{ per cent}$$

It can be seen that most of the redundancy is due to the intersymbol influence between A and B, the effect of symbol probabilities only reducing the information from 1.0 bits/symbol to 0.97 bits/symbol. The effect is even more pronounced in a practical language of more than the two symbols chosen here.

If intersymbol influence extends over several symbols, so that conditional probabilities of the form $p(k/ij)$ arise (that is, the probability of a k after the sequence i, j), the formulae are of the same general form. For example

$$H(k/ij) = - \sum_i \sum_j \sum_k p(i, j, k) \log p(k/ij) \text{ etc.}$$

2.3 Redundancy in Printed English

The redundancy in language arises in several ways. The letters have widely different probabilities (see exercise 3.7.4) and strong intersymbol influence exists not only over adjacent symbols but also over whole groups of symbols. Suppose we imagine that a word is being spelled out to us in a telephone conversation. There is a choice of 26 letters (though not equally probable) for the first letter, providing about 4 bits when received; suppose it was a D. The choices for the next letter are restricted, because of the construction of English, to about 7 letters, providing about 2.8 bits; assume it was an I. There is a greater choice next, of all letters, giving another 4 bits. However, if the next few letters were S, T, R the choice rapidly diminishes and after a further I, B, U the word can be reasonably guessed to be say DISTRIBUTION or DISTRIBUTIVE. The last few letters clearly provide very little information, because the probability of the next letters after the sequence DISTRIBU approaches unity.

Similarly, words are not equiprobable and intersymbol influence extends over groups of words, phrases, sentences etc., and the result is that the information content of language is very much less than the ideal 4.7 bits/symbol of a language of 26 equiprobable and independent symbols. It is likely that an optimum amount of redundancy is automatically achieved in the development of a language, such that it can be sufficiently understood in the presence of noise and errors. In some special cases the language does not have sufficient redundancy, and extra redundancy must be added, for example by the police when reading car registration numbers over radio (alpha, bravo etc.).

Shannon and Weaver (1949) studied the redundancy of printed English in a particularly interesting and instructive manner, by constructing successively closer approximations to complete text. Their zeroth approximation was a language consisting of 26 letters and a space symbol, all equiprobable, providing $\log_2 27 = 4.75$ bits/symbol. The space is actually the most probable symbol, so a sample of text from such a source looks wrong even from a distance (when the letters cannot be read). The first approximation consisted of putting in the correct letter probabilities; the information can then be calculated from

$$H = - \sum_i p_i \log p_i = 4.1 \text{ bits/symbol}$$

Such text looks correct from a distance, but is unpronounceable.

The second approximation involves using conditional probabilities over pairs of adjacent symbols, calculating the information from the formula

$$H(j/i) = - \Sigma\Sigma\, p(i, j) \log p(j/i) = 3.3 \text{ bits/symbol}$$

Tables of conditional probabilities are available, and it can be seen that a significant reduction of information occurs, the corresponding text being reasonably readable (though meaningless, of course). A third approximation, in which conditional probabilities over three symbols were considered, had a rather small effect, the information being calculated as 3.1 bits/symbol.

Further approximations involved using the correct probabilities for complete words (about 2.1 bits/symbol) and allowing for conditional probabilities between words. It becomes progressively more difficult to produce samples of text, and for the later approximations these were generated by picking letters or words out of a book (which automatically has the correct probabilities built into it).

Finally, in order to estimate the information in complete English text, 'volunteers' were used who were shown samples of text and asked to predict the next letters. This is a rather lengthy process but it was possible to show that the information varies between 0.6 and 1.3 bits/letter depending on the type of text. Presumably in some detective stories the content is rather low (since one can guess the outcome) whereas it is hoped that this book is at the higher end of the range!

A different approach was used by Bell (1953), who considered complete words (assumed equiprobable). Bell estimated the numbers of words of various lengths from a dictionary, as shown in table 2.1

Table 2.1

Number of letters	1	2	3	4	5	6	7	8	>8
Number of words	2	26	722	2166	3610	4765	4260	3861	8447
Entropy/letter	1.0	2.4	3.2	2.8	2.3	2.0	1.7	1.5	0.7

Finding 26 two-letter words would tax the imagination of most people (except players of a certain unmentionable word game) but, if equiprobable, each word provides log 26 = 4.7 bits or 2.35 bits/symbol. The information per letter rises with word length, reaching a maximum for three and four-letter words. Apparently expletives are very efficient at conveying information! The content then falls rapidly, as expected from the discussion above. An average over all word lengths gives 2.6 bits/letter, which is rather higher than Shannon's figure because of the assumption of independent and equiprobable words.

It thus appears that reasonable average values for the information content of English are about 2 bits/letter for complete words and about one bit per letter for text. The redundancy of text is therefore about (4.7 − 1)/4.7 = 80 per cent. As we saw above, this is probably an optimum for a spoken language, though a lower value may be appropriate for a written language. In particular, it can be seen that the storage of text in computers is very inefficient. Text is usually stored in ASCII form, in which each letter is stored as a 7-bit code. An 8-bit 'byte' is usually used for convenience, so nearly 8 times as much space is used as is ideally necessary. However, as will be shown in chapter 3, it is impractical to employ a code that provides a saving of more than about 50 per cent.

2.4   Exercises on Chapter 2

2.4.1. A binary source produces a sequence of Marks and Spaces such that

$$p(M/S) = \tfrac{1}{3}, \; p(S/S) = \tfrac{2}{3}, \; p(M/M) = \tfrac{5}{6}, \; p(S/M) = \tfrac{1}{6}$$

(a) Find $p(M), p(S), p(M, M), p(S, S), p(M, S), p(S, M)$.
(b) Find the conditional entropy and the redundancy.

2.4.2. A source produces three symbols A, B and C. After B the probability of a B is 1/2, of A 1/4 and of C 1/4. After A the probability of A is 5/8, of B 1/4 and of C 1/8. After C the probability of C is 5/8, of B 1/4, and of A 1/8. Find the redundancy of the system.

2.4.3. The joint entropy of a source is given by

$$H(i, j) = - \Sigma\Sigma p(i, j) \log p(i, j)$$
$$ i\ j$$

Show that $H(i, j) = H(i) + H(j/i)$ and demonstrate that this holds using the values in exercise 2.4.1. above.

2.4.4. A simple language consists of three symbols α, β, γ grouped into words of one, two or three symbols. The only single-letter word is α, two-letter words either begin or end with α and three-letter words always have α as the middle letter (and nowhere else). All words are equiprobable. Find the redundancy of the language.

2.4.5. Assume that the sequence below is part of a long sequence of a newly discovered language, comprising only two symbols A and B.

(a) Use the sequence to find the single, joint and conditional probabilities of the two symbols, assuming that conditional probabilities extend only over adjacent symbols.

(b) Hence find the average information per symbol and the redundancy of the language.

(c) How would you determine whether conditional probabilities extend over more than two symbols, and how would the redundancy be calculated if they do?

(d) Is the language likely to be spoken or written?

$$\text{A A A B A B A A B B A A A A B A A B A A} \vdots \text{A}$$

(*Note:* Assume that the 21st symbol is A, in order to obtain 20 pairs.)

3 Binary Coding in Noiseless Channels

3.1 Information Channels

The information produced by most sources of information is not in a suitable form for transmission via a channel, so that some type of coding procedure is necessary. The channel may be analogue or digital, and will have various characteristics such as bandwidth, transmitted power, error rate etc. Two important requirements of the system may be firstly that the information be transmitted as rapidly as possible and secondly that it be transmitted with as few errors as possible. These two requirements cannot easily be attained together; in order to increase the speed the redundancy of the code used has to be low, whereas to reduce the error rate the redundancy has to be high. However, we will see in chapter 5 that Information Theory offers a surprising compromise, whereby under certain conditions both can be achieved together.

In this chapter we will consider only the first requirement, that of speed of transmission, and assume that we are dealing with a noiseless digital channel (that is, there are no transmission errors). The channel will be a binary channel (unless otherwise specified) and will have a certain fixed bandwidth W. The bandwidth of a channel limits the rate at which the signal can change, so that the number of pulses per second that can be sent down the channel can be increased only at the expense of a reduction in transmitted amplitude. As will be shown in chapter 12 the maximum pulse rate for a channel of bandwidth W (without unacceptable attenuation) is known as the Nyquist rate of $2W$ pulses/s. A telephone channel of bandwidth 3000 Hz can thus accept up to 6000 pulses/s. This means that the only way the speed of transmission via a given channel of information can be increased is by the choice of an efficient coding system, with minimum redundancy, so that fewer binary digits need to be transmitted.

3.2 Binary Codes

We shall assume that we have a source of information, producing a *source alphabet* of symbols s_1, s_2 etc. of probabilities p_1, p_2 etc. One of the symbols may be a *space symbol* for separating groups of symbols. The symbols will be represented by a series of binary digits, the code for each symbol being known as a *code word*. A series of symbols, or the corresponding code words, will constitute a *message*. We shall deduce some of the important properties of binary codes by inspecting the five codes shown in table 3.1 for a set of four source symbols.

16

Table 3.1

Code no.	s_1	s_2	s_3	s_4
1	0	10	110	11
2	00	01	10	11
3	0	10	110	1110
4	0	01	011	0111
5	0	10	110	111

It can be seen that code 1 has an ambiguity, in that the code for the sequence s_4, s_1 is the same as that for s_3. This code does not have the required property of being *uniquely decodable* and is therefore not usable without modification. Code 2 is a simple equal length code; it should be noticed that, provided one starts at the beginning, no special space symbols are needed with this code since the binary digits can always be decoded in pairs. Code 3 is known as a *comma code* since the digit '0' is effectively used as a separator between code words. Such a system would clearly become very inefficient for a large source alphabet.

Codes 4 and 5 are both usable, but code 5 has an important property and is said to be *instantaneous*, whereas code 4 lacks this property. The distinction can be seen by considering the binary codes shown below for the sequence s_1, s_2, s_3, s_4, no space symbols being used.

    Code 4   0 0 1 0 1 1 0 1 1 1

    Code 5   0 1 0 1 1 0 1 1 1

With code 5, as soon as the code for a complete code word has been received, one can immediately decode that code word. However, for code 4, one has to look ahead at succeeding symbols before decoding is possible. An instantaneous code provides two important advantages; decoding is simple and no additional space symbols are required (provided that one starts at the beginning and that no errors occur). The required condition for an instantaneous code is that no code word be a prefix on another code word. Code 5 clearly satisfies this, whereas in code 4 each code word is a prefix of the succeeding one.

One may ask at this stage whether it would not be easier simply to use equal length codes, such as code 2. The answer is that it is precisely by using codes of different lengths that we can get an improvement in the efficiency of coding. All that has to be done is to represent the most probable symbols by the shortest code words, and use longer words for the less probable symbols. This is done to some extent in Morse Code, where the most probable letter 'E' is represented by a single dot. Such codes are said to be *compact*.

Suppose the probabilities of the four symbols s_1, s_2, s_3, s_4 above are 0.6, 0.2, 0.1 and 0.1 respectively. A message of ten symbols would require 20 binary digits using the equal length code 2. Using code 5 the message would require

$$10\,[(0.6 \times 1) + (0.2 \times 2) + (0.1 \times 3) + (0.1 \times 3)] = 16 \text{ binary digits}$$

The average length L of a code is an important parameter in determining the efficiency of a system. It is given by

$$L = \sum_i p_i \ell_i$$

where ℓ_i is the length (in binary digits) of the ith code word of probability p_i.

3.3 Compact Instantaneous Codes

The desirable properties of a code are clearly that it be uniquely decodable, instantaneous and compact and we therefore need a method of finding such codes. This is easy by trial and error in simple cases, but becomes very complicated for large alphabets.

3.3.1 A special case

There is an interesting special case, in which the symbol probabilities p_i are of the form $p_i = (\frac{1}{2})^{\alpha_i}$ where α_i is integral. It can be shown (Abramson, 1963) that perfect coding is obtained by setting the lengths of code words $\ell_i = \alpha_i$.

EXAMPLE 3.1

Four symbols s_1, s_2, s_3, s_4 have probabilities $1/2, 1/4, 1/8, 1/8$ respectively. Find an instantaneous compact code, and deduce its average length.
Using

$$p_i = (\tfrac{1}{2})^{\alpha_i}, \ell_1 = 1, \ell_2 = 2, \ell_3 = \ell_4 = 3$$

a suitable code would be $s_1 = 0, s_2 = 10, s_3 = 110, s_4 = 111$. The average length

$$L = \sum p_i \ell_i = (1 \times \tfrac{1}{2} + 2 \times \tfrac{1}{4} + 3 \times \tfrac{1}{8} + 3 \times \tfrac{1}{8}) = 1\tfrac{3}{4} \text{ binary digits}$$

The source entropy here is

$$H = -\sum p_i \log p_i = -(\tfrac{1}{2}\log \tfrac{1}{2} + \tfrac{1}{4}\log \tfrac{1}{4} + 2.\tfrac{1}{8}\log \tfrac{1}{8}) = 1\tfrac{3}{4} \text{ bits per symbol}$$

numerically equal to the average length. This is not a coincidence. If we consider the stream of 0s and 1s representing a message, this stream carries most information (1 bit/digit) when the 0s and 1s are equiprobable. If the average length is L binary digits then on average each symbol gives rise to L bits of information. This is the best that can be done. If the 0s and 1s are not equiprobable each symbol will produce on average more binary digits than are strictly necessary. The coding procedure can thus be seen to be essentially a matter of arranging that equal numbers of 0s and 1s are produced in the coded version of the message.

The efficiency of coding E is defined by

$$E = \frac{H}{L} \text{ and is always} \leqslant 1$$

It is equal to unity in the above example and can always be made so if the probabilities are integral powers of one-half. The same process can be applied to codes of any base n if $p_i = (1/n)^{\alpha_i}$.

3.4 Coding Methods

Although the above special case gives the required length of code words it does not actually produce the codes, though this is relatively easy knowing the lengths. A method of coding for any source was suggested by Shannon and Weaver (1949) and modified by Fano (1961). It involves writing the symbol probabilities in a table in descending order, and dividing them into pairs, as shown in example 3.2.

EXAMPLE 3.2

Find a code using Fano–Shannon coding for a source of five symbols of probabilities $0.5, 0.2, 0.1, 0.1, 0.1$. Find the efficiency.
Dividing lines are inserted to successively divide the probabilities into halves, quarters etc. (or as nearly as possible). A '0' and '1' are added to the code at each division and the final code obtained by reading from the right towards each symbol, writing down the appropriate sequence of 0s and 1s.

					code
s_1	0.5			0	0
s_2	0.2	0	0		100
s_3	0.1	1		1	101
s_4	0.1	0	1		110
s_5	0.1	1			111

$L = 0.5 \times 1 + 0.2 \times 3 + 3 \times 0.1 \times 3 = 2.0$

$H = 1.96$

$E = 0.98$

This coding procedure is very straightforward and can be applied easily to large source alphabets (see exercise 3.7.4). It is easy to implement by a computer program.

A rather more efficient scheme was developed by Huffman (1952), in which the probabilities are again placed in descending order but added in pairs from the bottom and re-ordered, as shown in example 3.3.

EXAMPLE 3.3

Use Huffman's method for the code in example 3.2.

$$L = 0.5 \times 1 + 0.2 \times 2 + 0.1 \times 3 + 2 \times 0.1 \times 4 = 2.0$$

$$H = 1.96$$

$$E = 0.98$$

A '0' or '1' is placed at each branch, and the code obtained by reading from the right towards the symbol required.

The code obtained is different from Fano–Shannon's but the efficiency turns out to be the same. The inherent improvement, due to the re-ordering, is only small and appears only in complicated systems. Huffman's method uses rather a lot of paper in such cases, though a computer solution is again easy to implement.

3.5 Shannon's First Theorem

Both the Fano–Shannon and Huffman methods usually produce efficient codes. However, a further increase in efficiency can be obtained by grouping the source symbols in pairs, threes etc., and applying the coding procedure to the relevant probabilities of the group chosen. If the symbols are independent (as assumed above) the probabilities of the groups are just the products of the single probabilities, but of course if intersymbol influence is present then the joint probabilities will reflect this.

Shannon proved formally that if the source symbols are coded in groups of n, then the average length per *single* symbol tends to the source entropy H as n tends to infinity. That is

$$\lim_{n \to \infty} \frac{L_n}{n} = H$$

where L_n is the average length of a group of n source symbols.

As before, the essence of the idea is that the coding procedure tends to produce equal numbers of 0s and 1s at the output, grouping in large groups simply making this more achievable. The coding process is sometimes known as 'matching the source to the channel', that is, making the output of the coder as suitable as possible for the channel used.

EXAMPLE 3.4

An information source produces a long sequence of three independent symbols A, B, C with probabilities 16/20, 3/20 and 1/20 respectively; 100 such symbols are produced per second. The information is to be transmitted via a noiseless binary channel which can transmit up to 100 binary digits per second. Design a suitable compact instantaneous code and find the probabilities of the binary digits produced.

It is a good idea to check whether the problem can be solved by finding the entropy of the source: $H = -\Sigma p_i \log p_i = 0.884$ bits. Thus, the source rate is 88.4 bits/s which is less than the channel capacity. Coding singly, using the Fano–Shannon method

A	16/20	0		0
B	3/20	0		10
C	1/20	1	$\Big\}$ 1	11

$L = 1.2$ bits/symbol and source rate = 120 binary digits/s. This is too great, so coding in pairs is necessary.

							code
AA	0.64					0	0
AB	0.12				0		10
BA	0.12			0			110
AC	0.04	0					11100
CA	0.04	1	0				11101
BB	0.02		0				11110
BC	0.01	0					111110
CB	0.01	0	1				1111110
CC	0.0025	1					1111111

$L = 1.865$ per pair = 0.9325 bits/symbol.

The source rate is now less than 100, and the efficiency $E = 93$ per cent. The probabilities of 0 and 1 in the coded stream are given by

$$\frac{p(0)}{p(1)} = \frac{0.64 \times 1 + 0.12 \times 2 + 0.04 \times 3 + 0.02 \times 1 + 0.01 \times 2}{0.12 \times 3 + 0.04 \times 7 + 0.02 \times 4 + 0.01 \times 11 + 0.0025 \times 7}$$

$$= \frac{1.03}{0.853}$$

Thus $p(0) = 0.547$, $p(1) = 0.453$.

The entropy of the output stream is $-(p(0) \log p(0) + p(1) \log p(1)) = 0.993$ bits, so the actual information rate is $0.993 \times 0.9325 \times 100 = 92.6$ binary digits/s. This gradually approaches the input rate as the efficiency increases, only becoming equal to it for perfect coding (when $p(0) = p(1)$), requiring infinitely long code groups.

3.6 Applications of Compact Codes

Although interesting and instructive, compact codes do not find much practical application. This is largely because errors occur owing to unavoidable random noise in most communication systems. Since compact codes are necessarily of unequal length and have minimum redundancy, they are very much affected by even a single error. Suppose we use code 5 again (section 3.2) to send the message below and that a single error occurs in the second binary digit

$$s_1 \ s_4 \ s_2 \ s_2 \ s_3 \ s_1 \ \xrightarrow{\text{coding}} \ 0\ 1\ 1\ 1\ 1\ 0\ 1\ 0\ 1\ 1\ 0\ 0$$

$$s_1 \ \underline{s_1} \ \underline{s_4} \ \underline{s_1} \ s_2 \ s_3 \ s_1 \ \xleftarrow{\text{decoding}} \ 0\ \underline{0}\ 1\ 1\ 1\ 0\ 1\ 0\ 1\ 1\ 0\ 0 \ (\text{errors underlined})$$

The sequence gets out of step as soon as the error occurs, and although it eventually recovers an extra symbol is actually received. It can be shown that the code does recover from an error in general and an expression for the error rate can be derived. However, this is rather an academic exercise and, as usual in such exercises, is not very instructive. Clearly these codes are inherently unsuitable when subject to error. Adding synchronisation bits tends to defeat the object of the code, of course.

However, the codes have recently found some application in the *storage* of text in computers, where errors can be assumed to be negligible. The directly addressable memory in most popular microprocessor-based computers is limited to 64K bytes and this is insufficient where the machine is to be used as a 'dictionary', in spelling check applications or for a certain unmentionable word game. Text is normally stored in ASCII form, which is a 7-bit code, and a whole 8-bit byte is usually used per character for convenience. We have seen previously that the information content of English text would be 4.7 bits/symbol for independent equiprobable letters, but falls to about 4 bits (as a result of letter probabilities), 3 bits (as a result of intersymbol influence over pairs of letters), 2 bits (complete words) and about 1 bit/symbol (overall). A saving with respect to ASCII code of about 50 per cent is thus possible by using a compact code taking account of letter probabilities (see exercise 3.7.4). In practice adjustments to the code are made so that a complete byte represents a whole number of characters and so that no characters require more than one byte. The coding and decoding procedures use a little memory, but the saving can still be considerable (for example, an extra 10,000 words).

A greater saving could be made by coding for pairs of symbols, using the appropriate probabilities, but this is less practical because of overlap between adjacent bytes and the length of the look-up table (26 × 26 pairs). A code could be designed for complete words, of course, but the look-up table would then exceed the storage space required for the code! Although English provides only about 1 bit/symbol, it is unfortunately impractical to code beyond single letter probabilities.

3.7 Exercises on Chapter 3

3.7.1. Construct a compact instantaneous code for five source symbols of probabilities $1/2, 1/4, 1/8, 1/16, 1/16$. Show that the average code length is equal to the source entropy.

3.7.2. The types and numbers of vehicles passing a point in a road are to be recorded automatically on a tape recorder. A binary code is to be assigned to each type of vehicle and the appropriate code recorded on the passage of that type. The average numbers of vehicles per hour are as follows:

Cars	: 500	Motorcycles	: 50	Buses	: 25
Lorries	: 200	Mopeds	: 50	Others	: 25
Vans	: 100	Cycles	: 50		

Design a suitable compact instantaneous code. Find its efficiency and compare it with that of a simple equal length binary code. Comment on the feasibility and usefulness of this system.

3.7.3. A source produces three symbols A, B, C with probabilities 0.6, 0.3, 0.1. Find a suitable binary code using Huffman's method,
  (i) using the source symbols separately
  (ii) using the source symbols in pairs.
Find the average code length and efficiency in each case.
Find the probabilities of the 0s and 1s in the output stream, and the entropy of the coded output.

3.7.4. Use Fano's procedure to find a compact code for the letters of the alphabet, using the probabilities overleaf, and estimate the saving in memory compared with standard ASCII code.

Percentage occurrence	Letter
18	space
11	E
8	T
7	A
6	H, I, O, S
5	N, R
3	D, L
2	C, F, M, U
1	B, G, K, V, W, Y, P
0.25	J, Q, X, Z

Note. These values have been rounded from the accepted probabilities.

4 Information Transfer in Noisy Channels

4.1 Information in Noisy Channels

In chapter 1 we saw that the quantity of information received from an event of probability p was given by $-\log p$ or $\log 1/p$. The probability of the event at the receiver changed from p before the event to unity after the event. However, in many practical situations the probability after the event will be a little less than unity, because there may be some uncertainty about the validity of the transmission. For example, if numerical data are read over a telephone line the listener may be unsure that he heard some of the values correctly, or in the transmission of data by binary pulses some of the pulses may be received in error.

Random noise

Random noise occurs in all physical processes. In order for a physical system to attain thermal equilibrium with its surroundings it must exchange energy and the result is a fluctuation in the energy of the system which gives rise to random noise in some form. (This is a statement of the Principle of Equipartition, which will be discussed further in chapter 7.) The fluctuations appear as Brownian motion in mechanical systems, as changes in temperature in thermal systems and as Johnson noise in electrical systems. Johnson noise occurs in any electrical component that dissipates power, so it occurs in resistors, in capacitors and inductors (because they have a non-zero ohmic resistance) and in transistors (because of their base resistance). Other types of electrical noise such as Shot noise (due to the discrete nature of electrical charge) and $1/f$ noise also occur in most semiconductor devices. It is clear that the amplifiers and receivers used in practical communication systems will be subject to random electrical noise, leading to the possibility of errors in the data transmitted.

Binary data may be transmitted as a succession of positive and negative electrical voltages as shown in figure 4.1. A '1' is represented by a positive level lasting one clock cycle and the level then remains the same for the next cycle if another '1' is transmitted, or falls to a negative value for a '0'. Such a signal is known as a *random telegraph signal*. The data are sent over the channel (not necessarily in this form) and 'reproduced' at the output of the channel. The receiver, which may be assumed to keep in step with the transmitter, must make a decision as to whether a '1' or a '0' is present. This is done by sampling the output at the centre of a clock cycle and decoding as '1' if the voltage is greater than zero or '0' if less than zero. Errors may occur because of

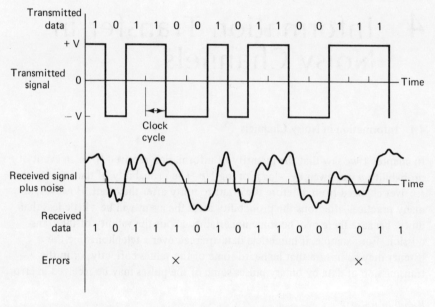

Figure 4.1 Errors due to random noise in a binary channel

the noise added to the signal in the transmission and reception processes. A simple binary channel is characterised by a certain mean binary error rate, which depends on the signal power transmission and bandwidth used.

Quantity of information in a noisy channel

Consider a hypothetical system consisting of a transmitter T, a receiver R and two channels, one of which is noisy and the other noiseless, as shown in figure 4.2.

An event of probability p_0 is transmitted over the noisy channel. At the receiver the probability after reception is p_1, a little less than unity because of

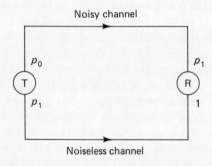

Figure 4.2 Quantity of information in a noisy channel

the possibility of error. A second transmission of the same event is now made via the noiseless channel and the probability at the receiver changes from p_1 before reception to unity after reception, as the channel is noiseless.

The total information transmitted is $I + \log(1/p_1)$, where I is the information in the noisy channel. Now the same information could have been obtained by a single transmission via the noiseless channel, the probabilities changing from p_0 to unity with information $+\log(1/p_0)$. Thus

$$I + \log \frac{1}{p_1} = \log \frac{1}{p_0}$$

or

$$I = \log \frac{p_1}{p_0}$$

p_0 is known as the *a priori* probability, the probability at the receiver of the event *before* transmission.

p_1 is known as the *a posteriori* probability, the probability at the receiver of the event *after* transmission.

It can be seen that for a noiseless system, p_1 would be unity and the expression would become $I = -\log p_0$ as before.

EXAMPLE 4.1

A binary system produces Marks and Spaces with equal probability, 1/8 of all pulses being received in error. Find the information received for all possible combinations of input and output.

There are four possibilities; M → M, M → S, S → M, S → S, though only the first two need be considered. For the case M → M, the probability at the receiver that an M was transmitted after an M has been received is 7/8. Thus

$$I(M \to M \text{ or } S \to S) = \log \frac{7/8}{1/2} = 0.81 \text{ bits}$$

Similarly, for the case M → S, the probability at the receiver that an M was transmitted after an S has been received is 1/8. Thus

$$I(M \to S \text{ or } S \to M) = \log \frac{1/8}{1/2} = -2.0 \text{ bits}$$

The average information received is

$$0.81 \times \tfrac{7}{8} + (-2.0) \times \tfrac{1}{8} = 0.46 \text{ bits}$$

A number of important observations can be made.

(a) Information is reduced even when the transmission is actually correct. In a noiseless system the information would have been one bit, but the *possibility* of error has reduced it to 0.81 bits. This can be seen to be reasonable, by considering transactions on the stock market. If there is some doubt about the validity of data received the investor will invest less than he might otherwise and therefore make less profit even if the data turn out to have been correct.

(b) An error leads to negative information. The receiver has no way of knowing which transmissions are in error, of course, so in the stock market example above the investor would lose if the data were wrong.

(c) The average information is always greater than (or equal to) zero. An error rate of 0.5 would make the average information zero. However, a greater error rate causes the information to increase again, because if every pulse was wrong the receiver would have totally correct data by a simple inversion.

This latter observation is greatly beloved of lecturers and authors, because it means that however bad their lecture or book it is almost certain to provide positive information on average! It also shows how politicians give nothing away; they lie exactly half the time but at random.

4.2 General Expression for Information Transfer

For a noiseless system we saw that the expression $I = -\log p$ for the quantity of information in a single event could be generalised to give the average information $H = -\sum_i p_i \log p_i$ over a set of events of probabilities p_i. We will do the same

thing for a noisy system, denoting inputs by x and outputs by y. Our previous formulae for conditional probabilities apply directly here, because p_1 (the probability at the receiver after the event) is clearly such a probability.

Suppose we have a set of input symbols x_i and a corresponding set of outputs y_i (so that $x_i \rightarrow y_i$ in the absence of error). The *a posteriori* probability p_1 is given by $\log p(x_i/y_i)$, that is, having received a certain symbol y_i the probability that a certain symbol x_i was transmitted. For this event we have

$$I(x_i\,y_i) = \log \frac{p(x_i/y_i)}{p(x_i)}$$

Since $p(x\,y) = p(x)\,p(y/x) = p(y)\,p(x/y) = p(yx)$, (the order of events does not matter, unlike the sequences considered earlier)

$$I(x_i\,y_i) = \log \frac{p(x_i/y_i)}{p(x_i)} = \log \frac{p(y_i/x_i)}{p(y_i)} = \log \frac{p(x_i\,y_i)}{p(x_i)\,p(y_i)}$$

To obtain the average information over all events we have only to multiply by the probability of the event $p(x_i\,y_i)$ and sum. The result is called the *Information Transfer $I(xy)$*:

$$I(xy) = \sum_x \sum_y p(xy) \log \frac{p(xy)}{p(x)\,p(y)}$$

(any of the previous three terms may be used, but this form is preferred).

This result is rather surprising in that it is symmetrical in x and y, that is, x and y are interchangeable! This gives us a rather different interpretation of information exchange; the information transferred is not unidirectional but is a measure of the degree of similarity between receiver and transmitter. In fact, the expression for information transfer is quite similar to the mathematical expression for the correlation coefficient between two sets of data.

Suppose one set up a system comprising a box with digital indicators (representing, say, some binary number) and a second similar box but arranged such that there were occasional random differences between the two numbers displayed. This could be a communication system with a certain error rate. A person entering the room would not know which was the receiver and which the transmitter, yet he could work out the information transfer (if he had read this book). Indeed, it would be physically unreasonable if he could tell which was which, as it would imply causality in random devices.

It can be seen that the general expression behaves satisfactorily, for if x and y are independent then $p(xy) = p(x) \times p(y)$ and the expression becomes

$$I(xy) = \sum_x \sum_y p(xy) \log \frac{p(x)\,p(y)}{p(x)\,p(y)} = 0$$

Similarly, if x and y are totally dependent (that is, in a noiseless system)

$$p(xy) \rightarrow p(x) = p(y) \text{ and } I \rightarrow -\sum p(x) \log p(x) = H(x)$$

EXAMPLE 4.2

A binary system produces Marks with probability 0.7 and Spaces with probability 0.3. 2/7 of the Marks are received in error and 1/3 of the Spaces. Find the information transfer.
This type of problem is best done by writing out a 'typical' sequence of M and S (that is, with the correct probabilities) and evaluating the required probabilities:

x M M M M M M M S S S

y M M M M M S S S S M

Table 4.1 shows the probabilities obtained by counting the required events. (Note that $p(x/y)$ and $p(yx)$ are not needed here, but are included for completeness and because they will be required later.)

Table 4.1

x	M	M	S	S
y	M	S	S	M
$p(x)$	0.7	0.7	0.3	0.3
$p(y)$	0.6	0.4	0.4	0.6
$p(x/y)$	$\frac{5}{6}$	$\frac{1}{2}$	$\frac{1}{2}$	$\frac{1}{6}$
$p(y/x)$	$\frac{5}{7}$	$\frac{2}{7}$	$\frac{2}{3}$	$\frac{1}{3}$
$p(xy)$	0.5	0.2	0.2	0.1
$I(xy)$	0.126	−0.097	0.147	−0.085

$$I(xy) = \underset{x\ y}{\Sigma\Sigma}\ p(xy) \log \frac{p(xy)}{p(x)\,p(y)}$$

$$\overbrace{= 0.5 \log \frac{0.5}{0.7 \times 0.6}}^{\text{MM}} + \overbrace{0.2 \log \frac{0.2}{0.7 \times 0.4}}^{\text{MS}} + \overbrace{0.2 \log \frac{0.2}{0.3 \times 0.4}}^{\text{SS}}$$

$$+ \overbrace{0.1 \log \frac{0.1}{0.3 \times 0.6}}^{\text{SM}}$$

$$= 0.091 \text{ bits/symbol}$$

Instead of using this expression one could use one with $p(x/y)$ or $p(y/x)$, but it is easier to work out the joint probabilities $p(xy)$ than conditional ones. The error rate in this example is impractically high of course and the error rates have been chosen to simplify computation. It can be seen that very little information is actually transmitted.

4.3 Equivocation

The idea of 'equivocation' provides another interpretation of information transfer. It represents the destructive effect of noise on information, or alternatively (which is the same thing) the additional information that the receiver requires in order to correct all his data. Consider a source and receiver again, connected by both a noisy and a noiseless channel as before, but this time with an 'observer' controlling the noiseless channel as in figure 4.3.

The observer looks at each pair of transmitted and received digits sent via the noiseless channel. If they are the same he sends the receiver a '1', if different a '0'. A sequence of transmissions could be as follows

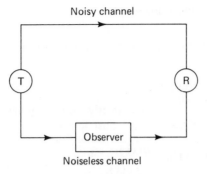

Figure 4.3   Noisy channel with hypothetical observer

x	M M S S M M M S M
y	M S S S M M M S S
observer	1 0 1 1 1 1 1 1 0

The information sent by the observer is easily evaluated. It is simply
$-(p(0) \log p(0) + p(1) \log p(1))$ applied to the binary stream sent. Moreover,
since he only sends a '0' for an error, the probability of '0' is just the channel
error probability p_e.

EXAMPLE 4.3

Find the information sent by the (hypothetical) observer for a binary system
with equiprobable inputs and an error rate of 1/8 (example 4.1 again). The
observer sends $7/8 \log (7/8) + 1/8 \log (1/8) = 0.55$ bits. Since the input information $H(x) = 1$ bit per symbol, the net information (without the observer)
is $1 - 0.55 = 0.45$ bits, agreeing with the previous result. Alternatively we can
say that noise in the system has destroyed 0.55 bits of information.

General expression for equivocation

Considering a specific pair of transmitted and received digits, the probability at
the receiver changes from $p(x)$ to $p(x/y)$ after reception down the noisy channel.
After receiving the observer's correcting data the probability changes to unity;
that is

the observer provides $- \log p(x/y)$

Averaging over all pairs as before, we obtain a general expression for equivocation $H(x/y)$

$$H(x/y) = - \underset{x\ y}{\Sigma\Sigma}\ p(xy) \log p(x/y)$$

The information transferred via the noisy channel (in the absence of the observer) must be

$$I(xy) = H(x) - H(x/y)$$

This expression can be deduced directly from our previous expressions for information transfer (since it clearly must agree):

$$I(xy) = \underset{x\ y}{\Sigma\Sigma}\ p(xy) \log \frac{p(xy)}{p(x)\,p(y)}$$

$$= \underset{x\ y}{\Sigma\Sigma}\ p(xy) \log \frac{p(x/y)}{p(x)} \quad (\text{since } p(xy) = p(y)\,p(x/y))$$

$$= \underset{x\ y}{\Sigma\Sigma}\ p(xy) \log p(x/y) - \underset{x\ y}{\Sigma\Sigma}\ p(xy) \log p(x)$$

$$= -H(x/y) + H(x) \quad (\text{since } \underset{y}{\Sigma}\ p(xy) = p(x))$$

A similar derivation gives

$$I(xy) = H(y) - H(y/x)$$

in which $H(y/x)$ is a 'backwards' equivocation.

EXAMPLE 4.4

Solve example 4.2 using the expression for equivocation.
In this case we have to work out the conditional probabilities. We need only either $p(x/y)$ or $p(y/x)$ but both will be used for completeness.
Referring again to table 4.1, in which $p(x/y)$ and $p(y/x)$ are evaluated:

$$H(x) = -\Sigma\ p(x) \log p(x) = -(0.7 \log 0.7 + 0.3 \log 0.3) = 0.881 \text{ bits}$$

$$H(y) = -\Sigma\ p(y) \log p(y) = -(0.6 \log 0.6 + 0.4 \log 0.4) = 0.970 \text{ bits}$$

$$H(x/y) = \Sigma\Sigma\ p(xy) \log p(x/y)$$

$$\overset{\text{MM}}{} \quad \overset{\text{MS}}{} \quad \overset{\text{SS}}{} \quad \overset{\text{SM}}{}$$

$$= 0.5 \log \tfrac{5}{6} + 0.2 \log \tfrac{1}{2} + 0.2 \log \tfrac{1}{2} + 0.1 \log \tfrac{1}{6}$$

$$= 0.790 \text{ bits}$$

$$\overset{\text{MM}}{} \quad \overset{\text{MS}}{} \quad \overset{\text{SS}}{} \quad \overset{\text{SM}}{}$$

$$H(y/x) = 0.5 \log \tfrac{5}{7} + 0.2 \log \tfrac{2}{7} + 0.2 \log \tfrac{2}{3} + 0.1 \log \tfrac{1}{3} = 0.879 \text{ bits}$$

Thus

$$I(xy) = H(x) - H(x/y) = 0.091 \text{ bits}$$

$$= H(y) - H(y/x) = 0.091 \text{ bits}$$

This agrees with the value found previously using the formula for information transfer. For completeness we can also calculate the joint entropy $H(xy)$ given by

$$H(xy) = \Sigma\Sigma\, p(xy) \log p(xy)$$

$$H(xy) = 0.5 \log 0.5 + 0.2 \log 0.2 + 0.2 \log 0.2 + 0.1 \log 0.1$$

$$= 1.76 \text{ bits}$$

It is easily proved that $H(xy) = H(x/y) + H(y/x) + I(xy)$ and the values above confirm this. However, the concept of joint entropy is not very important as it does not have any useful interpretation.

4.4 Summary of Basic Formulae by Venn Diagram

The various concepts and formulae discussed in this chapter, and the relations between them, can be usefully summarised in a Venn diagram. If we imagine that all possible information is represented by an unbounded plane, we can represent the information at the transmitter of a specific system by (say) a circle in the plane. The inside of the circle is the source entropy $H(x)$. If the system was noiseless the entropy $H(y)$ at the receiver would be represented by an identical circle coincident with that for $H(x)$. However, in a noisy system the two circles would intersect only partially and if x and y were independent they would not intersect at all. The area of intersection thus represents the information transfer $I(xy)$. Similarly, the equivocations $H(x/y)$ and $H(y/x)$ are represented by the remainder of the $H(x)$ and $H(y)$ circles respectively when $I(xy)$ is removed, and the joint entropy $H(xy)$ is the area bounded by the perimeter of the figure. The relations between the various measures can easily be seen (or remembered) from figure 4.4.

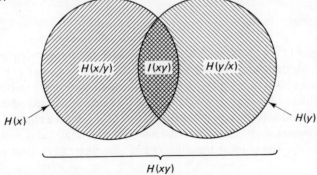

Figure 4.4   Venn diagram summarising basic formulae

Source entropy   : $H(x) = -\Sigma\, p(x) \log p(x)$

Receiver entropy   : $H(y) = -\Sigma\, p(y) \log p(y)$

Equivocations   : $H(x/y) = -\,\Sigma\Sigma\, p(xy) \log p(x/y)$

$$H(y/x) = -\,\Sigma\Sigma\, p(xy) \log p(y/x)$$

Information transfer : $I(xy) = +\,\Sigma\Sigma\, p(xy) \log \dfrac{p(xy)}{p(x)\, p(y)}$

$$= H(x) - H(x/y)$$

$$= H(y) - H(y/x)$$

Joint entropy   : $H(xy) = -\,\Sigma\Sigma\, p(xy) \log p(xy)$

$$= H(x/y) + H(y/x) + I(xy)$$

4.5 Channel Capacity

An information channel will normally have a fixed known bandwidth and a fixed known (or measurable) error probability. The *capacity* C of the channel is defined as the maximum information transfer, with respect to the probabilities of the input symbols (which are the only variables), that is

$$C \equiv \max. I(xy)$$

The relations between input and output in a general channel can be conveniently represented in matrix form, the elements of the matrix giving the conditional probabilities ($p(x/y)$ or $p(y/x)$ etc.). One can then calculate the capacity of a specific channel by finding the distribution of input probabilities that gives the maximum transfer. This would be very tedious in most cases. However, binary channels are by far the most common type, and of these the binary symmetric channel is the most usual. We will therefore concentrate only on this type of channel.

Binary symmetric channels

Referring again to the binary system shown in figure 4.1, the decision level at the receiver, which determines whether the received digit is a '0' or a '1', is usually chosen at 0 V for a bipolar system. If the noise in the system is random the probabilities of errors in '0' and '1' will be the same (a different choice of decision level could clearly give more errors in 0s or 1s). Such a channel is known as a *binary symmetric channel* and is characterised by a single value p of binary error probability. The possible transitions from transmitter to receiver are shown in figure 4.5.

p = binary error probability = $1 - \bar{p}$

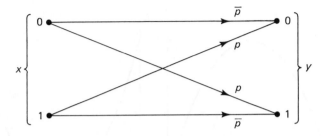

Figure 4.5   Binary symmetric channel

The capacity of this channel has a very simple form and can be deduced as follows:

$$I(xy) = H(y) - H(y/x)$$

$$= H(y) + \Sigma\Sigma_{x\ y}\ p(xy) \log p(y/x)$$

$$= H(y) + \Sigma_x\ p(x)\ (\Sigma_y\ p(y/x) \log p(y/x))$$

Considering the summation over y, for a given x one of the values of y represents an error and the other represents a correct transmission, so the two probabilities are just p and $\bar{p}$. Therefore

$$I(xy) = H(y) + \Sigma_x\ p(x)\ (p \log p + \bar{p}\ \log \bar{p})$$

$$= H(y) - H(p)\quad \text{where } H(p) = -(p \log p + \bar{p}\ \log \bar{p})$$

$H(p)$ is an equivocation and its formula is just like that for the entropy of a noiseless binary system with probabilities p and $\bar{p}$.

Now $I(xy)$ will be a maximum when $H(y)$ is a maximum, since p and therefore $H(p)$ is fixed. This will occur when $p(0) = p(1)$ at the receiver, and since the system is symmetric, when $p(0) = p(1)$ at the transmitter. The channel capacity is therefore

$$C = 1 - H(p)$$

and is obtained for equiprobable input symbols.

Figure 4.6(a) shows how $I(xy)$ varies with probability of input digits, reaching a maximum (when it becomes the channel capacity) of $1 - H(p)$ for $p(0) = p(1)$. Figure 4.6(b) shows how the capacity C varies with binary error probability p, being unity for $p = 0$ or $p = 1$ and zero for $p = \frac{1}{2}$.

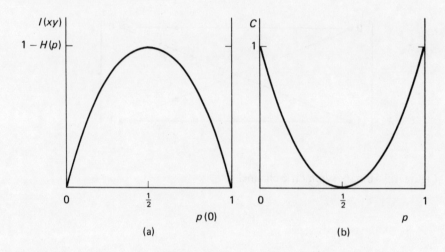

Figure 4.6   (a) Variation of information transfer with input probability,
(b) variation of channel capacity with error probability

EXAMPLE 4.5

Find the capacity of a binary symmetric channel with a binary error rate of
0.125.
This is a thinly disguised example 4.1 yet again.

$$H(p) = -(p \log p + \bar{p} \log \bar{p}) = -(\tfrac{1}{8} \log \tfrac{1}{8} + \tfrac{7}{8} \log \tfrac{7}{8}) = 0.55$$

$$C = 0.45 \text{ bits}$$

4.6   Exercises on Chapter 4

4.6.1. Symbols A, B and C occur with equal probability. Two-thirds of A's are
received as A, one-sixth as B and one-sixth as C. C behaves in a corresponding manner and no errors occur in B. Find the information transfer.

4.6.2. A binary symmetric channel has a binary error probability of 1/3. Two
equiprobable input symbols A and B are to be transmitted, coded as 11
and 00 respectively. Determine:

(a) the channel capacity;

(b) the information transfer through the channel, assuming that the
receiver interprets 11 as A, 00 as B and makes no decision for 01
or 10;

(c) the information transfer if the receiver interprets 11, 01 or 10 as A,
and 00 as B;

(d) the information transfer if the receiver interprets 01 and 10 randomly
as A or B.

Explain the reasons for the different values in (b), (c) and (d).

Note. The probabilities of A being received as 11, 01, 10 or 00 are respectively 4/9, 2/9, 2/9 and 1/9.

4.6.3. Two binary symmetric channels are to be cascaded. The first has a binary error probability of 0.02 and the second of 0.04. Assuming that the input symbols are equiprobable find the information transfer:

(a) through the first channel alone,

(b) through the second channel alone;

(c) through both channels in cascade.

Comment on the general effect of cascading noisy channels.

4.6.4. An information source produces three symbols A, B and C with probabilities 1/4, 1/4 and 1/2 respectively. Errors occur in transmission as shown in the table below. Find the probabilities of A, B and C at the receiver and hence deduce the information transfer.

Input	Output		
	A	B	C
A	$\frac{2}{3}$	$\frac{1}{3}$	0
B	0	1	0
C	0	$\frac{1}{3}$	$\frac{2}{3}$

4.6.5. An information source produces three symbols A, B and C with probabilities 1/2, 1/4 and 1/4 respectively. The symbols are transmitted via a binary symmetric channel of binary error probability 1/4; A is coded as '00', B and '01' and C as '10'.

The system is viewed by an observer who has noiseless communication channels between source and receiver. When a symbol is correct the observer sends '11', but if incorrect the correct code (above) for the symbol is sent.

Calculate how much information the observer sends and compare with the equivocation of the channel. Explain the difference between the two values, and what is wrong with the observer.

Note. The probabilities of $00 \rightarrow 00$, $00 \rightarrow 01$, $00 \rightarrow 10$ and $00 \rightarrow 11$ are 9/16, 3/16, 3/16 and 1/16 respectively.

5 Binary Coding in Noisy Channels

5.1 Introduction

We have seen previously that in a communication system we may be concerned either with the speed of transmission of information, or with the accuracy of transmission. In chapter 3 we considered speed of transmission in noiseless systems, and noted that the efficiency of coding was a measure of the redundancy of the system, perfect efficiency implying zero redundancy. In this chapter we will consider the accuracy of transmission in a noisy system. Clearly, redundancy will have to be added to give protection against errors. For example, in a system with two input symbols A and B, coding A = 000 and B = 111 gives a reduction in the overall error rate (compared with A = 0, B = 1) since single errors can be tolerated. Unfortunately the redundancy is greatly increased, and it appears at first sight that there is bound to be a simple exchange between error rate and redundancy. However, it will be shown that Information Theory predicts that the situation is not as bad as this, and that, subject to certain restrictions, a low error rate can be achieved together with a high data rate (or low redundancy).

We will assume that we are dealing with a binary symmetric channel with binary error probability p. The symbols to be transmitted will be coded as groups of binary digits (code words) and we will need to evaluate the symbol error probability $p(e)$ for a given coding system. It is important to distinguish this from the binary error probability; in the above example $p(e)$ is the sum of the probabilities of two and three binary errors in a sequence of three binary digits, whereas the binary error probability is simply the probability that a given binary digit is received in error.

The information rate R is the information per digit produced by the source before transmission, so in the above example $R = 1/3$ bit per binary digit (since three digits are used to carry one bit of information). The relation between R and $p(e)$ will be our main concern in this chapter.

5.2 The Binomial Probability Distribution

In order to find $p(e)$ we need to find the probability of getting a given number of errors in a given number of binary digits. The binomial distribution provides precisely what we require. It refers to a process with two outcomes of probabilities p (for success, say) and $\bar{p}$ (for failure), and states that the probability

38

$p(r)$ of getting r successes in n trials is given by the $(r+1)^{\text{th}}$ term of the binomial expansion of $(\bar{p}+p)^n$; that is

$$p(r) = \frac{n!}{(n-r)!\,r!}\; p^r\,\bar{p}^{\,(n-r)}$$

EXAMPLE 5.1

A dice is thrown four times; find the probabilities of throwing 0, 1, 2, 3 and 4 sixes.

Although most dice have more than two outcomes, we can consider success to be throwing a six and failure to be anything else, so $p = 1/6$ and $\bar{p} = 5/6$.

$$(\bar{p}+p)^4 = \bar{p}^4 + 4\bar{p}^3 p + 6\bar{p}^2 p^2 + 4\bar{p}\,p^3 + p^4$$

r	0	1	2	3	4
$p(r)$	0.4823	0.3858	0.1157	0.0154	0.0008

It is obvious that the probability of getting four sixes is $(1/6)^4$ and of getting no sixes is $(5/6)^4$, but the other probabilities are not intuitively obvious though they are easily found from the expression. Since $(\bar{p}+p) = 1$ the sum of the probabilities on the right-hand side must also be unity.

The distribution will be considered further in chapter 7, in connection with probability distributions.

5.3 Binary Coding for Error Protection

We will assume in this section that we are coding symbols for transmission in a binary symmetric channel of binary error probability $p = 0.01$. We will use code words that are five binary digits in length in all cases.

5.3.1 Coding by repetition

Suppose we code for two symbols A and B only, taking A = 00000, B = 11111. It is necessary to interpret received symbols according to a *decision rule* fixed in advance; in this case we will use a simple majority rule, so that the received sequence is interpreted as A if it has more 0s than 1s and vice-versa. Two errors can be tolerated without producing a symbol error and $p(e)$ is given by the sum of the probabilities of three, four and five errors (in five trials):

$$(\bar{p}+p)^5 = \bar{p}^5 + 5\bar{p}^4 p + 10\bar{p}^3 p^2 + 10\bar{p}^2 p^3 + 5\bar{p}\,p^4 + p^5$$

$p(r)$	$p(0)$	$p(1)$	$p(2)$	$p(3)$	$p(4)$	$p(5)$

Thus

$$p(e) = p(3) + p(4) + p(5)$$

$$\approx p(3)$$

$$\approx 9.8 \times 10^{-6}$$

The information rate $R = 1/5$ bits/binary digit.

Clearly, we can decrease $p(e)$ only at the expense of decreasing R; if we used 7 binary digits we would find $p(e) = 3.5 \times 10^{-9}$ and $R = 1/7$.

5.3.2   Coding by selection of code words

A more powerful and general approach is to select only certain code words for use out of all the possible code words. Using five digits there are 32 possible code words. We can view the repetition method above as a selection of only two of the possible code words.

(i) Two selections (that is, repetition)
   A = 00000, B = 11111
   This gives $p(e) = 9.8 \times 10^{-6}$, $R = 1/5$ as above.

(ii) Thirty-two selections
   At the other extreme we could elect to use all 32 code words (permitting some punctuation besides the 26 upper case letters), so A = 00000, B = 00001, C = 00010, . . ., "-" = 11111 etc. Since all combinations are used, a single binary error will produce a symbol error.
   Therefore

$$p(e) = p(1) + p(2) + p(3) + p(4) + p(5)$$

$$= 1 - p(0)$$

$$\approx 0.049$$

   The information rate $R = 1$ bit/binary digit (assuming 32 equiprobable symbols, each requiring 5 digits).

(iii) Four selections
   A compromise between these two extremes is possible, by selecting a number between two and thirty-two. To obtain a reasonable data rate we want to use a lot of code words, but to keep the symbol error rate low those selected should be as different from one another as possible. Consider the selection

$$A = 0\,0\,0\,0\,0$$

$$B = 0\,0\,1\,1\,1$$

$$C = 1\,1\,0\,0\,1$$

$$D = 1\,1\,1\,1\,0$$

Every code word differs from all the others in at least three digit positions. There are many other possible choices, but only four such code words are possible in each case. The number of digit positions in which two code words differ is known as the Hamming Distance, and the least difference between any members of a given set of code words is called the minimum Hamming Distance, MHD. It is clear that single errors can be tolerated, since a received code word with one error will still be closer to the transmitted code word than to any of the other *selected* code words. However, symbol errors will occur for two or more errors.

Thus

$$p(e) = p(2) + p(3) + p(4) + p(5)$$

$$\approx p(2)$$

$$= 9.7 \times 10^{-4}$$

The information rate $R = 2/5$ bits/binary digit.

A comparison of the three cases is given in table 5.1.

Table 5.1

No. of selections	$p(e)$	R
2	9.8×10^{-6}	0.2
4	9.7×10^{-4}	0.4
32	0.049	1

The discussion above suggests that a compromise between low error rate and high data rate may be possible by using long groups of digits (more than five, say) so that there are a large number of possible code words, and by selecting a sufficient number for use to keep the R values reasonable but sufficiently different from one another to make $p(e)$ acceptably low. This is the principle of Shannon's second theorem.

5.3.3 Shannon's second theorem

Shannon showed (see Shannon and Weaver, 1949) that if coding is in long groups of n binary digits, then provided that the number of selected groups M is less than or equal to 2^{nC}, where C is the channel capacity, the symbol error rate $p(e)$ can be made *arbitrarily small* as n tends to infinity.

Assuming that the M selected code words are equiprobable, the information rate $R = \log M/n$ bits/symbol; that is

$$R \leqslant \frac{\log 2^{nC}}{n} \leqslant C$$

In other words, provided $R \leqslant C$ then $p(e)$ tends to zero as n tends to infinity. We thus have the surprising result that, irrespective of the binary error probability, information can be transmitted at any rate up to and including the channel capacity with *no net errors* (that is, symbol errors).

Applying this to the system discussed above, the capacity C with $p = 0.01$ is 0.919 bits. Choosing 2 or 4 code words gives $R/C = 0.22$ and 0.44 respectively, whereas choosing 32 code words gives $R/C > 1$. However, $p(e)$ does not tend to zero since n is not sufficiently large. Of course, what the theorem does not tell us is how large the group of binary digits needs to be to give a specified symbol error rate. Unfortunately n has to be rather large in practice, as can be seen from the examples below.

EXAMPLE 5.2

Suppose $n = 10$ (with $p = 0.01$ and $C = 0.919$ as above). The total number of possible combinations is $2^n = 1024$. The number of selected code words M must be less than $2^{nC} \approx 2^9$, so choosing $M = 2^9$ (so $R/C = 1$) we would be using 512 symbols or 1 in 2 of the possible code words as symbols. There would be no way of selecting symbols so as to get a low error rate. On the other hand, if we chose $M = 32$ (so $R/C = 0.5/0.919 = 0.54$) we would have a choice of 1 in 32 of code words, which could be chosen to differ from one another in several digit positions.

Suppose now that $n = 100$; the total number of combinations is now 2^{100} and if we choose $R = C$ we have $M \approx 2^{90}$. Only 1 in 1000 of the possible code words are used, so they can be chosen to give a very low error rate. Making $R \ll C$ makes the position even more favourable. Unfortunately $M = 2^{90}$ ($\approx 10^{27}$) is considerably more than the vocabulary of even the most ardent player of that unmentionable word game, so such a system is totally impracticable.

Shannon's theorem points us in the right direction, showing what the theoretical limit is and indicating that the error rate falls as n increases to an extent depending on R/C. However, it does not help much in finding suitable codes and its direct application is not practical. It is nevertheless of great importance and has led to considerable developments in coding theory. Some of the codes developed will be outlined later in this chapter, but we will next consider some practical coding systems, viewing them in the light of Shannon's theorem.

5.4 Practical Codes for Error Detection and Correction

It is important to distinguish between error detection and error correction. Suppose we have a set of code words with an MHD of two. A single binary error will produce a code word not in the list of those selected, so that the presence of a (binary) error will be *detected*, but there will be no way of knowing which code word was actually transmitted. However, if a set of code words has an MHD of three, a single error will produce a code word nearest to the 'correct' code word (as seen above) so that single errors can be said to have been *corrected*. In general it can be seen that to detect E errors we need an MHD of $(E + 1)$ and to correct E errors we need MHD = $(2E + 1)$.

5.4.1 Error-detecting codes

(i) Double-difference codes

Single errors can be detected if the MHD is 2, and a simple way of constructing such a code with $n = 5$ is to use all the combinations in which exactly two 'ones' appear (the MHD is bound to be 2, since the worst case is where two code words have one 'one' in the same position). This is known as a 'two out of five' code, and there are ten possible combinations as shown in table 5.2.

Table 5.2

0	1 1 0 0 0	5	0 1 0 1 0
1	1 0 1 0 0	6	0 1 0 0 1
2	1 0 0 1 0	7	0 0 1 1 0
3	1 0 0 0 1	8	0 0 1 0 1
4	0 1 1 0 0	9	0 0 0 1 1

Another more useful version is a 'three out of seven' code, which has 35 combinations.

These codes detect single errors but fail for two or more errors. It can be arranged that a detected error automatically leads to retransmission of the erroneous symbol. Such systems are known as ARQ (automatic request repeat) systems.

(ii) Parity codes

The parity of a code word is defined as the sum of the binary digits, being even or odd. A parity digit is an extra digit added to a code word such that the overall parity (that is, including the parity digit) is even or odd as desired. For example, if a symbol S is initially coded as 0 0 1 1 1 an extra '1' will produce even parity or a '0' odd parity. Assuming 'even on 1s' parity, S = 0 0 1 1 1 1, and a single error will produce odd parity and is therefore detectable. The code will fail for an even number of errors, but will detect any odd number of errors.

Such codes are easily implemented, since the parity digit can be generated by exclusively OR-ing the information digits, and detected in a similar manner. They are widely used in computers and data systems, and are more useful and powerful than double-difference methods. ARQ systems can conveniently be used with parity codes.

5.4.2   Error-correcting codes

There are two distinct types of error-correcting codes, block codes and convolution codes. A block code consists of a number of information digits together with a number of checking digits (for example, parity checks on selected information digits). A convolution code consists of a stream of alternate information and check digits, the latter being effectively derived from several code words.

5.4.2.1   Block codes

A given code word comprises i information digits and c checking digits, so the length $n = i + c$ and the information rate $R = i/n$ (the redundancy is $(n - i)/n$). The best known and most instructive example of such codes is the code developed by Hamming (1950).

(i) Hamming code   This is a single-error-detecting block code (with MHD = 3). It comprises the required number of information digits (for example, 5 for 32 symbols) interspersed with parity check digits. Each parity digit checks a unique selection of information digits. If a single error occurs in transmission some of the parity checks will be found to fail. A 'checking number' is formed at the receiver, being a binary combination of the individual parity checks (writing '1' if it fails and '0' if it tallies). The selection of information digits checked by each parity digit is such that the checking number gives the actual position in the code word of the incorrect digit.

The positions in the final code word, and the selection of digits checked for each parity digit, are shown in table 5.3.

Table 5.3

Parity digit	Position in code word	Digit positions checked
C_0	1	1, 3, 5, 7, 9 . . .
C_1	2	2, 3, 6, 7, 10, 11 . . .
C_2	4	4, 5, 6, 7, 12, 13, 14, 15 . . .
C_3	8	8, 9, 10, 11, 12, 13, 14, 15 . . .

The checking number (in binary) is (C_3, C_2, C_1, C_0) with $C = 1$ for failure and $C = 0$ for a tally. The reason for the particular selection of digit positions will become clearer after considering an example.

EXAMPLE 5.3

Deduce a single-error-correcting/double-error-detecting Hamming code for 16 symbols.

We will ignore the double-error-detecting requirement initially. For 16 symbols we require 4 information digits (2^4 = 16). Since the check digits go in positions 1, 2, 4, 8 etc., we will have to put our information digits in positions 3, 5, 6 and 7 so three check digits are needed (in positions 1, 2 and 4). Any suitable code can be used for the information digits, but a simple binary code has been used below in table 5.4.

The binary code is first written out in digit positions 3, 5, 6 and 7, leaving positions 1, 2 and 4 blank. C_0 is then placed in position 1, being an even-on-1s parity check on digit positions 1, 3, 5 and 7. The process is repeated for C_1 and C_2 using the combinations in table 5.3 (ignore the digit shown in position 8 for the time being).

Table 5.4

	(C_0)	(C_1)		(C_2)				P
	1	2	3	4	5	6	7	8
(1) A	0	0	0	0	0	0	0	0
B	1	1	0	1	0	0	1	0
C	0	1	0	1	0	1	0	1
D	1	0	0	0	0	1	1	1
.								
.								
.								
O	0	0	0	0	1	1	0	1
(16)P	1	1	1	1	1	1	1	1

Suppose D(= 1 0 0 0 0 1 1) was transmitted and received as 1 0 1 0 0 1 1, that is, with the third digit in error. The parity checks are shown in figure 5.1.

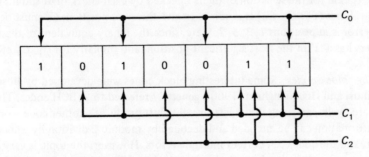

Figure 5.1   Parity checks for Hamming code

The binary checking number $(C_2, C_1, C_0) = 0\ 1\ 1 =$ decimal 3. The third digit is in error and is therefore complemented and 'D' decoded. If no errors occur the checking number will be zero, but if two or more occur it will not provide meaningful results. The code can be made to *detect* double errors if an extra overall parity digit is added, and this has been placed in position 8 above. Note that this is outside the Hamming process and must not be included in the error-correcting process. The decoding process is shown in figure 5.2.

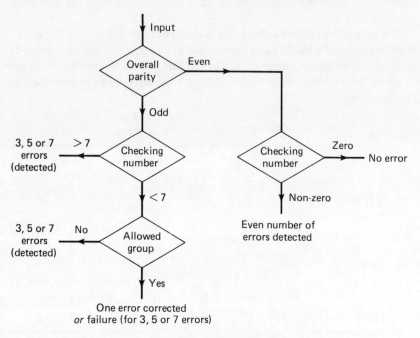

Figure 5.2   Flow diagram for decoding Hamming code

The reason for the selection of digits checked by each check digit should now be clear. Since (C_2, C_1, C_0) is required to give the error position, C_0 must be 1 if the error is in positions 1, 3, 5, 7, 9 etc. since the binary equivalent of these numbers has a '1' in the least significant position, and similarly for C_1, C_2 etc.

(ii) Other block codes   Some interesting block codes were developed by Bose, Chandhuri and Hocquenghem (1960), generally referred to as BCH codes. These codes are cyclic, meaning that a left or right shift produces another code word. The information can be encoded and decoded by modulo 2 division by a special divisor, and the codes can correct multiple errors. However, the topic is very mathematical and the implementation is rather complicated, and the codes have found little practical application so far.

Most block codes are intended to give protection against randomly occurring errors, as a result of random electrical noise for example. However, Fire (1959) developed a series of cyclic block codes capable of correcting up to three consecutive errors in a block. The mathematics and implementation are again somewhat complicated and they have similarly not yet found much practical application.

5.4.2.2 Convolution codes

Convolution codes are intended to give protection against bursts of errors, in which several consecutive bits in the data stream may be corrupted owing to a short burst of electrical interference. This type of error is in fact more common in many communication systems than the random errors that most block codes seek to correct.

The principle of convolution codes is that the check digits are on relatively widely spaced digits, so that an error burst of less than this length does not affect both the digits in the check. Several such codes were devised by Hagelburger (1959).

Hagelburger's code This code is able to correct bursts of errors of up to 6 digits in length, provided that there are at least 19 correct digits between the bursts. The information digits are fed to a shift register and a parity check carried out between the first and fourth positions, as shown in figure 5.3. The parity digit is then interleaved between successive information digits by means of the switch S.

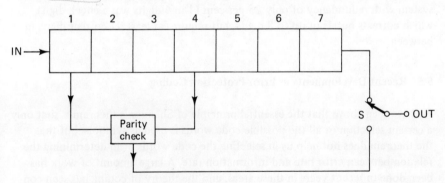

Figure 5.3 Hagelburger's coding system

Suppose that the information digits are 1 0 1 0 1 1 and that the shift register initially contains zeros. The first check will yield a zero, but when the first information digit is placed in register position 1 the check digit will be a 1 (assuming even-on-1s parity again). Figure 5.4 shows the contents of the shift register and the corresponding check digits for several cycles.

```
1 2 3 4 5 6 7  Check              Output stream
                digit
0 0 0 0 0 0 0    0    0 0
1 0 0 0 0 0 0    1    0 0 1 0
1 1 0 0 0 0 0    1    0 0 1 0 1 0
0 1 1 0 0 0 0    0    0 0 1 0 1 0 0 0
1 0 1 1 0 0 0    0    0 0 1 0 1 0 0 0 0 0
0 1 0 1 1 0 0    1    0 0 1 0 1 0 0 0 0 0 1 0
1 0 1 0 1 1 0    1    0 0 1 0 1 0 0 0 0 0 1 0 1 0
0 1 0 1 0 1 1    1    0 0 1 0 1 0 0 0 0 0 1 0 1 0 1 1
0 0 1 0 1 0 1    0    0 0 1 0 1 0 0 0 0 0 1 0 1 0 1 1 0 1
```

Figure 5.4

Because of the separation between the checked digit positions, the outgoing stream is such that the separation between any two information digits covered by a given parity check, or between any digit and a check digit covering it, is always greater than six digit positions, so that error bursts of up to six digits cannot defeat the system.

Decoding is somewhat more complicated, requiring the digits to be switched into data and check registers, with parity checks carried out at appropriate points. It can be shown that correct decoding is possible provided that there are at least 19 correct digits after a burst of errors.

This system has a redundancy of 50 per cent. Hagelburger described another system with redundancy of only 25 per cent (1 in 4 digits was a check digit) which corrects bursts of up to 8 digits, but requires at least 91 correct digits in between.

5.5 Recent Developments in Error-Protection Coding

We have seen above that the essential principle of Shannon's theorem is that only a certain selection of all the possible code words is used as symbols, but that the theorem does not help us in selecting the code words or in determining the relation between error rate and information rate. A large amount of work has been done in recent years in these areas, and the theory of coding has seen considerable developments such as in the BCH and Fire codes mentioned above.

However, it is only very recently that some of the coding schemes have found practical application. The course on which this book is based has always included Hamming's code, but until about 1980 it was necessary to say that error-correction schemes were of considerable theoretical interest but were too difficult to implement in practice. Recent technological developments have changed matters of course, and the coding and decoding required for a Hamming-type system can readily be implemented in an IC or the required program stored in a ROM. Error-correction schemes are important where data are to be transmitted, as opposed to text, and the Oracle and Ceefax systems employ such methods. Technology has caught up with Information Theory and there is no doubt that many interesting developments will become possible in the next few years.

One particularly promising area appears to be in Sequential Decoding (Fano, 1963; Wozencroft and Jacobs, 1965). The coding or decoding procedure can be thought of as involving a 'tree', with branches leading to a particular code. For example, if there are i information digits to be encoded then the tree will have 2^i terminating branches. The decoding process involves trying to find the correct path through a tree with 0s and 1s assigned to each junction. The decoder examines a predetermined number of digits at a time. At each junction it makes a decision as to which branch to follow based on say the minimum Hamming distance between the received digits and those corresponding to its position in the tree. It keeps a running count of the correspondence between the two sets. If an incorrect branch is chosen the decoder will eventually detect this, since the count will tend to fall, and it is able to go back and try another branch. The decoder can be thought of as a goal-seeking device employing feedback, and there is clearly great scope for intelligent decoders of this type. Considerable success has already been achieved in some space communication applications.

5.6 Exercises on Chapter 5

5.6.1. A simple language consists of four independent and equiprobable symbols A, B, C and D. The symbols are to be transmitted as a sequence of marks and spaces through a binary symmetric channel of error probability 0.1. A, B, C and D are coded as 00, 01, 10 and 11 respectively; each '1' is transmitted as a sequence of three successive marks and each '0' as a sequence of three successive spaces. The receiver interprets each group of three received digits as '1' or '0' on a simple majority basis.

Find the mean error rate for symbols.

5.6.2. (a) English text is to be transmitted via a binary symmetric channel that has a capacity of 50 binary digits per second and a binary error probability of 0.05. A non-redundant five-digit code is to be used for the symbols and punctuation (32 characters). Find the symbol error probability and comment on the quality of the received text.

(b) A single parity digit is added to the above five-digit code and the system arranged such that a detected symbol error automatically leads to the immediate retransmission of that symbol until no error is detected. Find the symbol error probability and the effective rate of transmission of symbols, and comment on the quality of the received text.

5.6.3. (a) A single-error-correcting and double-error-detecting binary Hamming code is required for 32 symbols, comprising letters and punctuation of English. Derive the first five code groups and find the efficiency of your code assuming that the symbols are equiprobable.

(b) The above code is to be used in a binary symmetric channel of error probability 0.01. Find the probabilities of:

  (i) a parity failure

  (ii) two or more errors being detected

  (iii) a symbol error.

6 Introduction to Signal Theory

6.1 Classification of Signals

Information Theory is concerned with the quantification, coding and transmission of information. So far we have discussed the quantification and coding in only rather special cases where we had a set of discrete events, such as the letters of the alphabet. We want to be able to analyse the information content of much more general situations, such as the amplitude modulated sine wave of figure 6.1(a) or the set of samples of a speech waveform of figure 6.1(b). This leads to the study of signals and signal theory.

A dictionary definition of 'signal' is 'a transmitted effect conveying a message'. In the general communication system of figure 1.1 the information to be trans-

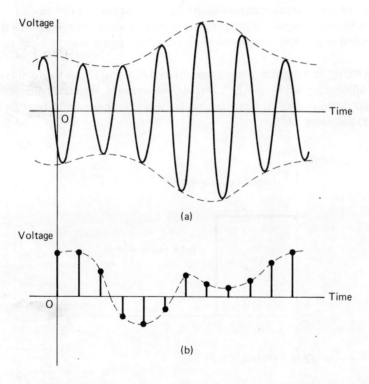

(a)

(b)

Figure 6.1   (a) Amplitude-modulated sine wave, (b) sampled speech signal

51

mitted was known as the *message* and this was encoded and transmitted in the channel as a *signal*. Signal Theory is thus a very basic part of Information Theory; it is concerned with the characteristics and properties of signals, and in particular with their information content.

An essential characteristic of a signal is that of change, since it must be capable of carrying information. We have seen that a stream of digits that are all ones carries no information, and similarly a constant quantity cannot carry information. Signals may be functions of time (temporal signals), as in the electrical signal in a telephone line, or functions of space (spatial signals), as in the case of a newspaper picture. They may be both spatial and temporal, as in a television picture, but the important element in each case is that of change. Most of the signals that we have to deal with will be temporal and although the equations for both temporal and spatial signals are identical in form we will use the notation $f(t)$ for all such signals.

An important classification of signals is into 'finite energy' and 'finite power' signals. The instantaneous power in a signal $f(t)$ is defined as $f^2(t)$. The signal will usually represent either voltage or current, and the units will be mean square volts or mean square current. In Signal Theory such quantities are always collectively referred to as 'power', although the units are usually not Watts. If $f(t)$ represented the percentage transmission of a transparency as a function of position the power would be mean square transmission, or if it represented the distribution of political inclinations in Finchley* the power may be mean square tories.

The energy in a signal in a small time interval δt is $f^2(t)\,\delta t$ so the total energy E over all time is given by $E = \int_{-\infty}^{+\infty} f^2(t)\,dt$. For example, the rectangular pulse of height A and width θ of figure 6.2 has instantaneous power A^2 (from $t = 0$ to $t = \theta$) and energy $A^2\theta$.

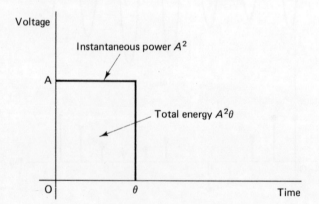

Figure 6.2   Energy in a rectangular pulse

*The constituency of a well-known female politician.

In contrast, the repetitive pulses of figure 6.3 have infinite energy, since each pulse contributes $A^2\theta$ and they are without limit. However, the pulses have a finite mean power $(A^2\theta/T)$ since power is energy per unit time, whereas the single pulse of figure 6.2 has zero mean power. Mean power is formally defined in the next section (6.2).

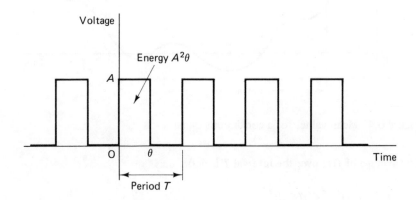

Figure 6.3   Power in an infinite train of pulses

It can be seen that the description of signals in terms of energy or power depends on their form. The most important forms are as follows:

(i) *Discrete* or *Transient* signals have finite energy and zero mean power. They usually last for a finite time, but an exception is an exponentially decaying waveform which in a sense lasts for all time but nevertheless has finite energy.

(ii) *Repetitive* or *Periodic* signals have infinite energy and finite mean power. They last for all time and are referred to as 'determinate' if their defining equations are known (for example, a sine wave).

(iii) *Continuous Random* signals similarly have infinite energy and finite mean power, but their exact amplitude cannot be predicted.

Signals may be analysed in the *time domain*, by considering various types of time average, or in the *frequency domain*, by considering the distribution of power or energy with frequency.

6.2 Time Domain Averages

(a) Finite mean power signals

Consider the continuous signal $f(t)$ shown in figure 6.4.

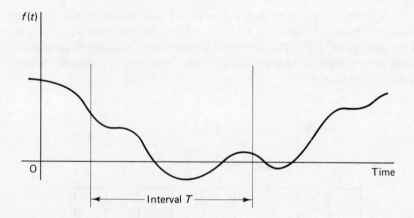

Figure 6.4 Mean values for a continuous signal

The average of $f(t)$ over the interval T is defined as

$$\bar{f}_T = \frac{1}{T} \int_{-T/2}^{T/2} f(t)\, dt$$

and the time average (over all time), known as the *mean value* is

$$\bar{f} = \lim_{T \to \infty} \frac{1}{T} \int_{-T/2}^{T/2} f(t)\, dt$$

For a repetitive waveform of period T_0 it is sufficient to average over only one period; so

$$\bar{f}_{T_0} = \bar{f} = \frac{1}{T_0} \int_{-T_0/2}^{T_0/2} f(t)\, dt$$

The *mean square value* or *mean power* is

$$\overline{f^2} = \lim_{T \to \infty} \frac{1}{T} \int_{-T/2}^{T/2} f^2(t)\, dt$$

$$\left(= \frac{1}{T_0} \int_{-T_0/2}^{T_0/2} f^2(t)\, dt \text{ if periodic} \right)$$

The *instantaneous power* is $f^2(t)$ (as above) so

$$\int_{-T/2}^{T/2} f^2(t)\, dt$$

is the energy in time T and

$$\frac{1}{T} \int_{-T/2}^{T/2} f^2(t)\, dt$$

the power averaged over time T.

The term 'mean power' implies an average over all time.

The *variance* is given by

$$\sigma^2 = \lim_{T \to \infty} \frac{1}{T} \int_{-T/2}^{T/2} (f(t) - \bar{f})^2\, dt$$

$$\left(= \frac{1}{T_0} \int_{-T_0/2}^{T_0/2} (f(t) - \bar{f})^2\, dt \text{ if periodic} \right)$$

$f(t) - \bar{f}$ is the instantaneous difference between $f(t)$ and its mean value $\bar{f}$, so σ^2 represents the mean square deviation from the mean value. The square root of this is usually called the standard deviation. The integral can be expanded into $[f^2(t) - 2f(t)\bar{f} + (\bar{f})^2]$ and it is easy to show that

$$\sigma^2 = \overline{f^2} - (\bar{f})^2$$

The relationship between these three quantities can be seen by considering the detection of a signal represented by a steady voltage in the presence of random noise, as in figure 6.5.

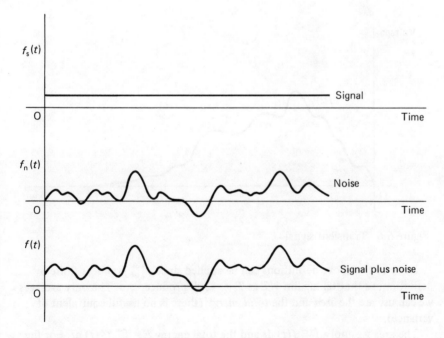

Figure 6.5 Detection of steady signal in noise

If the noise is random it will have a zero mean value. The mean value of $f(t)$ will thus be the required signal. The mean square value will give the total power of signal and noise together, and the variance will give the noise power; that is

$$\text{total power } \overline{f^2} = \text{signal power } (\overline{f})^2 + \text{noise power } \sigma^2$$

EXAMPLE 6.1

Find the mean value, mean square value and variance for a sine wave
$f(t) = A \sin \omega_0 t$.
The mean value f is clearly zero, so $\overline{f^2} = \sigma^2$.

$$\overline{f^2} = \frac{1}{T_0} \int_{-T_0/2}^{T_0/2} (A \sin \omega_0 t)^2 \, dt \quad \text{where } T_0 = \frac{2\pi}{\omega_0}$$

$$= \frac{A^2}{T_0} \int_{-T_0/2}^{T_0/2} (\tfrac{1}{2} - \tfrac{1}{2} \cos 2\omega_0 t) \, dt = A^2/2$$

(b) Finite energy signals

Consider the transient signal $f(t)$ of figure 6.6.

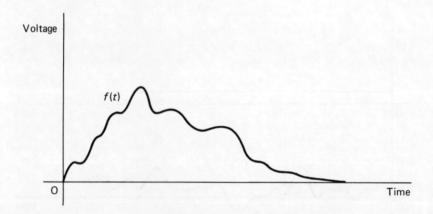

Figure 6.6   Transient signal

None of the above definitions can be applied since $\int_{-\infty}^{+\infty} f(t) \, dt$ is finite by definition, so that taking $\lim 1/T$ as $T \to \infty$ will produce zero. The only averages we can use are the *area* and the *total energy* (there is no useful equivalent of variance).

The area is simply $\int_{-\infty}^{+\infty} f(t) \, dt$ and the total energy $E = \int_0^\infty f^2(t) \, dt$. For the pulse of figure 6.2 the values are $A\theta$ and $A^2\theta$ respectively.

6.3 Frequency Domain Averages

(a) Finite mean power signals

Consider the continuous signal of figure 6.4 again and suppose it is fed to a tuneable filter and mean square meter as in figure 6.7 (most meters measure the root mean square value, but we require the square of this here).

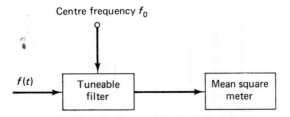

Figure 6.7   Apparatus for measuring power spectrum

We will assume that the filter passes a narrow band of frequencies of bandwidth Δf around a centre frequency f_0, which can be varied over a wide range without affecting Δf, and that the gain is unity.

For a continuous random signal the plot of meter reading versus centre frequency f would be similar to figure 6.8.

If $f(t)$ represented a voltage the units would be mean square volts per bandwidth Δf. The *power spectrum* (sometimes called power spectral density) $P(f)$ is the distribution of mean power per unit bandwidth, with units of mean square volts/Hz in this case. Clearly, the total mean power f^2 (or P) is given by

$$P = \int_0^\infty P(f) \, \mathrm{d}f$$

that is, the integral of $P(f)$ over all frequencies.

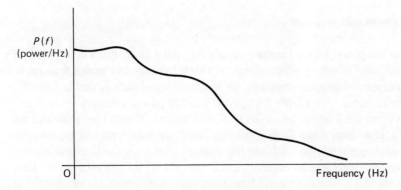

Figure 6.8   Power spectrum of a continuous signal

In the case of a repetitive signal, such as in figure 6.3, the power spectrum is found to consist of discrete lines spaced at multiples of the repetition period T_0, as in figure 6.9.

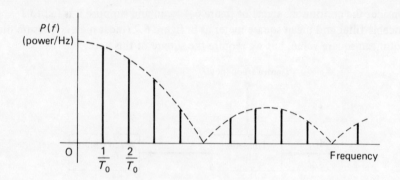

Figure 6.9   Power spectrum of a repetitive signal

The line at zero frequency is simply the square of the mean value, that is, $(A\theta/T_0)^2$, and is known as the zeroth harmonic. That at frequency $1/T_0$ is the fundamental or first harmonic, and that at $2/T_0$ is the second harmonic etc. (Many people confuse the first and second harmonics, particularly those with some musical knowledge. In music the first overtone is actually the second harmonic (for an open tube). Much musical notation appears to be almost designed to confuse or trap the unwary, but it was of course developed prior to Information Theory.)

The total mean power is just the sum of the power P_n in the lines; that is

$$P = \sum_{n=0}^{\infty} P_n$$

(b) Finite energy signals

Since the power is zero for these signals they must be analysed in terms of their distribution of energy with frequency. This is less easy to visualise than for finite power signals. Suppose, however, we imagine a signal such as that in figure 6.6 to be repeated with a fairly long period T_0. The power spectrum for such a repetitive signal would be similar to that in figure 6.9, with lines separated by $1/T_0$. If we now make T_0 progressively longer the waveform will approach the transient signal of figure 6.6 and the separation between the lines will become correspondingly less. In the limit, as $T_0 \to \infty$, the separation between the lines will approach zero and we will have a continuous spectrum. Unfortunately, in the limit, the power spectrum will have a value of zero everywhere! This is, of course, because one cannot analyse a finite energy signal in terms of power.

However, the above approach helps us to see that the *energy* distribution of a finite energy signal must be *continuous*, such as that in figure 6.10. If $f(t)$ represents a voltage the units will be (mean square volts/Hz) × time or mean square volts/(Hz)^2. The square root of the Energy spectrum is called *amplitude density* and has units of root mean square volts/Hz (in this case).

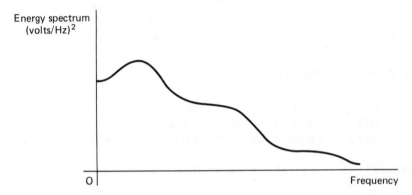

Figure 6.10 Energy spectrum of a discrete signal

Clearly, the total energy E is related to the Energy spectrum $E(f)$ by

$$E = \int_0^{+\infty} E(f)\,\mathrm{d}f$$

6.4 Summary of Time and Frequency Averages

The results deduced above are summarised in table 6.1.

Table 6.1

Type of signal	Time domain	Frequency domain
Repetitive (finite mean power)	$\bar{f} = \dfrac{1}{T_0} \displaystyle\int_{-T_0/2}^{T_0/2} f(t)\,\mathrm{d}t$ etc.	Discrete power spectrum of lines P_n spaced at intervals $1/T_0$. $P = \sum\limits_n P_n$
Continuous random (finite mean power)	$P = \overline{f^2} = \lim\limits_{T \to \infty} \dfrac{1}{T} \displaystyle\int_{-T/2}^{T/2} f^2(t)\,\mathrm{d}t$ etc.	Continuous power spectrum $P(f)$ $P = \int_0^\infty P(f)\,\mathrm{d}f$
Transient (finite energy)	$E = \displaystyle\int_{-\infty}^{+\infty} f^2(t)\,\mathrm{d}t$	Continuous energy spectrum $E(f)$ $E = \int_0^\infty E(f)\,\mathrm{d}f$

It is important to note that the simple time averages introduced here do not give any information about the frequency content of the signals that they describe. More advanced time averages, which do not have this limitation, are discussed in chapter 8. In addition, both the time domain averages and the frequency domain averages so far considered are in no sense unique to a particular signal, since many different signals could have the same mean value or power spectrum. However, a unique relation between the time domain and frequency domain representations of signals does exist, and is introduced in chapter 9.

6.5   Exercises on Chapter 6

6.5.1. Figure 6.11 shows a repetitive triangular waveform.
　　　　(i) Find the area and total energy of one pulse of the waveform.
　　　　(ii) Find the mean, mean square and variance of the repetitive waveform.

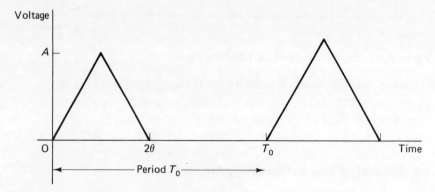

Figure 6.11   Repetitive triangular waveform

6.5.2. Figure 6.12 shows a pseudo-random binary sequence which repeats after a period T_0. Find the mean value, mean square value and variance, and discuss (and sketch) the form of its power spectrum.

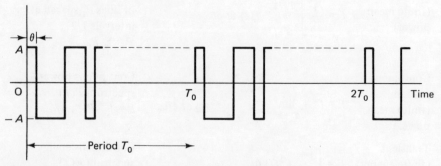

Figure 6.12   Repetitive pseudo-random sequence

7 Electrical Noise

7.1 Types of Electrical Noise

Random electrical noise occurs in any practical information transmission system. Although its general characteristics such as mean square value and power spectrum may be known, its essential characteristic is that its value at any instant (amplitude or frequency) is unpredictable. Electrical noise can, of course, be considered to be a signal, and is capable of carrying information; in fact it will be shown later that noise-like waveforms have the greatest information capacity. However, in practical systems electrical noise is an unwanted signal, producing errors or changes in amplitude of the wanted signal, and reducing the overall information transfer.

(i) Johnson noise

Johnson noise is the most basic type of electrical noise. It was discovered by Johnson (1928) and the expression for its power spectrum deduced by Nyquist (1928). Johnson noise occurs in any device that dissipates power, such as a resistor, but since all devices have some resistance (for example, capacitors, inductors, transistors) its occurrence is universal. It is the electrical equivalent of mechanical Brownian motion, and the defining equations are identical in form.

The Principle of Equipartition of Energy states that the mean kinetic energy of each degree of freedom of a system in thermal equilibrium with its surroundings in $\frac{1}{2}kT$, where k = Boltzmann's constant (1.4×10^{-23} J/K) and T is the absolute temperature. The electrons in a conductor thus have a mean square velocity (in one direction) that is dependent on temperature and given by $\frac{1}{2}m\overline{v^2} = \frac{1}{2}kT$. Since an electron is a charged particle, a moving electron constitutes a current and Johnson noise is the net effect, at any instant, of the current pulses due to all the electrons in the conductor.

The process is actually rather more subtle than this. An electron moving through the conductor with a velocity V produces a steady current eV. Other electrons moving in different directions with different velocities similarly produce steady currents, and the net effect of all these currents would average zero. However, the essential point is that electrons do not flow freely through conductors; they collide with the crystal lattice and in doing so change their velocities. Johnson noise is the net effect of the *current pulses due to collisions*, as illustrated in figure 7.1. The mean value averages to zero but the mean square value does not. In a perfect conductor there would be no collisions and no noise; however, collisions with the crystal lattice are the mechanism whereby thermal equilibrium is achieved, so a perfect conductor could not attain thermal equili-

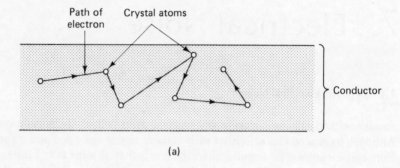

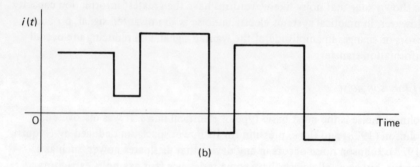

Figure 7.1   (a) Movement of electron in crystal lattice, (b) current pulses corresponding to (a)

brium in any case. It can be said that dissipation is the cause of fluctuations, since thermal equilibrium occurs via dissipation and fluctuations result from it.

It can be shown that the power spectrum (in mean square volts) for the Johnson noise in a resistor R is given by

$$P_v(f) = 4RkT$$

This is constant up to very high frequencies, and is referred to as *white noise*, since it contains all frequencies, in analogy to white light, which contains all colours.

(ii) Shot noise

Shot noise is less universal than Johnson noise, but occurs in diodes and hence in transistors, so in practice it is often the main source of noise. It was first studied in thermionic diodes, in which the emission of electrons from the cathode is a random process, so that the number of electrons reaching the anode per second fluctuates about its mean value. The effect occurs similarly in semiconductor diodes, since the passage of an electron across the potential barrier in a p-n diode is again a statistical process, leading to a fluctuation in the current. The expression for the power spectrum (in terms of mean square current) is

$$P_i(f) = 2\,e\,I$$

where I is the mean current and e the electronic charge (1.6×10^{-19} C).

The spectrum is again constant up to very high frequencies. Unlike Johnson noise, Shot noise depends specifically on the magnitude of e. If electricity were continuous there would be no Shot noise, but the formula for Johnson noise would be unchanged.

(iii) 1/f noise

It is found that most semiconductor devices produce more noise, particularly at low frequencies, than is predicted by Johnson or Shot noise. This is attributed to $1/f$ noise, which has a power spectrum inversely proportional to frequency, given by

$$P_v(f) = K\,\frac{I^2}{f}$$

in which I is the current in the device and K is a constant that depends on the device. A number of theories have been put forward to account for $1/f$ noise, but there is no satisfactory single quantitative explanation. The effect does not occur in pure metals, but has been observed over many decades of frequency in semi-conductors. It is apparently due to fluctuations in the numbers of electrons in the conduction band and 'queueing' theories have been favoured.

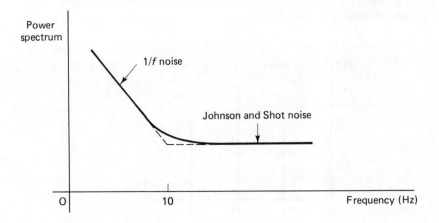

Figure 7.2   Noise power spectrum of operational amplifier

The formula is a little disturbing in that it predicts infinite noise at zero frequency. In practice, of course, one is rarely interested in averaging over periods greater than a few seconds, and even a day (10^5 s or 10^{-5} Hz) is far from zero frequency. Interestingly, $1/f$ noise has the property that the noise power in equal frequency ratios (decades, octaves etc.) is the same, unlike white noise where the power is the same in equal intervals. There is therefore five times as much $1/f$ noise between 1 Hz and 10^{-5} Hz as between 10 Hz and 1 Hz. A power spectrum for the noise from a typical operational amplifier is shown in figure 7.2.

7.2 Probability Distributions

Our particular interest in random noise is in determining its effect on the transmission of information; this requires a determination of the error rate due to noise, which involves a discussion of the probability distributions for noise. This section is equally applicable to signals, of course.

7.2.1 Discrete probability distributions

(i) The binomial distribution

We have already met this distribution in chapter 4, where we saw that in a process with two outcomes p (for success) and $\bar{p}$ (for failure) the probability of r successes in n trials is given by the $(r + 1)^{\text{th}}$ term of the binomial expansion of $(\bar{p} + p)^n$; that is

$$p(r) = \frac{n!}{(n-r)!\, r!}\, p^r\, \bar{p}^{(n-r)}$$

A plot of $p(r)$ versus r is called a probability distribution, and figure 7.3 is the distribution for $p = \bar{p} = \frac{1}{2}, n = 4$.

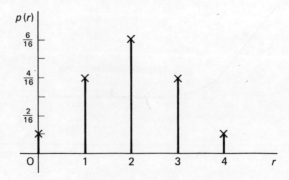

Figure 7.3   Binomial probability distribution for $p = 1/2, n = 4$

The *mean value* $\bar{r}$ of the distribution is the average number of successes. Clearly $\bar{r} = \Sigma r\, p(r) = np$.

The *mean square value* $\overline{r^2}$ can be shown to be

$$\overline{r^2} = \Sigma r^2\, p(r) = \bar{r}^2 + np\bar{p}$$

and the variance $\sigma^2 = \Sigma(r - \bar{r})^2\, p(r) = np\bar{p}\ (= \overline{r^2} - (\bar{r})^2$ as before).

(*Note:* The relation between these averages and the time averages of the same name discussed in chapter 6 will be deduced later.)

EXAMPLE 7.1

A random sample of 900 persons are asked 'Have you heard of Information Technology?'. Find the mean, mean square and variance of the expected distribution, assuming that over the whole population exactly one-third of the people would answer 'yes'. Comment on the result.

The mean value

$$\bar{r} = \tfrac{1}{3}.900 = 300$$

Similarly

$$\overline{r^2} = (900)^2.(\tfrac{1}{3})^2 + 900.\tfrac{1}{3}.\tfrac{2}{3} = 90200$$

and

$$\sigma^2 = 900.\tfrac{1}{3}.\tfrac{2}{3} = 200$$

The standard deviation is $\sqrt{200} \approx 14$. This is the order of the error to be expected statistically between the 'true' value (300) and the actual experimental value. Strictly, if many such samples were carried out the mean would be in the range 300 ± 14 for 68 per cent of the samples. Expressed as a percentage of the mean value, the error is just less than ± 5 per cent. This tends to undermine one's confidence in opinion polls (if one had any), where a swing of 5 per cent is hailed as a major event.

(ii) The Poisson distribution

It can be shown that if p is very small and n very large, the expression for $p(r)$ can be rewritten in the form

$$p(r) = \frac{\exp(-(\bar{r}))\,(\bar{r})^r}{r!}, \text{ depending on } \bar{r} \text{ only}$$

[It is a little surprising that the exponential (exp) should suddenly appear, but the proof involves replacing the factorials by a power series approximation and comparing the resulting series with that for $\exp(-(\bar{r}))$.]

The most relevant property of the Poisson distribution is that since p is very small $\bar{p}$ is very nearly unity so the variance $\sigma^2 = np = \bar{r}$; that is, the variance is equal to the mean value.

The Poisson distribution applies to many physical phenomena, such as radio-active decay, in which n (the number of atoms) is very large but p (the probability of a given atom decaying in a given time) is very low. In particular, it applies to Shot noise in diodes, since there are many electrons with a small probability of crossing the potential barrier.

EXAMPLE 7.2

Over a given period there are 10^6 cars on the roads, and the probability* of a given car having an accident is 10^{-4}. Find the mean number of accidents and the variance.

$$\bar{r} = np = 10^6 . 10^{-4} = 100$$

$$\sigma^2 = \bar{r^2} = 100 \text{ so the standard deviation is } 10$$

An increase of 10 per cent in the accident rate over a given period is apparently not necessarily indicative of any real effect, though such figures usually excite many media commentators and politicians.

(iii) The gaussian distribution

If the number of trials n becomes very large, without p necessarily being small, $p(r)$ can be written in the form

$$p(r) = \frac{1}{\sigma\sqrt{2\pi}} \ \exp\left(-\frac{(r-\bar{r})^2}{2\sigma^2}\right)$$

depending only on the variance σ^2.

One of the first practical applications of the gaussian distribution was that it was found to apply to the chest sizes of London guardsmen. It was then found to apply to many other physical characteristics and was soon thought to have some divine significance, though this view has declined somewhat in recent years. It was also found to apply to experimental errors, for example in the repeated measurement of some supposedly fixed quantity.

An explanation of its application to these two apparently different processes is that a given physical characteristic or experimental measurement can be thought of as being due to many small effects (for example, many different genetic factors or many small sources of error). The particular observed value is a particular selection from a binomial distribution (say r factors producing a tall person and $(n - r)$ tending to produce a short one), the gaussian being a special case of the binomial for large n.

*This rather low value is for male drivers over 25 only.

A similar argument applies to Johnson noise. There are many electrons moving in different directions and the observed noise at an instant depends on how many are moving one way and how many the other way (it also depends on their velocities, of course). The amplitude of Johnson noise follows a gaussian distribution, as expected.

Although we have introduced the gaussian distribution as a discrete distribution, it occurs frequently as a continuous distribution. Such distributions occur in many practical situations and will now be considered.

7.2.2 Continuous probability distributions

(i) Probability density

Suppose we sample the waveform of figure 7.4(a) with a digital voltmeter, taking a reading with a resolution of say 0.1 V in a time short compared with the rate of change of the waveform. We could produce a histogram giving the number of readings n_x versus range x as in figure 7.4(b). If we plot n_x/n, where n is the total number of readings, and let n become very large, our ordinate will represent the probability of getting a reading in a given range. The plot will become more symmetrical as n increases, but still jagged to an extent depending on the range interval. Of course, if we reduce the interval δx to 0.01 V or 0.001 V the plot will become more smooth, but will tend to disappear since n_x/n becomes very small. To avoid this, we can divide n_x/n by the interval δx, and let n tend to infinity and δx tend to zero. This process is shown in figure 7.4(b).

The resulting smooth curve is a plot of probability density $p(x)$ versus value x. The definition of $p(x)$ is

$$p(x) = \lim_{\substack{n \to \infty \\ \delta x \to 0}} \frac{n_x}{n} \cdot \frac{1}{\delta x}$$

Clearly $p(x).\delta x$ is the probability of a reading being in a small range δx, and the probability of a reading between two values x_1 and x_2 is

$$p(x_1 < x < x_2) = \int_{x_1}^{x_2} p(x)\, dx$$

Since any reading must have a value between $x = -\infty$ and $x = +\infty$

$$\int_{-\infty}^{+\infty} p(x)\, dx = 1$$

that is, the area under the curve is unity.

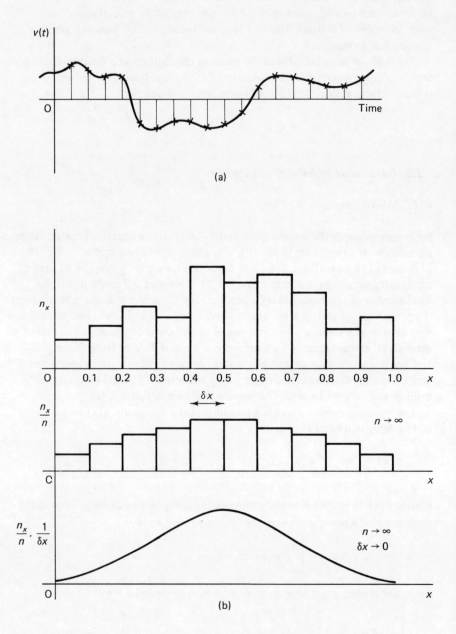

Figure 7.4   (a) Sampled waveform, (b) histograms and probability density distribution

Similar expressions to those above for the mean, mean square and variance apply. Referring to figure 7.5

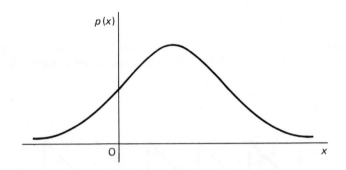

Figure 7.5   Probability density distribution

$$\bar{x} = \int_{-\infty}^{+\infty} x\,p(x)\,\mathrm{d}x$$

$$\overline{x^2} = \int_{-\infty}^{+\infty} x^2\,p(x)\,\mathrm{d}x$$

$$\sigma^2 = \int_{-\infty}^{+\infty} (x - \bar{x})^2\,p(x)\,\mathrm{d}x = \overline{x^2} - (\bar{x})^2$$

The *mode* is the value of x corresponding to maximum $p(x)$ and the *median* is the value of x dividing the plot into equal areas. The reason that we have to work in terms of probability density when dealing with continuous processes is that the probability of getting an exact value (for example, a reading of 1.100000001 V) tends to zero. Similarly, the probability of a man having a height of exactly 1.888888 m is very small. We therefore have to use the notion of probability density, and the probability of getting a value in a given range is given by the integral of $p(x)$ over this range, as above.

An expression for the probability density of a continuous waveform can be derived by noting that a waveform spends less time near a given value the greater its rate of change. It can be shown that

$$p(x) = \frac{1}{\text{slope}} \cdot \frac{1}{\text{period}}$$

though this has to be used with some care.

EXAMPLE 7.3

Deduce the probability density for the sawtooth waveform of figure 7.6(a).
Considering the waveform from 0 to T_0, the slope is A/T_0 so

$$p(x) = \frac{T_0}{A} \cdot \frac{1}{T_0} = \frac{1}{A}$$

The maximum value of amplitude is A, so $p(x)$ has the form shown in figure
7.6(b). This could be deduced intuitively in this case since the waveform moves

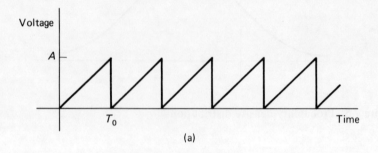

(a)

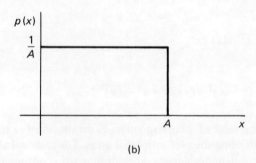

(b)

Figure 7.6   Sawtooth waveform (a) and its probability density distribution (b)

smoothly through all values between 0 and A. This is known as a *uniform*
distribution; triangular waves have the same distribution.

(ii) Important continuous distributions

(a) The gaussian distribution   A continuous gaussian distribution is shown in
figure 7.7

$$p(x) = \frac{1}{\sigma\sqrt{2\pi}} \exp\left(-(x - \bar{x})^2/2\sigma^2\right)$$

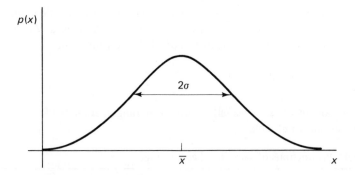

Figure 7.7   Gaussian distribution

The distribution is bell-shaped and symmetrical about its mean value $\bar{x}$. The width between the points of inflexion is 2σ. Since the amplitude of random noise has this distribution it is important to be able to calculate the probability that the noise exceeds a given value. Random noise has a zero mean value, so $\bar{x} = 0$ hence $\overline{x^2} = \sigma^2$ and $p(x) = (1/\sigma\sqrt{2\pi}) \exp(-x^2/2\sigma^2)$.

The probability that a given sample x exceeds a fixed value x_0 is given by

$$p(x > x_0) = \int_{x_0}^{\infty} p(x)\, dx = \int_{x_0}^{\infty} \frac{1}{\sigma\sqrt{2\pi}} \exp(-x^2/2\sigma^2)\, dx$$

and is represented by the shaded area in figure 7.8.

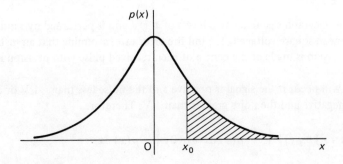

Figure 7.8   Probability of exceeding a given level for a gaussian distribution

Putting $t^2 = x^2/\sigma^2$ so $dt = dx/\sigma$

$$p(x > x_0) = \frac{1}{\sqrt{2\pi}} \int_{t_0}^{\infty} \exp(-t^2/2)\, dt$$

This integral cannot be evaluated in closed form (that is, in a simple expression containing functions of t) and numerical methods have to be used. Values are available in standard tables (Howatson *et al.*, 1972) usually in the form

$$\frac{1}{\sqrt{2\pi}} \int_{-\infty}^{x} \exp\left(-t^2/2\right) \mathrm{d}t$$

The proportions of samples falling into given ranges, evaluated from the above formula, are shown in table 7.1.

Table 7.1 Proportions of samples in given ranges

Range	Proportion within range	Proportion outside range
$\pm\,\sigma$	0.68	0.32
$\pm\,2\,\sigma$	0.95	0.05
$\pm\,3\,\sigma$	0.997	0.003
$\pm\,1.96\,\sigma$	95 per cent	5 per cent
$\pm\,2.58\,\sigma$	99 per cent	1 per cent
$\pm\,3.29\,\sigma$	99.9 per cent	0.1 per cent

When discussing the properties of noise one usually considers the range as an integral number times σ, whereas in specifying the accuracy of an experimental result one quotes *confidence limits*, being the range required such that, say, 95 per cent of values are within it.

EXAMPLE 7.4

A random telegraph signal has two levels of ± 1 V and is perturbed by random noise of mean square voltage 0.1. Find the error rate, assuming that an instantaneous decision is made at the centre of each received pulse with decision level zero.

An error will occur if the signal is positive and the noise less than -1 V or if the signal is negative and the noise greater than 1 V. Therefore

$$p(\text{error}) = p(1) \int_{-\infty}^{-1} p(x)\,\mathrm{d}x + p(0) \int_{1}^{\infty} p(x)\,\mathrm{d}x$$

$$= (p(0) + p(1)) \int_{-\infty}^{1} p(x)\,\mathrm{d}x$$

$$= \int_{-\infty}^{1} p(x)\,\mathrm{d}x$$

Proceeding as above, with $t = x/\sigma$ and $\sigma = 0.316$ (since $\sigma^2 = \overline{x}^2 = 0.1$)

$$p(\text{error}) = \frac{1}{\sqrt{2\pi}} \int_{-\infty}^{3.16} \exp(-t^2/2)\, dt$$

Using standard tables we find $p(\text{error}) = 8 \times 10^{-4}$.
(Note that $p(\text{error})$ is independent of $p(0)$ and $p(1)$, this being a binary symmetric system.)

This corresponds to a root mean square signal-to-noise (S/N) ratio of 3.16. The error rate falls very rapidly with increasing S/N and is sufficiently low for most practical applications with $\text{S/N} \approx 10$.

(b) The Rayleigh distribution When random noise is fed to a band-pass filter such that the ratio of centre frequency to bandwidth is greater than about ten, the resulting noise is known as narrow band noise and has the appearance of an amplitude-modulated sine wave as shown in figure 7.9(a).

The noise appears to have a constant frequency but its amplitude fluctuates. The instantaneous amplitude is known as the *envelope*, denoted by the dotted lines. It can be shown that the envelope follows a Rayleigh distribution, given by

$$p(x) = \frac{x}{\sigma^2} \exp\left(-x^2/2\sigma^2\right)$$

which is shown in figure 7.9(b).

The distribution is similar to the gaussian, but is not symmetrical (since the envelope cannot be less than zero but has no upper limit). It can be shown to be formed by the product of two gaussians. The distribution is important in communication systems, such as amplitude modulation, in which the envelope of a sine wave carries the information, since noise then perturbs the envelope.

(c) The uniform distribution It can be shown that the phase distribution of narrow band noise is *uniform*, as shown in figure 7.9(c).

An instantaneous measurement of phase (by comparison with a fixed sine wave) will give any value between $\pm \pi$ with equal probability.

7.3 Time and Ensemble Averages

The averages that we have dealt with in this chapter are known as *ensemble averages*, as opposed to the *time averages* that we considered in chapter 6. Using the previous notation in each case and considering a continuous random function

$$\text{Ensemble average: } \bar{x} = \int_{-\infty}^{+\infty} x\, p(x)\, dx \text{ etc.}$$

$$\text{Time average: } \bar{f} = \lim_{T \to \infty} \frac{1}{T} \int_{-T/2}^{T/2} f(t)\, dt \text{ etc.}$$

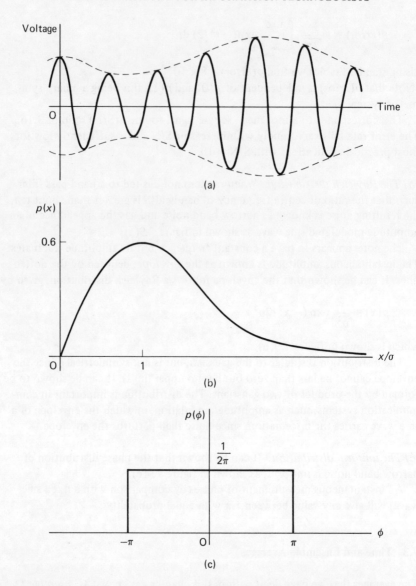

Figure 7.9   (a) Narrow band noise, (b) Rayleigh distribution, (c) uniform distribution

Both averages should clearly give the same result if applied to the same signal, and the relation between them can be seen by considering the Johnson noise produced by an infinite set of nominally identical resistors, as shown in figure 7.10.

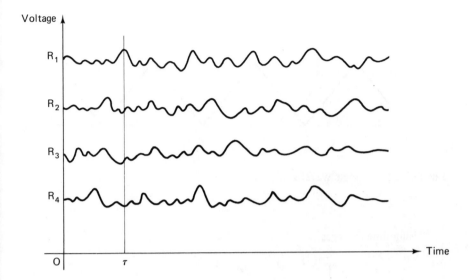

Figure 7.10 Noise waveforms from a set of 'identical' resistors

The ensemble average is effectively obtained from *the complete set* of resistors at any time τ; the voltages produce a probability density distribution from which $\bar{x}$ is evaluated. The time average is obtained from *any one resistor* in the set, averaging over all time. Clearly, the two values will be the same.

EXAMPLE 7.5

Find the mean, mean square and variance for (i) a sine wave, (ii) random noise and (iii) a triangle wave, using time averages or ensemble averages as appropriate.

(i) Sine wave. Since the equation for a sine wave is $x = a \sin \omega_0 t$ it is easier to use a time average. We obtain $\bar{x} = 0, \overline{x^2} = \sigma^2 = a^2/2$ as before. (*Note:* see exercise 7.5.4, in which an ensemble average is used.)

(ii) Random noise. $x(t)$ cannot be predicted in this case, so we have to use an ensemble average.

$$p(x) = \frac{1}{\sigma\sqrt{2\pi}} \exp(-x^2/2\sigma^2)$$

so $\bar{x} = 0, \overline{x^2} = \sigma^2$.

(iii) Triangle wave. Using the waveform of figure 7.11, $x(t)$ is given by

$$x = \frac{A}{T_0/2} \cdot t \quad \text{from 0 to } \frac{T_0}{2}$$

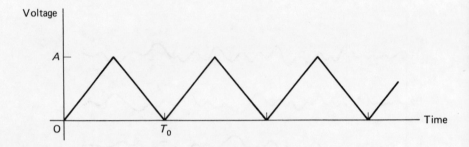

Figure 7.11   Triangle waveform

Using time averages

$$\bar{x} = \frac{1}{T_0/2} \int_0^{T_0/2} \frac{A}{T_0/2}\, t\, \mathrm{d}t = \frac{A}{2}$$

and similarly

$$\overline{x^2} = \frac{A^2}{3}$$

However, we can also use an ensemble average since $p(x) = 1/A$

$$\bar{x} = \int_0^A \frac{1}{A}\, x\, \mathrm{d}x = \frac{A}{2}, \ \overline{x^2} = \frac{A^2}{3}$$

7.4   Summary of the Properties of Electrical Noise

7.4.1   Time and frequency domains

The essential nature of electrical noise is that it is unpredictable in the time domain, its amplitude following a gaussian distribution; in the frequency domain it is white, that is, its power spectrum is constant. These two properties are really different ways of saying the same thing; unpredictability in the time domain implies flatness in the frequency domain, and vice versa. If the spectrum was not flat, but fell away at higher frequencies, it would be possible to predict accurately the amplitude a short time ahead. Of course, the spectrum does fall away eventually, otherwise the total power would be infinite, but for practical purposes it is considered to be flat.

Another way of looking at predictability is afforded by the concept of the autocorrelation of a waveform, introduced in the next chapter.

7.4.2 Representation of noise

Figure 7.12 shows the power spectrum of random noise, divided into strips, each of width δf.

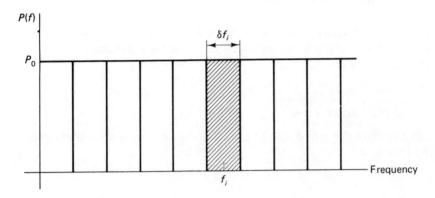

Figure 7.12   Power spectrum of random noise

One way of representing noise mathematically is to replace each strip by a single sinusoidal oscillator whose frequency is that of the centre of the strip and whose amplitude is equivalent to the power in the strip.

Thus, the ith strip is represented by an oscillator $a_i \cos(\omega_i t + \phi_i)$, where $\frac{1}{2}a^2_i = P_0 \delta f_i$, ϕ_i being the (random) phase. The noise waveform can be written as $v_n(t) = \Sigma a_i \cos(\omega_i t + \phi_i)$ and since all the amplitudes a_i are the same

$$v_n(t) = (2P_0 \delta f_i)^{\frac{1}{2}} \sum_i \cos(\omega_i t + \phi_i)$$

The effect of noise on a system can be found by combining the effects of sine waves over the required range of frequencies.

A more useful representation for narrow band noise can be obtained from this expression by writing the frequency of the ith strip as $f_i = f_0 + i\delta f_i$ and expanding $\sin(\omega_i t + \phi_i)$. The resulting expression can be written as

$$v_n(t) = r(t) \cos(\omega_0 t + \phi(t))$$

where $r(t)$ involves a summation but is in fact just the envelope of the noise discussed above, so $r(t)$ is Rayleigh distributed and $\phi(t)$ uniform. A further representation deducible from this is

$$v_n(t) = x(t) \cos \omega_0 t + y(t) \sin \omega_0 t$$

where $x(t)$ and $y(t)$ again involve summations, but are both gaussian distributed.

The importance of these two representations is that they involve only a single frequency f_0 (the centre frequency of the filter) so the effect of noise on a system can be found very easily. For example, if noise represented by the second equation is added to a sinusoidal carrier $a \cos \omega_0 t$, then $x(t)$ produces amplitude errors and $y(t)$ produces phase (or frequency) errors.

7.4.3 Addition of random generators

When two independent sources of noise are added, it is the mean square values which add, in contrast to two signal sources where the root mean square values are added. That is

Noise sources   : $\overline{v}^2_{\text{sum}} = \overline{v}^2_1 + \overline{v}^2_2$

Signal sources   : $\sqrt{\overline{v}^2_{\text{sum}}} = \sqrt{\overline{v}^2_1} + \sqrt{\overline{v}^2_2}$

The reason for this can be seen by considering the two noise sources of figure 7.13.

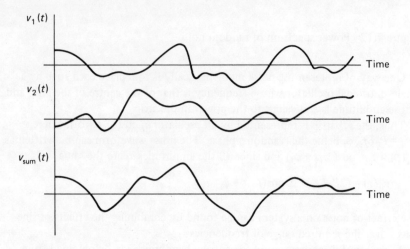

Figure 7.13   Waveforms of two independent noise sources

The instantaneous sum $v_{\text{sum}}(t) = v_1(t) + v_2(t)$. The mean square value is

$$\overline{v}^2_{\text{sum}} = \overline{v}^2_1 + \overline{v}^2_2 + 2\overline{v_1 v_2}$$

Since the noise sources are independent, the cross term $2\overline{v_1 v_2}$ averages to zero. However, for two signals of the same frequency and phase (but different amplitudes, say), $2\overline{v_1 v_2}$ would not be zero (the contributions at all times would be positive), so we would find $\overline{v}^2_{\text{sum}} = ((\overline{v}^2_1)^{\frac{1}{2}} + (\overline{v}^2_2)^{\frac{1}{2}})^2$; that is, the root mean square values add.

Noise sources are said to be *incoherent* and signal sources *coherent*.

EXAMPLE 7.6

A thermionic diode is connected in series with a resistor of 10 kΩ and carries a current of 0.1 mA, as shown in figure 7.14. Find the noise voltage at the output in a bandwidth of 1 MHz.

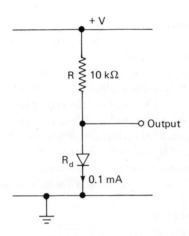

Figure 7.14   Diode and resistor network for noise analysis

The resistor produces Johnson noise $4RkT\Delta f$ in bandwidth Δf. Taking $kT = 4 \times 10^{-21}$ J at room temperature, $\overline{v}_J{}^2 = 4 \times 10^4 . 4 \times 10^{-21} . 10^6$

$$= 1.6 \times 10^{-10} \text{ V}^2$$

The diode produces a Shot noise current, which flows through the resistor, so the voltage produced is $\overline{v}_S{}^2 = 2eI\Delta f.R^2$

$$= 2. \ 1.6 \times 10^{-19} . 10^{-4} . 10^6 . 10^8$$
$$= 3.2 \times 10^{-9} \text{ V}^2$$

The total noise, the sum of the mean square values, is 3.4×10^{-9} V^2 or about 5.9×10^{-5} V root mean square.

Note: It may appear rather academic to consider a thermionic diode, which is little used in practice now. However, the reason for doing so is to simplify the calculations since the Johnson and Shot noise can be directly added. A thermionic diode has a very high impedance so that the noise voltages are measured across the 10 kΩ resistor. In contrast, a semiconductor diode has a low impedance (250 Ω at a current of 0.1 mA), so the noise voltage is determined by this small value, and is much smaller (see exercise 7.5.4).

7.5 Exercises on Chapter 7

7.5.1.   (i) Explain why Johnson noise increases with temperature. Does it occur at absolute zero?

(ii) Does Johnson noise depend on the direct current flowing in a resistor? Does it occur in semiconductors?

(iii) Does Shot noise depend on the current, on the temperature or on both in a semiconductor diode? Does Shot noise occur in a resistor carrying direct current?

7.5.2. A probability density distribution is given by $p(x) = a \exp(- |x|/b)$, where a and b are constants.

(i) Find the mean, mean square and variance in terms of b.

(ii) Noise having this distribution is added to a random binary telegraph signal of amplitude $\pm V$. Find the error probability, assuming the decision level is zero, and sketch as a function of V.

7.5.3. Many full-wave rectifier meters are calibrated so that the indicated root mean square value is correct for sine wave inputs. Find the ratio between the mean modulus and the root mean square value of a sine wave and hence deduce the percentage error when such a meter is used for the measurement of

(i) square waves and

(ii) gaussian noise.

Note: The mean modulus $|x|$ is the mean value *ignoring the sign.*

7.5.4. (a) Find and sketch the probability density amplitude distributions for a square wave, a triangle wave and a sine wave.

(b) Find the mean square values of these functions (i) as an ensemble average and (ii) as a time average.

7.5.5. Repeat *example 7.6* but using a semiconductor diode instead of the thermionic diode. What would be the effect on the noise if the current was increased by a factor of 10 for (i) the thermionic diode and (ii) the semiconductor diode?

(*Note:* The resistance of a silicon diode is 25 Ω at 1 mA, 250 Ω at 0.1 mA etc.)

8 Time Domain Properties of Signals

8.1 Correlation

In chapter 6 we saw that the simple time domain averages – the mean, mean square and variance – do not provide any information about the frequency content of signals; also, they do not uniquely specify a particular signal, since many different signals may have the same mean or mean square value. The process of correlation overcomes the first of these limitations, but not the second.

The general form of the correlation function between two signals $f_1(t)$ and $f_2(t)$ (which may, as a special case, be identical) is

$$f(\tau) = \int_{-\infty}^{+\infty} f_1(t) f_2(t + \tau)\, dt \quad \text{(finite energy signals)}$$

or

$$f(\tau) = \lim_{T \to \infty} \frac{1}{T} \int_{-T/2}^{T/2} f_1(t) f_2(t + \tau)\, dt \quad \text{(finite mean power signals)}$$

The representation $f(t + \tau)$ denotes a time-shifted version of a function $f(t)$, τ being the amount of shift. This idea is very important and is illustrated in figure 8.1 which shows a function $f(t)$ together with shifted versions of the same signal $f(t + \tau_1)$ and $f(t - \tau_2)$. The left-hand edge of $f(t + \tau_1)$ occurs earlier in time than the same edge of $f(t)$, so $f(t + \tau_1)$ is said to be *advanced* by τ_1; similarly $f(t - \tau_2)$ is *delayed* by τ_2.

It is easy to remember the sense of shift by sketching graphs of $y = t$, $y = t + 1$, $y = t - 1$ as shown in figure 8.2, when it can be seen that $f(t + 1)$ is just $f(t)$

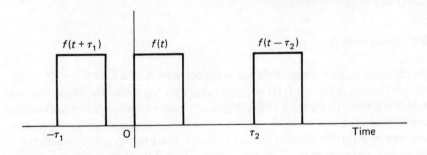

Figure 8.1 Delayed and advanced pulses

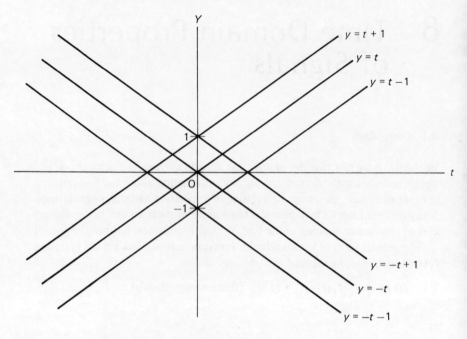

Figure 8.2 Delayed, advanced and reversed signals

shifted left (that is, advanced). Alternatively, plotting $y = -t$, $y = -t + 1$, $y = -t - 1$, shows that $f(-t)$ is the mirror image (in the y-axis) of $f(t)$ and that the shifts for $f(-t)$ are reversed in sense.

The meaning of the expression for correlation is thus that a function $f_1(t)$ is multiplied by a shifted version of a second function $f_2(t)$ and the result integrated over all time. This yields a particular value of the function $f(\tau)$ corresponding to the shift used, and $f(\tau)$ is just the set of values for all possible shifts.

We will confine our attention mainly to finite energy signals (partly because they are easier to sketch), though the equations and properties of finite mean power signals correspond exactly, of course.

8.2 Autocorrelation

As the name implies, autocorrelation is the correlation of a function with itself, so that the two functions $f_1(t)$ and $f_2(t)$ above are the same. The autocorrelation function provides a measure of the degree to which a future value of the function can be predicted, and is closely related to the energy spectrum of the signal. It is denoted by $R(\tau)$ (finite mean power) or $R_1(\tau)$ (finite energy), or alternatively by $\phi_{11}(\tau)$, and is given by $R_1(\tau) = \phi_{11}(\tau) = \int_{-\infty}^{+\infty} f(t) f(+\tau)\, dt$.

The correlation process is often denoted by ✪ so $\phi_{11}(\tau) = f_1 ✪ f_1$.

EXAMPLE 8.1

The autocorrelation of a rectangular pulse.

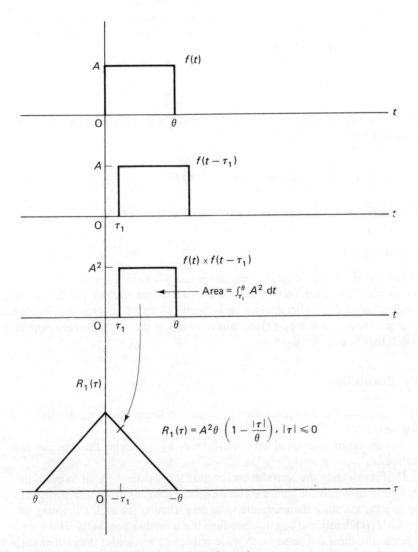

Figure 8.3 Autocorrelation of a rectangular pulse

The shift τ_1 shown produces a single point on the graph of $R_1(\tau)$. If the procedure is repeated for all τ, the complete function $R_1(\tau)$ is obtained. One simply imagines moving $f(t)$ over itself to the right and left, and plots below the area obtained at each shift. Since a shift left represents delay $(-\tau)$ it is easier to plot $R_1(\tau)$ with its axes reversed, that is, $-\tau$ to the right.

It is clear that $R_1(\tau)$ is always an even function (since shifting one version of $f(t)$ to the right is the same as shifting another version to the left). Also, $R_1(0)$ is the total energy (or mean power $\overline{f^2}$ for mean power signals).

It can easily be seen that $R(\tau)$ for a d.c. level is another d.c. level (implying perfect prediction), $R(\tau)$ for a sine wave is a cosine wave, and $R(\tau)$ for random noise is an impulse (zero prediction).

8.3 Cross-correlation

The cross-correlation function measures the similarity between two functions $f_1(t)$ and $f_2(t)$, and is given by

$$\phi_{12}(\tau) = \int_{-\infty}^{+\infty} f_1(t) f_2(t + \tau)\, \mathrm{d}t = f_1 \bigstar f_2$$

The order *does* matter here, so $f_1 \bigstar f_2$ means that f_2 is to be shifted.

EXAMPLE 8.2

The cross-correlation of two rectangular pulses is shown in figure 8.4.
As for autocorrelation, one function is slid to the right and left and the resulting area evaluated, $\phi_{12}(\tau)$ being most conveniently plotted with axes reversed. It can be seen that $\phi_{12}(\tau)$ and $\phi_{21}(\tau)$ are mirror images in the y-axis; this is a general result, that is, $\phi_{12}(\tau) = \phi_{21}(-\tau)$.

8.4 Convolution

The expression for the convolution between two finite energy signals $f_1(t)$ and $f_2(t)$ is $c_1(\tau) = \int_{-\infty}^{+\infty} f_1(t) f_2(-t + \tau)\, \mathrm{d}t$.

The operation is denoted by $*$ so $c_1(\tau) = f_1 * f_2$, f_2 being the function to be shifted.

On first meeting the convolution function it is a little difficult to avoid the thought that it must be a pure mathematician's delight (pure mathematicians have curious tastes), since there appears to be no particular reason for choosing to reverse $f_2(t)$ before shifting it, other than it is a further·possibility. However, convolution turns out to be much more important and useful than either auto-correlation or cross-correlation, and even better, its properties are relatively simple. Convolution is best thought of as a 'blurring' of one function by another.

EXAMPLE 8.3

The convolution of two rectangular pulses (the same two as in example 8.2) is shown in figure 8.5.
The procedure is similar to correlation, except that the second function must

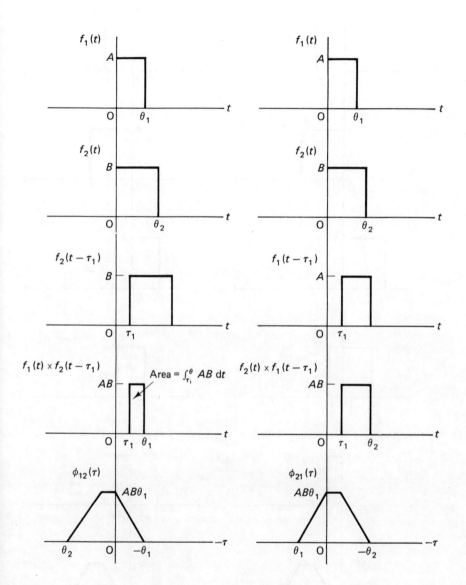

Figure 8.4 Cross-correlation of two rectangular pulses

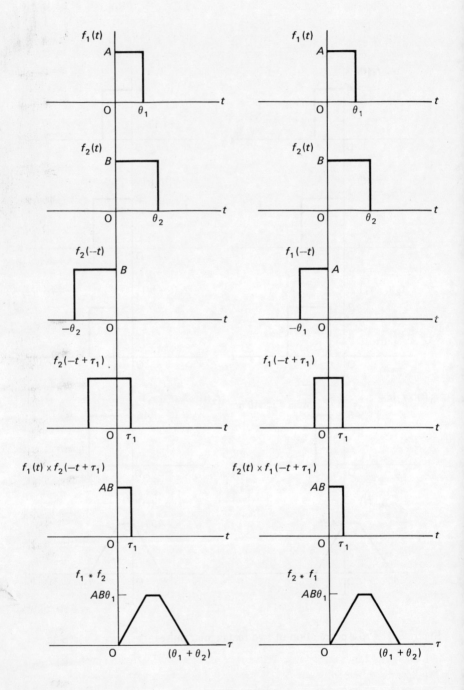

Figure 8.5   Convolution of two rectangular pulses

be reversed before being shifted. The reversal has the effect that a shift of $+\tau$ now produces movement to the right (that is, delay, instead of advance). However, all one has to do is slide the reversed function over the other and plot the area below, but now labelling the axes *without* reversal. One finds that, because of the time reversal, $f_1 * f_2$ is always the same as $f_2 * f_1$. See figure 8.5.

The idea of convolution as 'blurring' can be seen by convolving a rectangular pulse with successively narrower pulses. This is shown in figure 8.6.

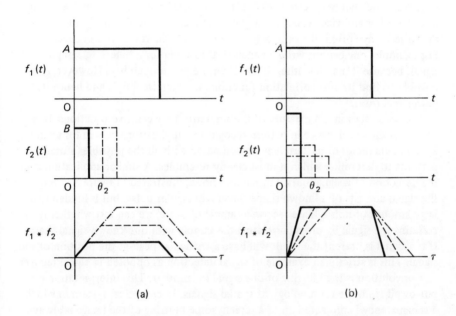

Figure 8.6   Convolution as 'blurring': (a) constant height, (b) constant area

To avoid $f_1 * f_2$ becoming small as $f_2(t)$ is decreased, the area of the pulse must be kept constant, that is, $B\theta_2$ = constant. As θ_2 approaches zero, B becomes very large, and in the limit we have $\theta_2 \rightarrow 0$, $B \rightarrow \infty$ but $B\theta_2$ = constant. This is known as an *impulse* of strength $B\theta_2$ units, being a *unit impulse* if $B\theta_2 = 1$.

We can see that if a function is convolved with a unit impulse it is *reproduced exactly* at the position of the impulse. The greater the departure from an impulse the more the function is 'distorted'. Also, we could construct a repetitive function by convolving one of our required pulses with a train of equally spaced impulses.

8.5 Applications of Correlation and Convolution

It has been necessary to introduce these functions in a fairly abstract manner at this point, since an understanding of them is required in later chapters, but it is appropriate to outline some of their applications here.

Autocorrelation is a measure of the extent to which the future value of a function can be predicted. Its main importance in Information Technology is that it is related to the energy spectrum of a signal (power spectrum for finite power signals). It will be shown in chapter 10 that the autocorrelation function $R_1(\tau)$ and the energy spectrum $E(f)$ form a Fourier pair; that is, one transforms into the other and vice versa. In many communications applications this provides the easiest way (often, the only way) of finding the energy or power spectrum. For example, one cannot write an analytical formula for a binary telegraph signal, because it may be either '0' or '1' with equal probability. However, it is possible to find its autocorrelation function (see exercise 8.6.3) and hence its power spectrum.

Cross-correlation is a measure of the similarity between two functions. It is clearly of direct relevance in pattern recognition applications, where for example a read-in character or pattern may be compared with all the possible (stored) patterns to determine which it most clearly resembles. A similar application is in the detection of a signal buried in random noise, illustrated in figure 8.7. Suppose the signal consists of a known shape, say a rectangular pulse, but is hidden in a large amount of noise. If we receive a sample of noise, we can test whether it contains the signal by cross-correlating the sample with our known signal shape. If the signal is present the result will have a triangular peak at the position of the signal. This is strictly an example of signal detection as opposed to signal recovery.

Convolution is the blurring of one signal by another. This interpretation is borrowed from the terminology of spatial signals. In an optical system in which a transparency is projected on to a screen, some blurring of the image is always present. If the transparency consisted of a very small central pinhole the system should produce a corresponding small bright point on the screen; in practice a small area of light will be seen. This is known as the *impulse response* of the system; that is, the output for an impulse as input, since the pinhole is the spatial equivalent of an impulse. An ideal impulse response is, of course, an impulse, but a practical one is a small roughly circular area in this case. When a transparency is used as input, the output on the screen is the convolution between the transparency and the impulse response of the system. Every point on the screen is blurred by the non-ideal impulse response of the system.

This is an example of one of the most fundamental properties of the convolution function; for any linear system the output is the convolution between the input and the impulse response. Another very important property is that when two functions are multiplied their Fourier Transforms are convolved, and vice versa. We will be amplifying and using both these properties in chapters 9 and 10.

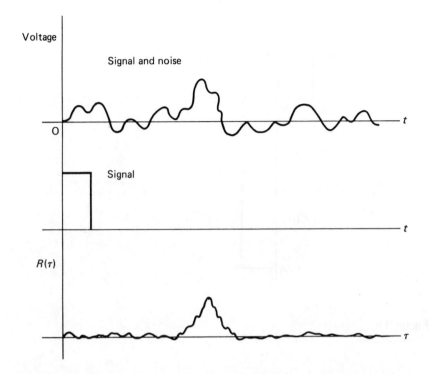

Voltage

Signal and noise

O

t

Signal

t

$R(\tau)$

τ

Figure 8.7   Detection of a signal in noise by cross-correlation

8.6   Exercises on chapter 8

8.6.1. Answer the following, illustrating by sketches as appropriate:
  (i) Is $f_1 ✪ f_1$ necessarily even and positive?
  (ii) What is the relation between $f_1 ✪ f_2$ and $f_2 ✪ f_1$?
  (iii) What is the relation between $f_1 * f_2$ and $f_2 * f_1$?
  (iv) Is $f_1 ✪ f_1$ the same as $f_1 * f_1$?

8.6.2. Sketch the convolution of an exponential decay ($\exp(-\alpha t), t > 0$) with
  (i) a rectangular pulse and (ii) a burst of sine waves. What is the physical
  significance of these results?
  (*Note.* The impulse response of a first-order system, such as an R–C low-
  pass filter, is an exponential decay.)

8.6.3. Sketch the autocorrelation function for a repetitive pseudo-random
  sequence (that is, a random binary telegraph signal) with levels of 0 V
  and 5 V, and length 8 clock pulses.

8.6.4. For the two functions $f_1(t)$ and $f_2(t)$ below, sketch $f_1 ✪ f_1, f_2 ✪ f_2,$
  $f_1 ✪ f_2, f_2 ✪ f_1, f_1 * f_1, f_2 * f_2, f_1 * f_2$ and $f_2 * f_1$.

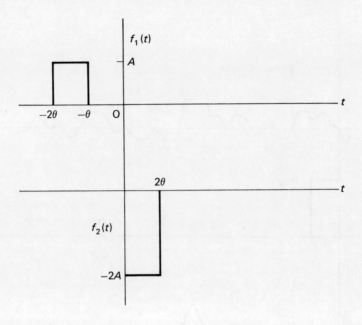

Figure 8.8

9 Frequency Domain Representation of Signals

9.1 Fourier Theory

Fourier Theory uniquely relates the time and frequency domain representations of signals. It is a particularly satisfying theory, being mathematically precise and elegant, and yet having a very clear physical interpretation and application. Like most worthwhile studies its understanding requires a certain amount of initial effort. It has been said that 'Fourier Theory grows on you' but unfortunately this is rather undermined by the reply 'like warts or spots'. Most subjects become easier with use, of course, but this is particularly true of Fourier Theory. It is very difficult to find an examination question that someone well versed in the subject cannot do in less than about ten minutes; indeed, this is probably the best academic reason for not teaching it!

The subject is beloved of mathematicians who, by their nature, are rather more interested in the mathematics than its application. Probably because of this it has not been much liked by engineers, who set great store by the rather similar Laplace Transform yet tend to shun the Fourier Transform. This is a pity, because the former is used mainly as a tool in finding the time domain response of systems but is much less elegant and has a far less obvious physical meaning than the latter.

It is, of course, possible to make some progress in Fourier Theory simply by learning the rules and turning the handle (as is often done with Laplace Transforms), but such an approach is ill advised. Understanding is everything in science. One can teach a dog all sorts of tricks, but as soon as some new situation occurs they are all useless. It is essential to make the effort necessary to understand basic scientific theory; it is well worth the effort and can be very rewarding. Otherwise, unfortunately, one always gets caught out sooner or later.

9.2 Finite Power Signals: Fourier Series

As we have seen above, it is usually necessary to deal differently with finite power and finite energy signals. In Fourier Theory it is possible to handle both types of signals using Fourier Transforms, which deal essentially with finite energy signals. However, their interpretation is less obvious than that of Fourier Series, which deal with finite power signals, and we will therefore consider this type of signal first.

91

The essential idea of Fourier Series is that a repetitive function of time $f(t)$ of period T can be represented as a sum of simple waveforms, that is

$$f(t) = a_0 + \sum_{n=1}^{\infty} a_n \cos n\omega_0 t + \sum_{n=1}^{\infty} b_n \sin n\omega_0 t \qquad (9.1)$$

where $\omega_0 = 2\pi/T$ and a_0, a_n, b_n are constants. The meaning becomes clearer if we combine the second and third terms, giving

$$f(t) = a_0 + \sum_{n=1}^{\infty} d_n \cos(n\omega_0 t + \phi_n) \qquad (9.2)$$

where

$$d_n = (a_n^2 + b_n^2)^{\frac{1}{2}} \quad \text{and} \quad \phi_n = \tan^{-1} - \frac{b_n}{a_n}$$

This equation means that a repetitive function of time is equivalent to the sum of a set of cosine waveforms at angular frequencies $\omega_0, 2\omega_0, 3\omega_0$ etc., each with different amplitude d_n and phase ϕ_n, plus a constant level a_0. The constituent waveforms are known as *harmonics*; the zeroth harmonic has zero frequency and amplitude a_0; the first harmonic has frequency $1/T (= 2\pi\omega_0)$, amplitude d_1 and phase ϕ_1; the second has frequency $2/T$, amplitude d_2 and phase ϕ_2 etc.

It can be shown (Stuart, 1966) that a_0, a_n and b_n are given by

$$a_0 = \frac{1}{T} \int_{-T/2}^{T/2} f(t) \, dt, \qquad a_n = \frac{2}{T} \int_{-T/2}^{T/2} f(t) \cos n\omega_0 t \, dt$$

$$b_n = \frac{2}{T} \int_{-T/2}^{T/2} f(t) \sin n\omega_0 t \, dt \qquad (9.3)$$

Equation (9.2) could have been written in terms of sine waves, of course, but cosines are preferable.

EXAMPLE 9.1

Find the coefficients a_0, a_n, b_n for the square wave of figure 9.1(a).

$$a_0 = \frac{1}{T} \int_{-T/2}^{T/2} f(t) \, dt = \frac{1}{T} \int_{-T/4}^{T/4} A \, dt = \frac{A}{2}$$

$b_n = 0$ since $f(t)$ is even and the integral is odd

$$a_n = \frac{2}{T} \int_{-T/4}^{T/4} A \cos n\omega_0 t \, dt = \frac{2A}{n\pi} \sin n \frac{\pi}{2}$$

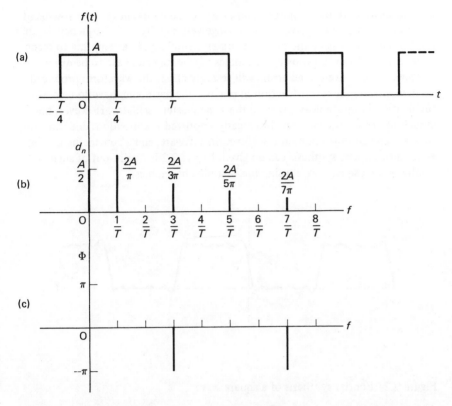

Figure 9.1 (a) Square wave, (b) amplitude spectrum, (c) phase spectrum

Thus

$$f(t) = \frac{A}{2} + \frac{2A}{\pi} \left[\cos \omega_0 t - \frac{1}{3} \cos 3\omega_0 t + \frac{1}{5} \cos 5\omega_0 t \ldots \right]$$

The plot of d_n versus f is known as the *amplitude spectrum*, and that of ϕ_n versus f is known as the *phase spectrum*. These are shown in figure 9.1(b) and (c).

The zeroth harmonic is just the mean value $\overline{f}$. For a square wave all the even harmonics are zero and the odd ones decrease uniformly in amplitude (as $1/n$) and alternate in phase between zero and $-\pi$.

Equation (9.2) is *reversible*. The time domain representation $f(t)$ is *completely equivalent* to its frequency domain representation d_n and ϕ_n, and each uniquely determines the other. A repetitive signal can be broken down into its harmonics by feeding it to a suitable narrow-band tuneable filter, and the same waveform can be reconstructed by adding together the appropriate harmonics. There are, however, some practical problems in demonstrating this experimentally. One must measure both the amplitude and phase of the harmonics but narrow-band filters have phase characteristics that change very rapidly with frequency, so that it is difficult to measure the phase accurately. Similarly, in attempting to reconstruct a signal from its (known) harmonics the frequencies have to be *exact* multiples of $1/T$; even small errors will severely affect the waveform produced. To demonstrate the reconstruction in practice the harmonics have to be derived (by division or multiplication) from the same master oscillator. However, the availability of microcomputers has greatly improved the situation; one can easily generate and add the required waveforms in software, and a convincing demonstration of Fourier synthesis can be given. Figure 9.2 is a print-out of such a synthesis for a square wave, using the first nine harmonics.

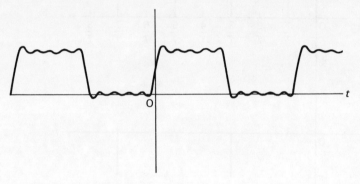

Figure 9.2   Fourier synthesis of a square wave

9.2.1   *Complex representation of Fourier Series*

The equations of Fourier synthesis (9.1 or 9.2) and the corresponding equations for the coefficients (9.3) can hardly be said to be very elegant or compact. Equation (9.1) has three terms on the right-hand side involving the three separate coefficients of equation (9.3). However, a considerable simplification can be achieved by replacing the sines and cosines by cisoids, using the relation $\exp(j\phi) = \cos\phi + j\sin\phi$. The word cisoid comes from $\cos + i\sin$ but most people now use j to represent $\sqrt{-1}$. After a little manipulation we obtain

$$f(t) = \sum_{n=-\infty}^{+\infty} c_n \exp(jn\omega_0 t), \quad c_n = \frac{1}{T} \int_{-T/2}^{T/2} f(t) \exp(-jn\omega_0 t) \, dt \quad (9.4)$$

$c_n = \frac{1}{2}(a_n - jb_n)$ is the *complex amplitude spectrum* and replaces d_n and ϕ_n above. Equations (9.4) are much the most satisfactory and compact statement of the Fourier Series relation, but require a little explanation. $f(t)$ is now represented by a sum of cisoids, over both positive and negative values, and c_n is given by a single integral again involving a cisoid.

Figure 9.3 shows the cisoids $\exp(j\omega_0 t)$ and $\exp(-j\omega_0 t)$ plotted on an Argand diagram; $\exp(j\omega_0 t)$ rotates anticlockwise with angular velocity ω_0 tracing out a circle of unit radius, and $\exp(-j\omega_0 t)$ rotates similarly clockwise.

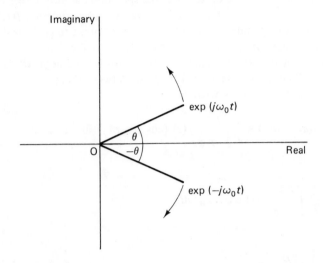

Figure 9.3   Positive and negative cisoids

It is well known that

$$\cos \omega_0 t = \tfrac{1}{2}\exp(j\omega_0 t) + \tfrac{1}{2}\exp(-j\omega_0 t)$$

and this is immediately evident from figure 9.3; if we add the two cisoids the imaginary components cancel and the real parts add (hence the factor $\frac{1}{2}$ as above).

Cisoids are very important basic functions in Signal Theory, much more so than simple sine waves and cosine waves. Any signal, whether real, imaginary or complex, can be constructed by adding cisoids, whereas sine and cosine waves are essentially real. However, many signals in information processing have to be expressed in complex form. If a signal has both amplitude and phase it can be expressed by a single complex number z; $z = x + jy = |z|\exp(j\phi)$, the real modulus $|z| (= (x^2 + y^2)^{\frac{1}{2}})$ and phase $\phi (= \tan^{-1} y/x)$ being both expressed by the complex z. This applies to the response of filters (having amplitude and phase response), to optical systems (transmission amplitude and phase) and to many other systems as well as to the basic Fourier Theory.

People sometimes claim that cisoids are 'abstract' and try to avoid using them. However, this is rather like trying to do something (such as make love) with both hands tied behind one's back; it may present something of a challenge but it considerably limits the possibilities. Most mathematical concepts are rather abstract but cisoids are hardly more so than the notion of a sine wave as the projection on the y-axis of a point moving in a circle!

The meaning of equation (9.4) is that any repetitive function $f(t)$ can be represented as a sum of cisoids, the amplitudes and phases of the various harmonics being given by the modulus and phase of the complex function c_n. Since cisoids may be either positive or negative, the spectrum has both positive and negative sides (n goes from $-\infty$ to $+\infty$). However, for a real function $f(t)$, the positive and negative cisoids for a given value of n combine to give a real cosine waveform, since $\exp(jn\omega_0 t) + \exp[j(-n)\omega_0 t] = 2\cos\omega_0 t$ as above. One can think of a real function $f(t)$ as comprising both positive and negative cisoids, but that we are physically unable to distinguish between them.

The equation for c_n can be written

$$c_n = \tfrac{1}{2}(a_n - jb_n) = \frac{1}{T}\int_{-T/2}^{T/2} f(t)\,[\cos n\omega_0 t - j\sin n\omega_0 t]\ \mathrm{d}t$$

so

$$a_n = \frac{2}{T}\int_{-T/2}^{T/2} f(t)\cos n\omega_0 t\ \mathrm{d}t \qquad\qquad (9.5a)$$

and

$$c_n = \frac{2}{T}\int_{-T/2}^{T/2} f(t)\sin n\omega_0 t\ \mathrm{d}t \qquad\qquad (9.5b)$$

agreeing with equation (9.3) (c_0 is identified with $2a_0$).

If $f(t)$ is even then $b_n = 0$ (since $\sin n\omega_0 t$ is odd) and similarly if $f(t)$ is odd then $a_n = 0$; in these cases one could use only equation (9.5a) or equation (9.5b), but the saving in calculation is small and usually it is easier to stick to equation (9.4).

EXAMPLE 9.2

Repeat example 9.1 using the complex representation.

$$c_n = \frac{1}{T}\int_{-T/4}^{T/4} A\exp(-jn\omega_0 t)\ \mathrm{d}t$$

$$= \frac{A}{n\pi}\sin\frac{n\pi}{2}$$

The spectrum is shown in figure 9.4 ($c_0 = A/2$ since $\lim_{n\to 0}(\sin n\pi/2)/n\pi/2 = 1$).

Having found c_n we simply have to find the modulus to get the amplitude spectrum and the argument to get the phase. The plots represent the distribution of cisoids, in terms of the (positive or negative) harmonic number n. However, it is usual to label the axis as frequency, so that lines appear at intervals of $1/T$. It should be noted that the above plot for the amplitude spectrum does not have an 'out of sequence' value at the origin, unlike that in figure 9.2, and that the amplitude spectrum is even and the phase spectrum odd.

This is always the case for a real function, because the imaginary parts of the constituent cisoids *must* cancel and they can do this only if $c(+n) = \dot{c}(-n)$ and $\phi(+n) = -\phi(-n)$, as can be seen by expanding equations (9.4). Physically, of course, we measure only positive frequencies, so the measured amplitude spectrum is the sum of the two sides (often thought of as a 'folding over' of the negative side on to the positive) and the measured phase spectrum is (by convention) the positive side.

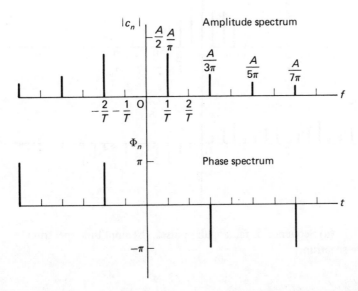

Figure 9.4 Spectrum of a square wave using complex form of Fourier Series

9.2.2 Sequence of rectangular pulses

The most instructive example in Fourier Series is probably an infinite sequence of rectangular pulses, since many important deductions can be made from it. In figure 9.5(a) the origin has been deliberately chosen at the left-hand edge of a pulse, to give a more interesting phase spectrum (the analysis is slightly easier with the origin in the centre of a pulse).

$$c_n = \frac{1}{T} \int_0^\tau A \exp(-jn\omega_0 t) \, dt$$

$$= \frac{A}{T} \cdot \frac{-1}{jn\omega_0} \left[\exp(-jn\omega_0 t)\right]_0^\tau$$

$$= \frac{A}{T} \cdot \frac{-1}{jn\omega_0} \left[\exp(-jn\omega_0) - 1\right]$$

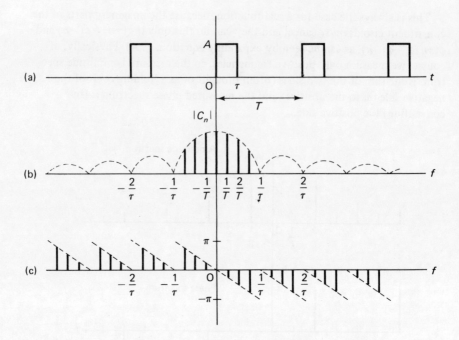

Figure 9.5   (a) Sequence of rectangular pulses, (b) amplitude spectrum, (c) phase spectrum

$$= \frac{A}{T} \cdot \frac{-1}{jn\omega_0} \cdot \exp\left(-jn\omega_0\tau/2\right)\left[\exp\left(-jn\omega_0\tau/2\right) - \exp\left(+jn\omega_0\tau/2\right)\right]$$

$$= \frac{A}{T} \cdot \frac{-1}{jn\omega_0} \cdot \exp\left(-jn\omega_0\tau/2\right). -2j \sin\left(n\omega_0\tau/2\right)$$

$$= \frac{A}{T} \cdot \frac{-1}{jn\omega_0} \cdot \exp\left(-jn\omega_0\tau/2\right). -2j \frac{\sin\left(\pi n\tau/T\right)}{\pi n\tau/T} \cdot \frac{\pi n\tau}{T}$$

which simplifies to

$$c_n = \frac{A\theta}{T} \cdot \exp\left(-jn\pi\tau/T\right). \operatorname{sinc} n\tau/T \tag{9.6}$$

The sinc function is defined by

$$\operatorname{sinc} x = \frac{\sin \pi x}{\pi x}$$

and is plotted in figure 9.6.

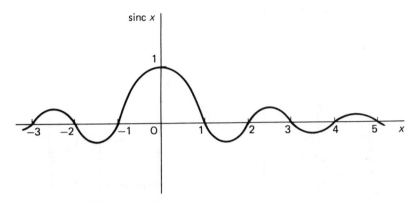

Figure 9.6   The sinc function

It is very important in Communication Theory and occurs whenever a rectangular-shaped signal occurs. It has the interesting property that it is zero for all integral values of x (other than $x = 0$) and that both $\int_{-\infty}^{+\infty} \text{sinc}\, x \; dx$ and $\int_{-\infty}^{+\infty} \text{sinc}^2 x \; dx = 1$. (These properties would not be so simple had it been defined as $\sin x/x$.) Evaluating the modulus and phase of c_n we obtain the spectra (b) and (c) in figure 9.5, which are plotted for a ratio of period to pulse width $T/\tau = 4$. The harmonics are spaced at intervals of $1/T$, their envelope following the (modulus of the) sinc function. A zero amplitude occurs whenever sinc $(n\tau/T)$ is integral so with $T/\tau = 4$ the fourth, eighth, twelfth lines etc. are zero; these zeros occur at frequencies $1/\tau, 2/\tau, 3/\tau$ etc., directly determined by the pulse width. There are clearly two factors that determine the spectrum; the repetition of the waveform produces lines every $1/T$ Hz and the envelope of the spectrum is determined by the shape of the waveform. The term $\exp(-jn\pi\tau/T)$ is a phase term dependent on the choice of origin and vanishes if the origin is chosen in the centre of a pulse. In general, a shift of origin of θ in time produces a phase term of $\exp(-jn\omega_0\theta)$ in the corresponding spectrum.

A number of useful deductions can be made and are illustrated in figure 9.7.

(i) For a given period T the value of τ determines the distribution of power in the spectrum.
(ii) For a given value of pulse width τ, the period T similarly determines the power distribution.
(iii) If we put $T = \tau$ we get a constant (d.c.) level. $|c_n|$ is then given by A sinc n so a single spectral line of height A occurs at zero frequency (one might possibly expect this).
(iv) Putting $\tau = T/2$ produces a square wave. Every second harmonic will be zero, as previously found in examples 9.1 and 9.2.
(v) If we let the repetition period T become very large, the line spacing $1/T$ becomes small. As T tends to infinity the spacing tends to zero and we get

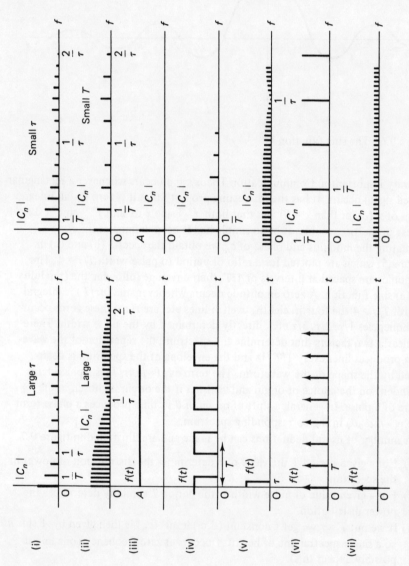

Figure 9.7 Deductions from the spectrum of figure 9.5

a *continuous* spectrum. Unfortunately, since $|c_n|$ is inversely proportional to T the spectrum vanishes everywhere. This is again because $f(t)$ becomes a finite energy signal if T is infinite, and such signals have zero mean power. This problem is avoided in the next section, but it is clear that finite energy signals will have continuous spectra.

(vi) Suppose we make τ small but keep the pulse area $A\tau$ constant. In the limit we get an impulse of strength $A\tau$, as discussed previously. The spectrum will simply be a set of lines of constant height A/T (or $1/T$ for unit impulses).

(vii) Finally, it is clear that a single impulse will have a constant but continuous spectrum, though the same problem as in (v) occurs again.

We have seen previously that a repetitive function can be constructed by convolving a single period of the waveform with a set of impulses spaced at the required repetition period. We will see later that convolution in the time domain is equivalent to multiplication in the frequency domain. The spectrum of the repetitive pulse is thus the product of the spectrum of a single pulse with that of a set of impulses, and therefore has lines spaced at $1/T$ (due to the impulses) with height governed by a sinc function (the shape of the spectrum of a single pulse). These properties will be discussed in more detail in the next section.

9.3 Finite Energy Signals: Fourier Transforms

We have seen that if we attempt to apply the Fourier Series equations to a finite energy signal, by letting the period T become very large, we can deduce that the spectrum will be continuous since the separation between the lines $1/T$ tends to zero. However, since the expression for c_n contains a $1/T$ outside the integral, c_n also tends to zero. In order to deal satisfactorily with finite energy signals, all we have to do is to modify equations (9.4) slightly. We can denote the (vanishingly small) line separation $1/T$ as a differential quantity δf, with the continuous frequency $f = n.\delta f$, replace the summation by an integral and define the complex spectrum as $F(f) = \lim_{T \to \infty} c_n \times T$. We obtain the Fourier Transform relations

$$f(t) = \int_{-\infty}^{+\infty} F(f) \exp(j\omega t)\, df$$

$$(9.7)$$

$$F(f) = \int_{-\infty}^{+\infty} f(t) \exp(-j\omega t)\, dt$$

The first equation is sometimes called the forward transform and the second the reverse transform, and $f(t)$ and $F(f)$ are said to constitute a transform pair. The equations are a very compact and pleasingly symmetrical statement of the essential idea of Fourier Theory. $f(t)$ is uniquely expressed as a sum of cisoids, of all frequencies, and the complex spectrum $F(f)$ determines their amplitude and phase. Similarly, $F(f)$ can also be thought of as a sum of cisoids, with $f(t)$ determining amplitude and phase. As for Fourier Series, the amplitude spectrum is the modulus of $F(f)$ and the phase spectrum its argument; real functions of time have an even amplitude spectrum and an odd phase spectrum. The units of the amplitude spectrum are amplitude density (the square root of energy density).

As in the case of Fourier Series, $F(f)$ can be written as

$$F(f) = a(f) - jb(f) = \int_{-\infty}^{+\infty} f(t) \left[\cos \omega t - j \sin \omega t\right] \, dt$$

so

$$a(f) = \int_{-\infty}^{+\infty} f(t) \cos \omega t \, dt \tag{9.8a}$$

and

$$b(f) = \int_{-\infty}^{+\infty} f(t) \sin \omega t \, dt \tag{9.8b}$$

These are known as the sine and cosine transforms.

If $f(t)$ is even then $b(f) = 0$ and similarly if $f(t)$ is odd then $a(f) = 0$, so some calculations can be simplified by using (9.8a) or (9.8b). However, we will see later that the manipulative rules of Fourier Transforms are so powerful that it is hardly ever necessary to evaluate the integral, so it is much better to think in terms of equations (9.7).

EXAMPLE 9.3

Find the spectrum of the rectangular pulse of figure 9.8(a).

$$F(f) = \int_{-\infty}^{+\infty} f(t) \exp(-j\omega t) \, dt$$

$$= \int_{-\theta/2}^{\theta/2} A \exp(-j\omega t) \, dt$$

$$= A . \frac{-1}{j\omega} \left[\exp(-j\omega t)\right]_{-\theta/2}^{\theta/2}$$

$$= \frac{2A}{\omega} \sin \omega\theta/2$$

Leading to

$$F(f) = A\theta \, \text{sinc} \, f\theta \tag{9.9}$$

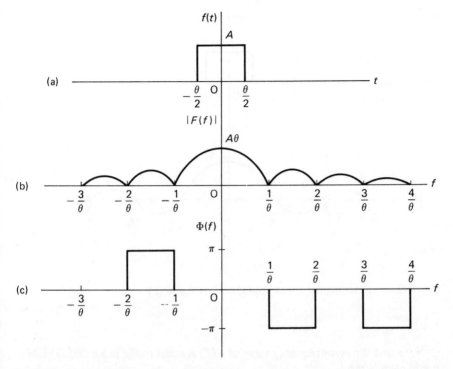

Figure 9.8   A rectangular signal (a) and its spectrum (b and c)

This is a very basic result and should be memorised. $F(f)$ is real in this case, so it could be plotted on a single diagram. However, the amplitude and phase spectra are shown separately in parts (b) and (c) of figure 9.8.

EXAMPLE 9.4

Find the signal corresponding to the rectangular spectrum of figure 9.9(a).

$$f(t) = \int_{-\infty}^{+\infty} F(f) \exp(j\omega t)\, \mathrm{d}f \rightarrow Bf_c \text{ sinc } f_c t$$

The examples illustrate the basic symmetry of the Fourier Transform relations; a function $f(t)$ can be converted to its spectrum $F(f)$ by the forward transform, the reverse transform being used for the reverse direction. (Logically one requires only a single transform, but it requires three applications of the forward transform to convert $F(f)$ back to $f(t)$, so the reverse transform is convenient.) A Fourier pair, that is, $f(t)$ and its corresponding $F(f)$ are often denoted by

$$f(t) \rightleftharpoons F(f)$$

(the British Rail sign indicates a lack of concern about direction of travel).

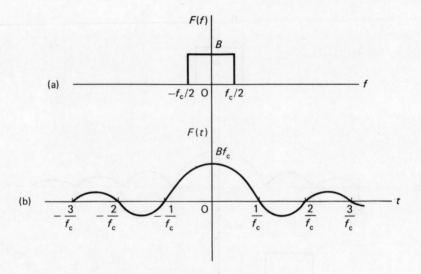

Figure 9.9   A rectangular spectrum (a) and its signal (b)

Note that the zero-frequency value of $F(f)$ is equal to the pulse area. This is a useful general result

$$\int_{-\infty}^{+\infty} f(t) = F(0) \tag{9.10}$$

Conversely, of course

$$\int_{-\infty}^{+\infty} F(f) \, \mathrm{d}f = f(0)$$

It can be seen from these examples that if a function is extended in one domain it is narrow in the other, and vice versa. This is known as the *principle of reciprocal spreading*. It has a direct application in optics, where the spectrum of light from an incandescent source is broad because the light is emitted in short bursts, whereas that from a laser is narrow because the wavetrains are very long. There is an approximate general relation between the 'width' of a function Δt in the time domain and its corresponding 'width' Δf in the frequency domain

$$\Delta f \times \Delta t \approx 1$$

(The 'width' really requires definition, and is the range from the origin to the first zero crossing in the above examples.)

One important class of functions, which has the same form in each domain, is the gaussian $\exp(-at^2)$ or $\exp(-Af^2)$. This again has an application in optics;

the intensity distribution across a laser beam is gaussian, and transforms performed on it (by lenses etc., see later) do not change the form (though they may change the scale).

We can also deduce the spectrum of an impulse, by letting A tend to infinity and θ tend to zero, but with the area A constant. $F(f)$ is constant with value equal to the strength, that is, unity for a unit impulse. It is therefore a useful function for measuring the frequency response of a system, because its application is equivalent to applying all frequencies simultaneously with equal amplitude and zero phase.

EXAMPLE 9.5

Find the spectrum of the exponential decay of figure 9.10(a).

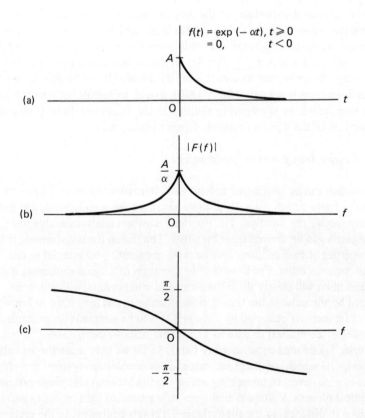

Figure 9.10   An exponential decay (a) and its spectrum (b and c)

This function is neither odd nor even, so we have no choice but to use the full transform here

$$F(f) = \int_0^\infty A \exp(-\alpha t) \exp(-j\omega t) \, dt$$

$$= \frac{A}{\alpha + j\omega}$$

Thus

$$|F(f)| = \frac{A}{(\alpha^2 + \omega^2)^{\frac{1}{2}}}$$

and

$$\Phi(f) = -\tan^{-1} \frac{\omega}{\alpha}$$

These are plotted in figure 9.10(b) and (c).

We can deduce the spectrum of the unit step function from this example, by letting α tend to zero, so $F(f) \to 1/j\omega$. This is not strictly correct; the Fourier Transform expressions (9.7) are valid only when the integrals converge, and a requirement for this is that $\int_{-\infty}^{+\infty} f(t) \, dt$ is finite. A unit step is not, of course, a finite energy function, and its area is similarly infinite. It can be shown that its Fourier Transform is actually $1/j\omega + \frac{1}{2}\delta(0)$, that is, an impulse of strength one-half at zero frequency is present in addition to the $1/j\omega$ term. In fact, $1/j\omega$ is the spectrum of the signum function, shown in figure 9.11.

9.3.1 Fourier Transforms of spatial signals

Any function can be considered to have two alternative representations – time domain or frequency domain. Both representations are equally valid, and both uniquely specify the function. The Fourier Transform relations enable one representation to be derived from the other. The reason for transforming is that the properties of the functions may be more apparent or meaningful in one domain than the other. For example, the spectrum of a signal containing a sine wave and noise will clearly show the sinusoidal components, which may be obscured by the noise in the time domain. Similarly, one may need to know the range of frequencies occupied by a signal if it is to be sampled (for example, for processing by computer) or used in a communication system.

Fourier Transforms occur in many fields. So far we have dealt almost entirely with temporal signals, of direct relevance to communication systems and electronics etc. However, an interesting analogy exists between electronic systems and optical systems. Voltage is analogous to transmitted light intensity and time analogous to distance, so the slit in figure 9.12(a) is equivalent to the rectangular pulse of 9.12(c).

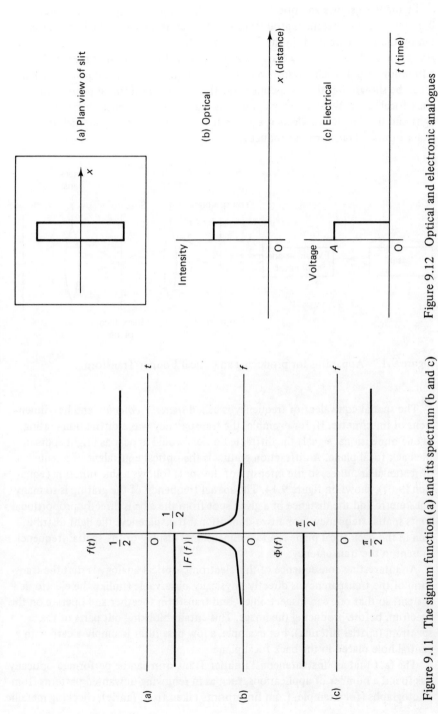

(a) Plan view of slit

(b) Optical

(c) Electrical

Figure 9.12   Optical and electronic analogues

Figure 9.11   The signum function (a) and its spectrum (b and c)

Figure 9.13 shows an optical system, in which coherent light from a laser illuminates a transparency, producing an image on the screen. The light transmitted by the transparency is in the form of a spatial distribution of light intensity $f(x, y)$; in each dimension a distance x (or y) is analogous to the time variable of a function $f(t)$. If such a transparency is placed in the front focal plane of a lens it can be shown that the (two-dimensional) Fourier Transform appears in the back focal plane. What actually happens is that the transparency diffracts the light and the first lens collects it again, but the path differences are such that an exact Fourier Transform is produced.

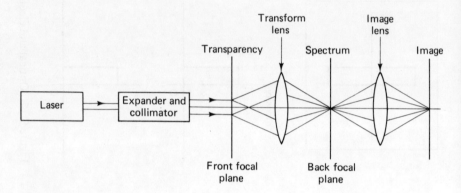

Figure 9.13   Apparatus for producing an optical Fourier Transform

The spatial equivalent of frequency is called *spatial frequency* and has dimensions of lines/metre. If, for example, the transparency was a diffraction grating (a one-dimensional signal) the diffracted orders would appear as bright spots in the back focal plane. A diffraction grating is the optical equivalent of a sequence of rectangular pulses, so the intensity of the spots follows a sinc function (equation (9.6)), shown in figure 9.14. The spatial frequency of the grating is so many lines/metre and the distance of a given spot from the axis is directly proportional to its spatial frequency. For a two-dimensional transparency, the light distribution in the back focal plane is a two-dimensional display of the spatial frequencies present in the transparency.

An interesting consequence of this electronic/optical analogy is that the transform of the transparency is directly physically observable (unlike the electronic system) so that one can inspect object and transform together and operate on the spectrum before producing the image. This entails blocking out parts of the spectrum (spatial filtering). For example, a low-pass filter is simply a card with a central hole placed in the back focal plane.

The fact that an 'instantaneous' Fourier Transform can be performed optically has found a number of applications, such as in removing unwanted patterns from photographs (for example, from fingerprints taken from fabric), checking metallic

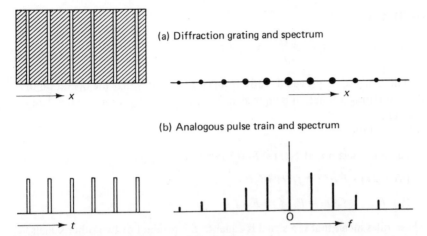

(a) Diffraction grating and spectrum

(b) Analogous pulse train and spectrum

Figure 9.14 Diffraction grating and its spectrum

gratings for use in image tubes, deblurring photographs, in character recognition and in data analysis. There are some experimental difficulties in that a laser must be used to produce the transform, and the data to be processed must be in a suitable form (such as a transparency). However, the technique is likely to grow in importance as input mechanisms are improved, and has inherent advantages over electronic systems.

9.3.2 Properties of Fourier Transforms

Fourier Transforms have a number of important and powerful properties, which greatly simplify the process of deducing transforms for most functions. The list given here is by no means exhaustive; only those essential to Information Technology are included. Proofs of the various rules are given in Stuart (1966).
(i) Addition

If $f_1(t) \rightleftharpoons F_1(f)$ and $f_2(t) \rightleftharpoons F_2(f)$ then $f_1(t) + f_2(t) \rightleftharpoons F_1(f) + F_2(f)$

This is embarrassingly obvious, but is included for completeness.
(ii) Multiplication by a constant

If $f(t) \rightleftharpoons F(f)$ then $af(t) \rightleftharpoons aF(f)$

This is even more embarrassing.
(iii) Time shift

If $f(t) \rightleftharpoons F(f)$ then $f(t - \tau) \rightleftharpoons F(f) \exp(-j\omega\tau)$

This can be proved formally from relationships (9.7) and can be verified, for example, by calculating the transform of a pulse such as in example 9.3 with its origin at the edge. The relation states that a delay or advance τ simply adds a phase term $\exp(j\omega\tau)$ to the spectrum.

(iv) Differentiation

If $f(t) \rightleftharpoons F(f)$ then $\dfrac{df(t)}{dt} \rightleftharpoons j\omega F(f)$

This can also be proved directly from (9.7). It states that the operation of differentiating a function is equivalent to multiplying by $j\omega$ in the frequency domain.

(v) Convolution

Assuming again that $f_1(t) \rightleftharpoons F_1(f)$ and $f_2(t) \rightleftharpoons F_2(f)$

(a) $F_1(f) \times F_2(f) \rightleftharpoons f_1(t) * f_2(t)$

(b) $f_1(t) \times f_2(t) \rightleftharpoons F_1(f) * F_2(f)$

These rules mean that if a signal is equal to the product of two other signals, then its spectrum is the convolution between the corresponding spectra, and similarly for the convolution of two signals. The operations of multiplication and convolution are complementary in Fourier Transforms.
(These can again be proved from (9.7), but the proof is somewhat lengthy and tedious.)
The following examples illustrate the various rules.

EXAMPLE 9.6

Find the spectrum of the pair of pulses of figure 9.15(a).

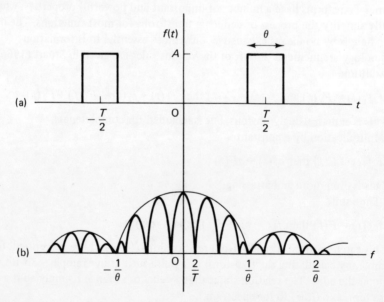

Figure 9.15   Two pulses (a) and their amplitude spectrum (b)

Using the rules for time shift and addition

$$F(f) = A\theta \text{ sinc } f\theta \exp\left(-j\omega T/2\right) + A\theta \text{ sinc } f\theta \exp\left(+j\omega T/2\right)$$

$$= A\theta \text{ sinc } f\theta . 2 \cos \pi fT$$

The spectrum is similar to that for a single pulse but with 'beats' due to the second pulse. In fact it is identical to the interference seen in optics between two slits illuminated by coherent light.

EXAMPLE 9.7

Find the spectrum of the triangular pulse of figure 9.16(a).

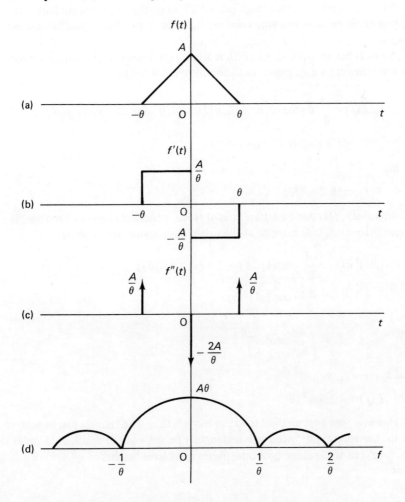

Figure 9.16 (a) Triangular pulse $f(t)$, (b) $f(t)$ differentiated once, (c) $f(t)$ differentiated twice, (d) spectrum of $f(t)$

There are at least four different ways of doing this example. The most obvious is to let

$$f(t) = A \left(1 - \frac{|t|}{\theta} \right), \ |t| < \theta$$

for the triangle and use the standard formula; that is

$$F(f) = \int_{-\theta}^{\theta} A \left(1 - \frac{|t|}{\theta} \right) \exp(-j\omega t) \, dt$$

This is without doubt the world's worst way of solving this problem! Although the integral is not very difficult the working takes about a page of A4 and the probability of error is rather high (about 99.9 per cent for most students). It should *never* be done this way (another instance of two hands tied behind the back).

A much better method is to differentiate $f(t)$, producing rectangular pulses whose transforms are known, as shown in figure 9.16(b).

$$j\omega F(f) = \frac{A}{\theta}.\theta \ \text{sinc} \ f\theta . \exp(j\omega\theta/2) - \frac{A}{\theta}.\theta. \ \text{sinc} \ f\theta . \exp(-j\omega\theta/2)$$

$$= A \ \text{sinc} \ f\theta \ (2j \sin \omega\theta/2)$$

giving

$$F(f) = A\theta \ \text{sinc}^2 f\theta$$

Alternatively, $f(t)$ can be differentiated twice, when only impulses remain, as in figure 9.16(c). A unit impulse at the origin has a transform of unity.

$$(j\omega)^2 F(f) = \frac{A}{\theta} (\exp(j\omega\theta) - 2 + \exp(-j\omega\theta))$$

$$= \frac{2A}{\theta} (\cos \omega\theta - 1)$$

$$= \frac{-4A}{\theta} \sin^2 \frac{\omega\theta}{2}$$

and again

$$F(f) = A\theta \ \text{sinc}^2 f\theta$$

However, the best method is to use convolution. The triangle can be seen to be the convolution between two rectangular pulses, each of width θ. In order that the height of the traingle be A, the pulses must have heights of $\sqrt{(A/\theta)}$. We thus have

$$F(f) = \sqrt{\frac{A}{\theta}} . \ \theta \ \text{sinc} \ f\theta . \sqrt{\frac{A}{\theta}} . \ \theta \ \text{sinc} \ f\theta = A\theta \ \text{sinc}^2 f\theta$$

Actually it is even easier than this. We do not have to bother about the height of the pulses since we know from equation (9.10) that the area of the triangle must be equal to the zero-frequency component of its spectrum. In one line, therefore

$$F(f) = (\text{area}) \operatorname{sinc} f\theta \,.\, \operatorname{sinc} f\theta = A\theta \operatorname{sinc}^2 f\theta$$

9.3.3 Repetitive signals

Since a repetitive signal of period T can be thought of as the convolution between a single cycle and a set of impulses spaced by T, we can find the Fourier Transform of a repetitive signal if we know that of a set of impulses. We saw previously that the Fourier Series spectrum of a set of unit impulses is a set of lines of height $1/T$ spaced at $1/T$. It can be shown that the Fourier Transform equivalent is simply a set of impulses of strength $1/T$ spaced at $1/T$. In fact, if we have the Fourier Series representation of a repetitive signal (always a set of lines spaced at $1/T$) then the Fourier Transform representation is the same, but with impulses replacing the lines. This is obvious from our definition of $F(f)$; we multiplied c_n by T and the units became amplitude density instead of amplitude (a line at a particular frequency has an infinite amplitude density). We thus have the important result shown in figure 9.17.

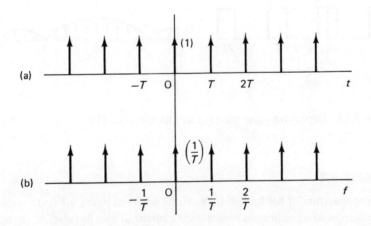

Figure 9.17   Sequence of impulses (a) and its spectrum (b)

It is thus not necessary to use Fourier Series methods at all. The reason for dealing with them is that Fourier Series are easier to understand initially, especially as Fourier synthesis is so easy to demonstrate by computer. However, having moved on to Fourier Transforms they are no longer required. Fourier Transform methods are so powerful and easy to apply that it is usually much quicker and easier to construct any repetitive function by convolution.

EXAMPLE 9.8

Find the spectrum of the repetitive pulse train of figure 9.18(a).
The repetitive train is the convolution between a set of impulses and a single
rectangular pulse. The spectrum is therefore the product between the spectrum
of the impulses (impulses of strength $1/T$ and spacing $1/T$) and that of the single
pulse (a sinc function). The result obtained is of course just that of section 9.2.2,
but with impulses replacing the lines.

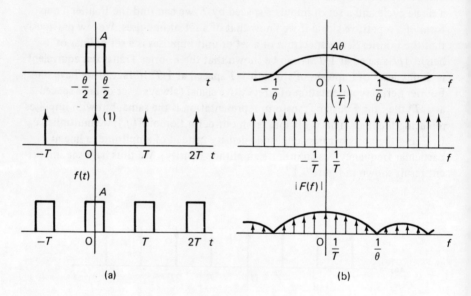

Figure 9.18   Repetitive pulse train (a) and its spectrum (b)

EXAMPLE 9.9

Find the spectrum of the limited train of sine waves of figure 9.19(a).
The spectrum of a continuous cosine wave consists of two impulses of strength
one-half, since $\cos \omega_0 t = \frac{1}{2}(\exp(j\omega_0 t) + \exp(-j\omega_0 t))$ and the Fourier Transform
is simply a plot of cisoids. A limited train of sine waves of length θ can be obtained by multiplying a continuous train by a rectangular pulse of length θ. The
spectrum of the limited train is therefore the convolution between the spectrum
of the continuous train (two impulses) and that of the rectangular pulse (a sinc
function)

$$F(f) = \frac{A\theta}{2}\left[\operatorname{sinc}\theta\left(f + \frac{1}{T}\right) + \operatorname{sinc}\theta\left(f - \frac{1}{T}\right) \right]$$

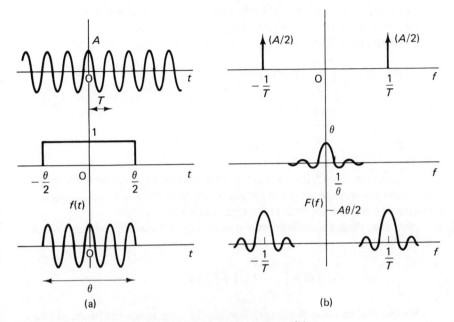

Figure 9.19   Burst of sine waves (a) and its spectrum (b)

9.3.4 Energy spectrum and autocorrelation

The ideas of Energy Spectrum and Autocorrelation were introduced in earlier chapters. We can now relate them to our Fourier Theory expressions.

The energy E in a finite energy signal is given by

$$E = \int_{-\infty}^{+\infty} f^2(t) \, dt = \int_{-\infty}^{+\infty} E(f) \, df \quad \text{(taking } E(f) \text{ two-sided)}$$

Therefore

$$E = \int_{-\infty}^{+\infty} f(t) \left[\int_{-\infty}^{+\infty} F(f) \exp (j\omega t) \, df \right] dt$$

$$= \int_{-\infty}^{+\infty} F(f) \left[\int_{-\infty}^{+\infty} f(t) \exp (j\omega t) \, dt \right] df$$

$$= \int_{-\infty}^{+\infty} F(f) \times F^*(f) \, df$$

where

$$F^*(f) = \int_{-\infty}^{+\infty} f(t) \exp (j\omega t) \, dt$$

and is the *complex conjugate* of $F(f)$.

Thus, $E(f) = |F(f)|^2$, so $E(f)$ is just the squared modulus of the Fourier Transform (the phase information in $F(f)$ is therefore lost).

Similarly, for a finite power signal we have signal power P given by

$$P = \lim_{T \to \infty} \frac{1}{T} \int_{-T/2}^{T/2} f^2(t)\, dt = \int_{-\infty}^{+\infty} P(f)\, df$$

For a repetitive signal we find

$$P = \sum_{n=-\infty}^{+\infty} |c_n|^2, \quad P_n = |c_n|^2$$

so the power in the nth line is $|c_n|^2$. Continuous finite power signals have a continuous power spectrum but cannot be expressed in terms of a complex Fourier spectrum, since their phase spectrum is random (uniform).

Note that these expressions are a special case of Parseval's Theorem, which states that

$$\int_{-\infty}^{+\infty} f_1(t) f_2(t)\, dt = \int_{-\infty}^{+\infty} F(f) . F_2^*(f)\, df$$

We can find an important expression for the autocorrelation function of a finite energy signal in a similar manner.

$$R_1(\tau) = \int_{-\infty}^{+\infty} f(t) f(t + \tau)\, dt$$

and replacing $f(t + \tau)$ by $F(f) \exp(j\omega\tau)$ and changing the order of integration as above, we find

$$R_1(\tau) = \int_{-\infty}^{+\infty} E(f) \exp(j\omega\tau)\, df$$

This is exactly the Fourier Transform relation between $R_1(\tau)$ and $E(f)$, so $R_1(\tau)$ and $E(f)$ are a Fourier pair. That is

$$R_1(\tau) \rightleftharpoons E(f)$$

Similarly, for finite power signals

$$R(\tau) \rightleftharpoons P(f)$$

[Alternatively, since $R_1(\tau) = f(t) \bigstar f(t) = f(t) * f(-t)$, the Fourier Transform of $R_1(\tau)$ must be $F(f) \times F(-f) = F(f) \times F^*(f) = E(f)$.]

Some examples of power spectra and autocorrelation functions for finite power signals are shown in figure 9.20.

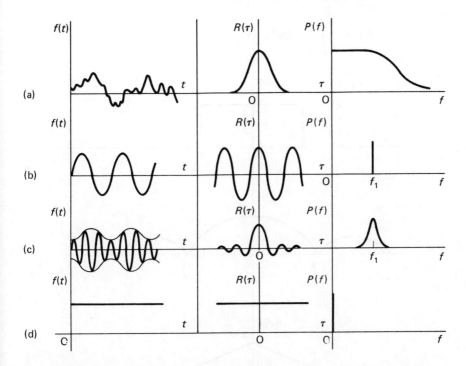

Figure 9.20 Power spectrum and autocorrelation for various signals: (a) noise, (b) sine wave, (c) noise + sine wave, (d) d.c. level

EXAMPLE 9.10

Verify the above relations for the rectangular pulse of figure 9.21.

We have $F(f) = A\theta$ sinc $f\theta$ as before, so $E(f) = A^2\theta^2$ sinc^2 $f\theta$. Also $R_1(\tau) = A^2\theta(1 - |\tau|/\theta)$; $|\tau| \leqslant \theta$. Now $E(f) \rightleftharpoons R_1(\tau)$, and since $R_1(\tau)$ is triangular we can use the result derived above, so $E(f) = $ (area) sinc^2 $f\theta = (A\theta)^2$ sinc$^2 f\theta$, as above. Unfortunately we cannot easily evaluate the Fourier Transform of $E(f)$, so we cannot formally show that it is equal to $R_1(\tau)$.

Finally, the total energy

$$E = \int_{-\infty}^{+\infty} f^2(t)\,\mathrm{d}t = A^2\theta$$

As an integral over frequency

$$E = \int_{-\infty}^{+\infty} E(f)\,\mathrm{d}f$$

$$= \int_{-\infty}^{+\infty} (A\theta)^2 \text{ sinc}^2 f\theta \; \mathrm{d}\theta$$

$$\to A^2\theta \ \left(\text{since} \int_{-\infty}^{+\infty} \text{sinc}^2 x \ dx = 1\right.$$

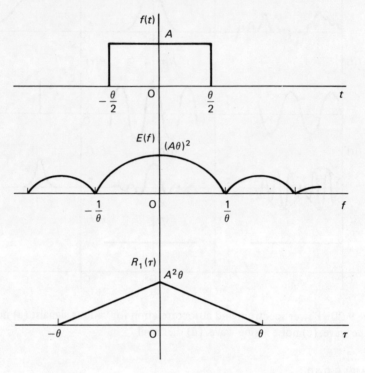

Figure 9.21   Power spectrum and autocorrelation function of a rectangular pulse

9.3.5 Linear systems

Fourier Theory provides a valuable insight into the behaviour of linear systems, and we will conclude this chapter by giving a brief summary of the important relations.

A linear system obeys the *principle of superposition*, which means that if an input i_1 produces an output o_1 and an input i_2 produces an output o_2 then $(i_1$ and $i_2)$ together produce $(o_1 + o_2)$. Essentially, no frequencies are present at the output that were not present at the input.

Consider the system of figure 9.22 in which an input $f(t)$ produces an output $g(t)$.

In the frequency domain we have an input spectrum $F(f)$ and an output spectrum $G(f)$ related by the system transfer function $H(f)$. That is

$$G(f) = H(f) \times F(f)$$

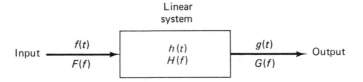

Figure 9.22   Fourier relations in a linear system

$H(f)$ is complex; its modulus is the amplitude response of the system, and its argument the phase response, that is $H(f) = A(f) \exp (j\phi(f))$. The time-equivalent of $H(f)$ has been labelled $h(t)$. To see its significance, let $f(t)$ be a unit impulse. We have $F(f) = 1$ so $G(f) = H(f)$. The output time response is $g(t) = h(t)$; in other words $h(t)$ is the *impulse response* of the system and $h(t) \rightleftharpoons H(f)$. The impulse response of a system is a particularly important parameter. It is more fundamental that the widely used step response (preferred by engineers because it is more easily realised in practice), being the Fourier Transform of the transfer function.

Since $G(f)$ is the product of $H(f)$ and $F(f)$ we can immediately deduce that

$$g(t) = h(t) * f(t)$$

that is, the output is the convolution between input and impulse response.

The impulse response has the significance of representing the system's 'memory' of past inputs. A 'broad' impulse response means that the output at a given instant is determined by previous inputs stretching backwards in time; an ideal system has an impulse response that is an impulse and the output depends only on the present input.

We therefore have two methods for finding the response of a system; we can use a convolution in the time domain, or we can use a product in the frequency domain and then carry out a Fourier Transform if we want the time response.

EXAMPLE 9.11

Step response of a low-pass filter.
For the filter of figure 9.23

$$H(f) = \frac{v_{out}}{v_{in}} = \frac{\dfrac{1}{j\omega C}}{R + \dfrac{1}{j\omega C}} = \frac{\alpha}{\alpha + j\omega}$$

where $\alpha = 1/RC$.

The impulse response $h(t) \rightleftharpoons H(f)$ so $h(t) = \exp (-\alpha t)$ (since we know the transform of the exponential decay).

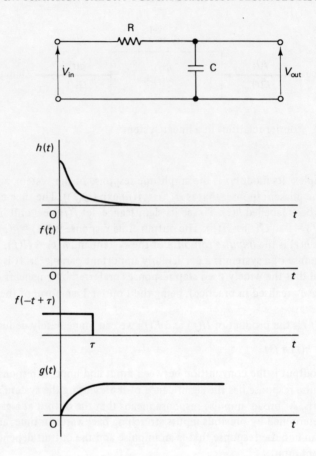

Figure 9.23   Step response of a low-pass filter

Since $g(t) = h(t) * f(t)$ we can see geometrically that $g(t) = 1 - \exp(-\alpha t)$.
(Alternatively, $g(\tau) = \int_{-\infty}^{+\infty} f(\tau - t) h(t) \, dt = \int_0^\tau h(t) \, dt$ from figure 9.23.)
In the frequency domain

$$G(f) = H(f) \times F(f)$$

$$= \frac{1}{j\omega} \cdot \frac{\alpha}{\alpha + j\omega}$$

$$= \frac{1}{j\omega} - \frac{1}{\alpha + j\omega}$$

Taking the Fourier Transform, $g(t) = 1 - \exp(-\alpha t)$ (for $t > 0$), taking the transform of the unit step to be $1/j\omega$ (see example 9.5).

9.4 Summary

We have seen that Fourier Theory provides a unique relationship between a function and its spectrum. Although expressed in mathematical terms, it is the meaning of the relationship that is so important. Mathematics is used as a tool, and it enables us to express neatly and compactly the basic idea of the relationship, which would take (and has taken) many pages of words to describe.

A particular application of Fourier Theory in Information Technology is discussed in the next chapter, namely sampling theory, which is absolutely essential in modern information transmission systems. However, a proper understanding of Fourier Theory is important before proceeding and the reader is encouraged to attempt the exercises at the end of this chapter (or at least to read through the solutions), since some important points arise that may not be apparent from the text.

It is very helpful to memorise some of the basic results. These days, of course, anything that remotely resembles rote learning is strongly discouraged, in contrast to the educational methods built up over many previous years in which it was strongly encouraged! Unfortunately the almost complete emphasis now based on trying to teach understanding in the U.K. educational system has its drawbacks. Many people are unsuited to such a singular approach, understanding slowly being acquired over a period of time, often stemming directly from facts learned though not understood at the time. The result is that students arrive at University often lacking not only the very understanding their teachers have tried so hard to give them, but also lacking the basic factual knowledge that could have led to that understanding.

9.5 Exercises on Chapter 9

9.5.1.   Use the complex form of Fourier Series to find the coefficients c_n for the square waves of figure 9.24, taking the origins as shown. Sketch the amplitude and phase spectrum in each case.

9.5.2.   Show that the complex Fourier Coefficients c_n for the repetitive waveform $f_1(t)$ of figure 9.25(a) are given by

$$c_n = \frac{A}{T} \text{ sinc } \frac{n\tau}{T}$$

Show how the repetitive waveform $f_2(t)$ of figure 9.25(b) can be derived from $f_1(t)$ by simple operations such as addition, inversion and lateral shift, and hence deduce the complex Fourier Coefficients for $f_2(t)$.

Sketch the amplitude and phase spectra for the first eight harmonics of $f_1(t)$ and $f_2(t)$, assuming that $T = 4\tau$.

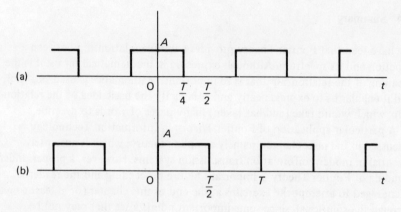

Figure 9.24

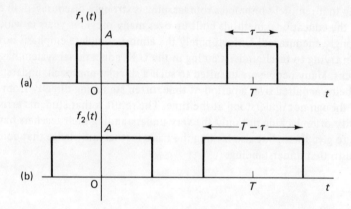

Figure 9.25

9.5.3.   (i) What is the effect of the zeroth harmonic?
         (ii) Are the even harmonics of a square wave necessarily zero?
        (iii) Are the even harmonics of an even function necessarily zero?
         (iv) What is special about the phase of the harmonics of an even
               function? And an odd function?
          (v) What is the effect on the harmonics of inverting a function?
         (vi) What is the effect on the harmonics of shifting the origin of a
               function?
        (vii) How can the harmonics be changed so as to reverse a function
               (that is, mirror image it in the y-axis)?
       (viii) If a rectangle wave has a period of 120 units and a pulse width of
               20 units, which is the lowest harmonic of zero magnitude? Does
               this depend on the origin chosen?

(ix) What is the effect of adding together many harmonics all of the same magnitude and phase?

(x) How should one select harmonics to produce an approximation to random noise?

9.5.4. Find the spectrum of the 'half cosine' pulse of figure 9.26 and sketch its amplitude spectrum

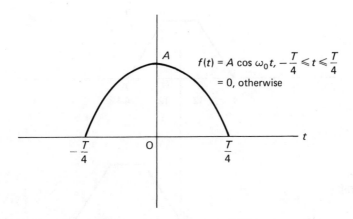

$$f(t) = A \cos \omega_0 t, \quad -\frac{T}{4} \leqslant t \leqslant \frac{T}{4}$$
$$= 0, \text{ otherwise}$$

Figure 9.26   Half-cosine pulse

9.5.5. Find the spectrum of the double pulse of figure 9.27. Sketch the amplitude spectrum for $T = 2\tau$ and $T = \tau/2$.

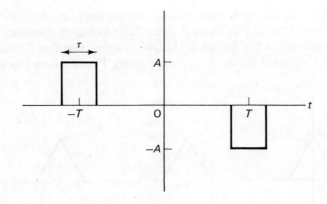

Figure 9.27

9.5.6.   (i) Find the spectrum of the single pulse of figure 9.28(a). Hence, deduce and sketch the modulus of the spectrum of the single pulse of figure 9.28(b).

(ii) The waveform of figure 9.28(b) is repeated continuously with period T. Find the ratio of the amplitudes of the first six harmonics.

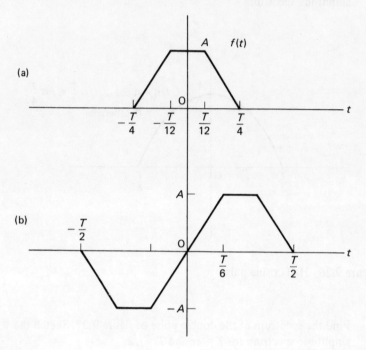

Figure 9.28

9.5.7.   A simple electronic organ produces a repetitive triangular pulse waveform of period T as shown in figure 9.29. At a given frequency the base-width of the triangle can be changed over the range 0 to T to simulate the sounds of chosen musical instruments. Find a general expression for

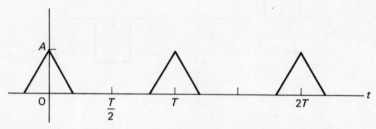

Figure 9.29

the amplitude spectrum of the waveform and sketch it for $\theta = T/4$. Estimate the values of θ, as fractions of T, to make reasonable simulations of the three instruments, whose relative harmonic content should be assumed to be as shown below.

Harmonic	Clarinet	Trumpet	Flute
1	10	10	10
2	0.1	5	1.0
3	1.1	1.1	0.4
4	0.1	0.1	0.6
5	0.4	0.4	0.1
6	0.1	0.6	0.2
7	0.2	0.2	0.1
8	0.1	0.1	0.1

9.5.8. A function of time $f(t)$ is shown in figure 9.30. It consists of a series of equally spaced triangles, all of the same base-width $2a/3$, with heights determined by a larger triangle. Express $f(t)$ in terms of products and convolutions between simpler functions, and hence sketch the modulus of the Fourier Transform of $f(t)$ versus frequency.

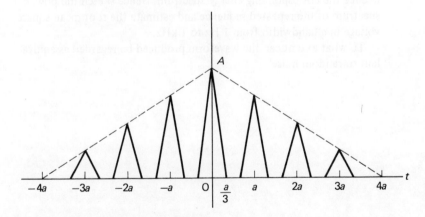

Figure 9.30 The triangle of triangles

9.5.9. Find the finite autocorrelation function $R_1(r)$ for the function $f(t)$ defined by

$$f(t) = A \exp(-\alpha t), (t > 0)$$
$$= 0, \qquad (t < 0)$$

and hence find the energy spectrum $E(f)$ and the total energy E.

Find the Fourier transform $F(f)$ of $f(t)$ and show that $|F(f)|^2 = E(f)$, and that $\int_{-\infty}^{+\infty} f^2(t)\,dt = E$.

Sketch the graphs of $E(f)$ and $R_1(r)$.

9.5.10. Figure 9.31 shows part of the sequence of binary pulses produced by a pseudo-random generator. The basic pulses have amplitude 5 V and duration 1 μs, and the complete sequence is repeated once per second.

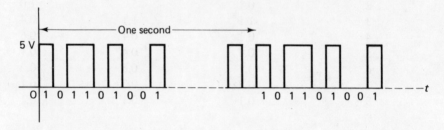

Figure 9.31

The succession of pulses in each sequence may be assumed to be random.

Sketch the finite autocorrelation function for the basic sequence and deduce the corresponding energy spectrum. Hence sketch the power spectrum of the repeated sequence and estimate the root mean square voltage in a bandwidth from 1 Hz to 1 kHz.

To what extent can the waveform produced be regarded as equivalent to random noise?

10 Sampling Theory

10.1 Sampled Signals

There are many applications in Information Technology in which the signal of interest has to be sampled at discrete intervals. For example, in order to transmit several telephone conversations down a single channel, the signals may be sampled in turn at a suitable rate, the succession of samples transmitted in sequence, and the individual conversations reconstructed from the samples at the receiver. Similarly, if an analogue signal is to be processed by a computer, an 'instantaneous' value of the signal must be digitised (fed to an analogue-to-digital convertor or ADC), the required processing carried out, and an analogue value produced at the output via a digital-to-analogue convertor or DAC.

Figure 10.1(b) shows such a system. For simplicity the computer simply reads in the values and immediately puts them out again, with a short time delay. The output value from the DAC is held constant until updated at the next output.

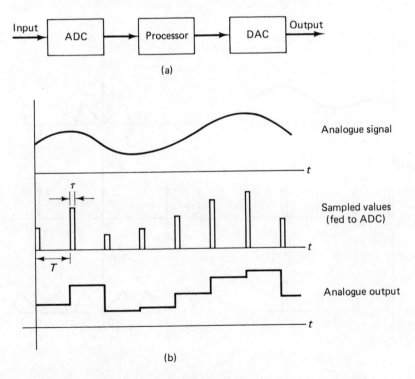

Figure 10.1   (a) Digital processing system, (b) input and output signals

Clearly we need to know what effect the sampling process has on the reconstructed signal, and how it is related to the sampling interval T, the sampling pulse width τ and the holding time.

10.2 The Spectrum of Sampled Signals

The process of sampling an analogue signal is illustrated in figure 10.2, in which a switch S is periodically connected to the signal for a short time τ.

The sampling process can be thought of as the product between the signal $f(t)$ and a switching waveform $s(t)$, as shown in figure 10.3. It follows, therefore, that

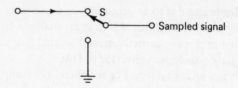

Figure 10.2 The sampling process

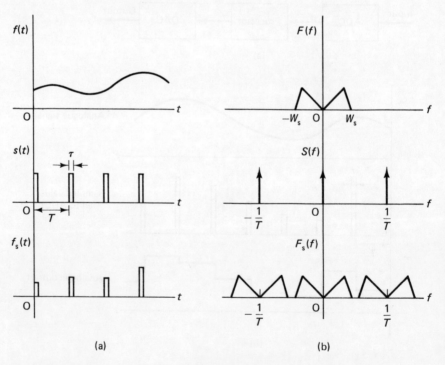

(a)   (b)

Figure 10.3 Sampled signal (a) and its spectrum (b)

the spectrum of the sampled waveform is the convolution between the spectrum of $f(t)$ and the spectrum of $s(t)$. The former has been assumed to be triangular for convenience, with bandwidth W_s, whereas the latter is a set of impulses with envelope determined by a sinc function (dependent on the pulse width τ).

The spectrum of the sampled signal $F_s(f)$ is just a series of repetitions of the original spectrum $F(f)$, spaced at intervals of $1/T$ and decreasing in height according to the sinc function. It is clear that *any one of these repetitions contains all the information in the original signal*. For example, a low pass filter of bandwidth a little more than W_s would extract the central section of $F_s(f)$, or a bandpass filter centred on $1/T$ (with similar bandwidth) would extract the first repeated section (strictly the pair at $1/T$ and $-1/T$).

It appears, therefore, that we can completely recover the original signal from the sampled version, without any loss of information at all! However, there is a critical restriction; the repeated spectra must not overlap with one another. This requires that the separation between spectra is greater than twice the bandwidth of the signal; that is

$$\frac{1}{T} > 2W_s$$

This is the well-known sampling theorem, usually stated as follows.
Sampling Theorem: If a signal contains no frequencies outside the range zero to W_s Hz, it is completely determined by the values of its ordinates spaced at less than or equal to $1/2W_s$ seconds.

Expressed slightly differently, if a signal has a bandwidth W_s we need to take at least $2W_s$ samples per second to retain all the information in the signal. If we take fewer than $2W_s$ samples/s the signal cannot be reconstructed, whereas if we take more its reconstruction is easier, since the tolerances on the filter required are less. This is illustrated in figure 10.4.

When the sampling rate is insufficient, so that the repeated spectra overlap, an important effect known as *aliasing* occurs. This is the appearance of frequencies in the 'recovered' signal that were not in the original signal. This can be seen better by considering a sine wave, as in figure 10.5. If the frequency is f_0 it should be sampled at a rate of at least $2f_0$. However, the figure shows that sampling at intervals of slightly greater than T_0 ($= 1/f_0$) causes a low-frequency sine wave to appear. By considering the frequency domain representation as in figure 10.6, we can see that we do indeed have an unwanted component at frequency $(1/T) - (1/T_0)$ or $(f - f_0)$ where f is the sampling frequency. In practical systems *anti-aliasing filters* are always used to prevent such effects from occurring, by limiting the signal bandwidth appropriately.

The version of the sampling theorem discussed above is the most useful, but there are various extensions, for example to bandpass signals and also to 'sampling' in the frequency domain, to which one would expect that a similar theorem applies.

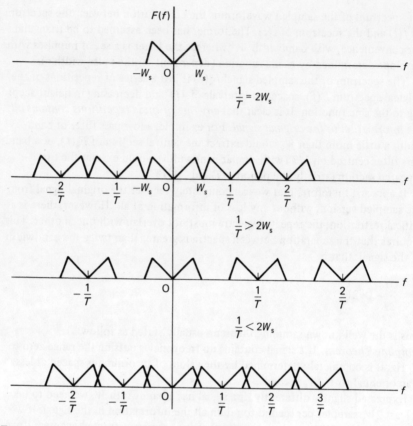

Figure 10.4   Effect of sampling rate on spectrum

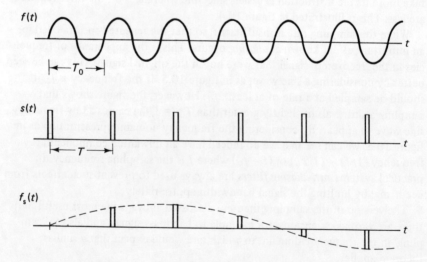

Figure 10.5   The phenomenon of 'aliasing'

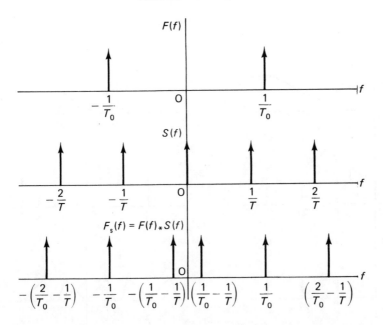

Figure 10.6 Spectrum of 'aliased' signal. Note that convolutions with the $2/T$ and $-2/T$ components of $S(f)$ have been omitted for the sake of clarity

10.3 Impulse Sampling

The sampling process was illustrated above by means of a switch closing for a short time τ, producing a series of pulses proportional to the height of the signal and of width τ. Ideally we would like the pulse width to tend to zero, giving an 'instantaneous' sample, but the power in the pulse train would then tend to zero. Mathematically we can overcome the difficulty by considering that the sampling process is equivalent to multiplying the signal by a train of unit impulses, producing another train of impulses of strengths proportional to the signal values, as in figure 10.7.

Mathematically, the process of taking a sample at a time τ is known as the *sampling property of impulses* (or sifting property), whereby the value of a function $f(t)$ at a time τ is given by

$$f(\tau) = \int_{-\infty}^{+\infty} f(t)\,\delta(t-\tau)\,dt$$

that is, multiplying $f(t)$ by a unit impulse at time τ. The periodic sampling by a series of impulses is denoted by a sampling train

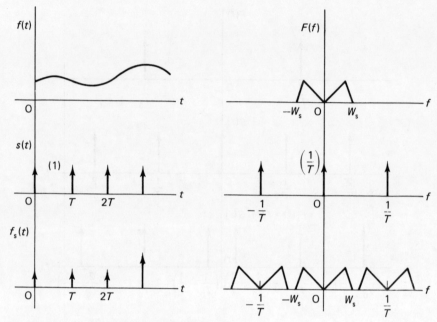

Figure 10.7 Impulse sampling and its spectrum

$$s(t) = \sum_{n=-\infty}^{+\infty} \delta(t - nT)$$

so the sampled waveform $f_s(t)$ is given by

$$f_s(t) = f(t) \sum_{n=-\infty}^{+\infty} \delta(t - nT)$$

The spectrum is similar to that of figure 10.3, except that the repetitions are now all of the same height.

Unfortunately one cannot easily make a good approximation to an impulse, since a pulse of great height would be needed. However, the technique usually used is known as *sample and hold* (strictly the arrangement is known as 'zero-order hold') whereby the 'instantaneous' value of one sample is held at a constant value (for example, by an integrator) until the next sample is taken, as illustrated in figure 10.8. A train of broad pulses is produced, as at the output of the DAC in figure 10.1.

The spectrum of the sample and hold output can be obtained easily from the convolution theorems (surprise, surprise!) since the hold signal is just the convolution between the train of impulses (from the impulse sampler) and a single rectangular 'hold' pulse. The spectrum is therefore the product between the spectra of the impulse train (impulses) and the hold pulse (a sinc function), as shown in figure 10.9.

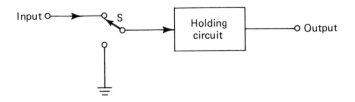

Figure 10.8   Sample and hold circuit

We have

$$f_s(t) = f(t) \times s(t) \text{ and } f_{sh}(t) = f_s(t) * h(t)$$

Therefore

$$F_s(f) = F(f) * S(f) \text{ and } F_{sh}(f) = F_s(f) \times H(f)$$

The spectrum is slightly distorted by the sinc function due to the hold pulse, but it can be recovered completely (provided $1/T > 2W_s$) by a filter with the required gain characteristic (that is, a slight rise with frequency, up to W_s).

The concept of 'impulse sampling' is thus very useful, since although it is difficult to implement directly it permits us to analyse the waveforms actually produced in practice.

10.4   Recovery of Signal from Samples

We have seen above that complete recovery of the signal from its samples is possible in principle provided that we have at least $2W_s$ samples per second. The result is really rather surprising, since one tends to think that the waveform of a signal *between* samples cannot possibly be known *exactly*. However, by transforming to the frequency domain we have seen that it must be completely recoverable at all times, that is, even between samples. In reconstructing the waveform in the time domain each value is determined in part by all the infinite set of impulses, and it is this, together with the fact that $f(t)$ is specifically limited in bandwidth (which limits its rate of change) that makes complete recovery possible.

$f(t)$ is recovered by a filter, as shown in figure 10.10, where an ideal filter is assumed whose response falls immediately to zero at $1/2T$, and with no phase shift. Such a response cannot be obtained in practice, of course, so that sampling at a rate greater than $2W_s$ is necessary (typically 8000/s for a 3 kHz telephone channel) to ease the filter constraints.

The time equivalent of the ideal filter characteristic is a sinc function, with zeros at T, $2T$, $3T$ etc. (it is actually the impulse response of the filter, of course). Multiplying $F_s(f)$ by $H(f)$ gives $F(f)$, so in the time domain we obtain $f(t)$ by convolving the sinc function $h(t)$ with the impulses $f_s(t)$. This produces a set of sinc functions centred on 0, T, $2T$ etc., with heights governed by the appropriate

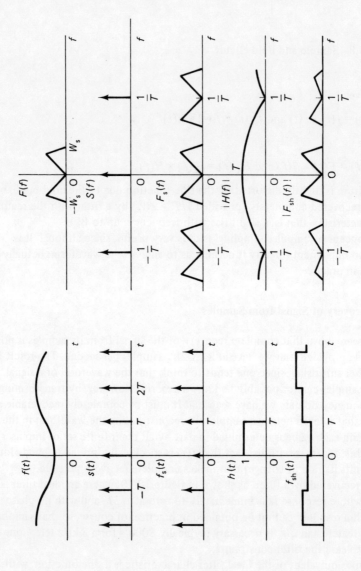

Figure 10.9   Spectrum of sample and hold system

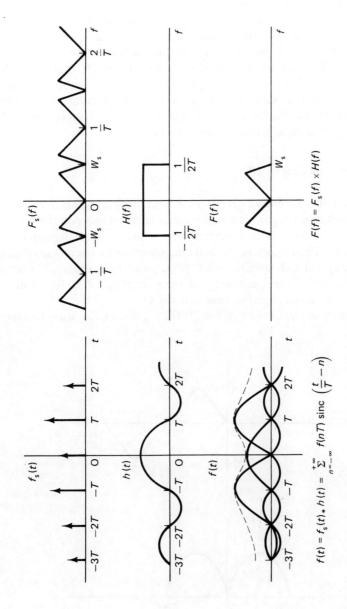

Figure 10.10 Recovery of a signal from samples

sample values. For a given sample the sinc function has a peak height equal to its own sample value and is zero *at all other sample points*. $f(t)$ is thus reconstructed by adding sinc functions centred on all the sample values. In the particular case sketched, where the filter bandwidth is $1/2T\,(= W_s)$, the sinc functions determine only their own sample value, so that the samples are (just) independent of one another. However, with more rapid sampling this would no longer be the case.

In practice, therefore, one samples at a rate greater than $2W_s$ (having specifically limited the signal bandwidth to W_s by means of an anti-aliasing filter) so that a practical filter can be designed to recover $f(t)$. Its operation is equivalent to the addition of the sinc functions, fitting in the 'correct' values between samples and permitting a 'perfect' reconstruction of $f(t)$.

10.5 Exercises on Chapter 10

10.5.1. A waveform is given by $f(t) = \frac{1}{2}\cos 3\omega_0 t - \cos \omega_0 t$. Simulate the sampling process by plotting the values of $f(t)$ at intervals of $\pi/3$ from zero to 2π (that is, sampling interval = period/6 = twice frequency of the third harmonic). Reconstruct the waveform by erecting sinc functions (by eye) at each sampling point, of maximum value equal to the sample value at that point, and zero at all other sampling points. Why is the reconstruction imperfect near zero and 2π?

10.5.2. The signal $f(t)$ band-limited to 2000 Hz is sketched in figure 10.11(a)

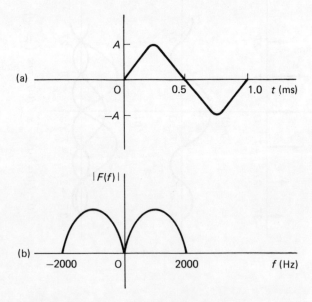

Figure 10.11   Band-limited signal (a) and its spectrum (b)

and the modulus of its spectrum in figure 10.11(b). It is impulsively sampled at a rate of 5,000 samples per second, and the sampled signal fed to a zero-order hold circuit of hold time 0.2 ms.

(i) Sketch the impulsively sampled signal and its spectrum, and explain how $f(t)$ could be recovered.

(ii) Sketch the output of the hold circuit and its spectrum, and explain how $f(t)$ could be recovered.

(iii) Discuss the recovery of $f(t)$ when:

(a) the sampling rate is reduced to 3000 samples/s;

(b) the holding time is reduced to 0.1 ms (sampling rate 5000 samples/s).

11 Information in Continuous Signals

11.1 Continuous Signals

We are now in a position to consider the information content of much more general signals than we discussed in chapters 1–5. We restricted our attention there to discrete signals, such as letters of the alphabet or streams of binary digits. However, many practical signals are essentially analogue (that is, continuous) in practice, such as a speech signal from a microphone or a radio signal (although they are often digitised later for processing by computer), and we need to be able to deduce their information capacity.

A typical analogue signal is shown in figure 11.1.

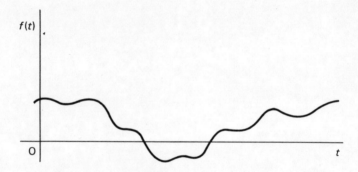

Figure 11.1   Continuous analogue signal

A simple way of estimating its information content is to remember that such a signal can be converted into samples with no loss of information provided that we take at least $2W$ samples/s, W being the signal bandwidth. The information per second R provided by the signal is therefore given by

$$R = (\text{number of samples/s} \times \text{information per sample}) \tag{11.1}$$

There are a number of possible objections to this equation. Firstly we can, of course, take as many samples as we wish, not just $2W$/s. What is really required is the *maximum number of independent samples/s*. Fortunately this is just the value provided by the sampling theorem. If we take more than $2W$/s the waveform will be easily reproducible from the samples, but the samples will not be independent. In contrast, if we take fewer than $2W/s$ the waveform will not be reproducible but the samples will be independent. The critical number $2W/s$ is the value required and is known as the Nyquist signalling rate.

The second objection is more serious. From our previous definition of information in discrete signals as the logarithm of the probability of an event, the information per sample can be taken as the logarithm of the number of distinguishable levels (assuming for the present that all levels are equiprobable). However, if the signal is not perturbed by noise the number of possible levels is infinite. In principle, if we have a sufficiently good meter we can measure the amplitude of a given sample as accurately as we wish, so there is no limit to the number of levels, even if the maximum amplitude is fixed. The information per sample is therefore infinite! This is unfortunate. One intuitively feels that different types of continuous signal should have different information capacity, a random signal being capable of carrying more information than say a mainly sinusoidal signal. However, apparently they do all have the same capacity — infinity!

The solution lies in recognising that any practical system will be perturbed by random noise, and that this will limit the number of distinguishable levels. If the root mean square noise level is σ_n the meter will read σ_n for zero signal. It is found practically that the smallest detectable signal has amplitude about σ_n (that is, root mean square signal-to-noise ratio unity), the next about $2\sigma_n$ etc., so if the maximum signal amplitude is S the number of distinguishable levels is about S/σ_n. (One could argue that it is $S/\sigma_n + 1$, including the zero signal case, but the approach here is only approximate in any case.) We thus obtain an expression for the information per second, usually identified with the channel capacity C, of

$$C = 2W \times \log\left(\frac{S}{\sigma_n}\right)$$

This is often rewritten in terms of signal-power-to-noise-ratio P/N where $P = S^2$ and $N = \sigma_n^2$, giving

$$C = 2W \log\left(\frac{P}{N}\right)^{\frac{1}{2}} = W \log\left(\frac{P}{N}\right)$$

Our intuitive approach has thus yielded a simple yet specific result, almost identical to the result of a more thorough analysis which we shall now consider.

11.2 Relative Entropy of Continuous Signals

We have shown previously that the entropy of a discrete set of events of probability p_i is given by $H = -\sum_i p_i \log p_i$. When dealing with continuous signals probability densities $p(v)$ replace discrete probabilities p_i, such that $p_i = p(v)\delta v$ is the probability of the signal being in the range δv. A continuous version of the equation for entropy can be obtained by letting v tend to zero, giving

$$H(v) = - \lim_{\delta v \to 0} \sum_i p(v)\delta v \log (p(v)\delta v)$$

$$= - \int_{-\infty}^{\infty} p(v) \log p(v) \, dv - \lim_{\delta v \to 0} \sum_i p(v) \log (\delta v) \, \delta v$$

$$= \int_{-\infty}^{+\infty} p(v) \log p(v) \, dv - \lim_{\delta v \to 0} (\log \delta v) \qquad (11.2)$$

The second term tends to infinity and corresponds to the effect of having no limit to the number of distinguishable levels. In practice, where noise is always present, the capacity of signal and noise together will be the difference between two expressions like (11.2), one for signal and one for noise. The two second (infinite) terms will always cancel one another, since the term involves δv only and not $p(v)$. We are therefore left only with the first term, which we will call the *relative entropy* $H_r(v)$ of a continuous signal.

$$H_r(v) = - \int_{-\infty}^{+\infty} p(v) \log p(v) \, dv \qquad (11.3)$$

It represents the information per sample of a continuous waveform, ignoring the infinite term, and depends on $p(v)$ as we intuitively require. Its use will not cause any difficulties provided we remember that all practical signals are perturbed by noise, but the expression must not be used blindly in isolation.

The type of signal having greatest information capacity will clearly have a probability density distribution $p(v)$ which maximises $H_r(v)$. One might expect this to be a uniform distribution (since H for a discrete system is greatest when all the probabilities are equal), but a better guess would be a gaussian distribution (since there is no limit to amplitude and it applies to random noise). There are mathematical techniques for obtaining the maximising distribution, but they will not be reproduced here as they add nothing (except about a page of working) to the subject. We will therefore simply evaluate $H_r(v)$ for a gaussian, taking $p(v) = (1/\sigma\sqrt{2\pi}) \exp(-v^2/2\sigma^2)$, assuming zero mean, and this will be the maximum possible value of $H_r(v)$. The integral is easier to evaluate if we work in natural units (nats), taking logs to base e.

$$H_r(v) = - \int_{-\infty}^{+\infty} p(v) \log_e p(v) \, dv \text{ nats}$$

$$= \int_{-\infty}^{+\infty} p(v) \log_e(\sigma\sqrt{2\pi}) \, dv + \int_{-\infty}^{+\infty} p(v) . \frac{v^2}{2\sigma^2} \, dv$$

$$= \log_e(\sigma\sqrt{2\pi}) + \tfrac{1}{2}$$

$$= \log_e(\sigma\sqrt{2\pi e}) \text{ nats} \quad (\text{since } \tfrac{1}{2} = \log_e(e^{\frac{1}{2}}))$$

We can now change the base back to 2 and the units simply change to bits! Thus

$$H_r(v) = \log_2(\sigma\sqrt{2\pi e}) \text{ bits}$$

Writing signal power $P = \sigma^2$, the final expression becomes

$$H_r(v) = \log(2\pi e P)^{\frac{1}{2}} \text{ bits} \tag{11.4}$$

This derivation is much admired by those who are peculiarly appreciative of any results that can be obtained without doing any real work!

EXAMPLE 11.1

Compare $H_r(v)$ for the following waveforms, normalising such that all waveforms have a variance of unity: (i) gaussian distributed, (ii) repetitive triangular, (iii) square.
  (i) The gaussian gives $\log_2(\sigma\sqrt{2\pi e})$ bits as shown above.
  (ii) Figure 11.2(a) and (b) shows a typical triangular wave and its probability density distribution.

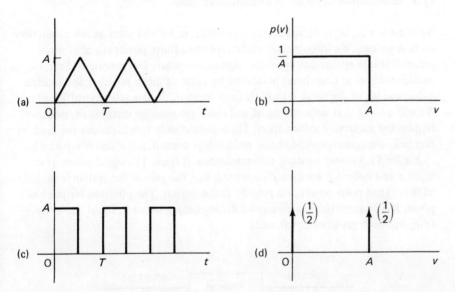

Figure 11.2 Triangle waveform (a) and its probability density distribution (b). Square wave (c) and its probability density distribution (d)

$$\bar{v}^2 = \int_0^A v^2 p(v)\, dv = \frac{A^2}{3}, \quad \bar{v} = \frac{A}{2}, \quad \sigma^2 = \frac{A^2}{12}$$

$$H_r(v) = -\int_0^A \frac{1}{A} \log \frac{1}{A}\, dv = \log A = \log(\sigma\sqrt{12})$$

(the same value will be found for any triangle wave).

(iii) Figure 11.2(c) and (d) shows a square wave and its probability density distribution. $p(v)$ consists of two impulses, each of strength one-half, at O and A.

$$H_r(v) = - \int_{-\infty}^{+\infty} p(v) \log p(v) \, dv = - (\tfrac{1}{2} \log \tfrac{1}{2} + \tfrac{1}{2} \log \tfrac{1}{2}) = 1 \text{ bit}$$

(since the only contributions to the integral are at $v = O$ and $v = A$, and $p(v)$ is then $\tfrac{1}{2}$).

Note that this is the same result we get for a discrete system with two levels, and that the height of the levels does not matter. The ratios of $H_r(v)$ for the three cases are $1:0.87:0.49$, showing that the gaussian distribution carries more information than the uniform distribution, as expected. The term 'entropy power' is sometimes used in comparing $H_r(v)$ for different waveforms.

11.3 Information Capacity of Continuous Signals

We want our signal to be as general as possible, so we will place as few restrictions on it as we can. We will consider a non-repetitive finite power signal of mean power P (finite energy and repetitive signals are clearly less general and can be considered special cases here) perturbed by noise of mean power N and limited in bandwidth to the range 0 to W Hz (*any* bandwidth W is actually sufficient). We will assume that both the signal and noise are gaussian distributed, since we require the maximum information. These are the only specifications required; in fact only the signal-power-to-noise ratio P/N is needed, not P and N separately.

Figure 11.3 shows a simple communication system. The signal power at the input x and output y are both P (assuming that the gain in the system is suitably adjusted) but noise power N is present at the output. The observed output has power $P + N$, since there is no way of distinguishing between signal and noise (they are both gaussian distributed).

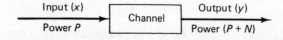

Figure 11.3 Information transfer in a continuous channel

From our previous formulae the information transfer $I(xy)$ is

$$I(xy) = H(y) - H(y/x)$$

The equivocation $H(y/x)$ represents the effect of noise, since x and y would be identical in a noiseless system, so we can replace it by $H(n)$, meaning the noise entropy, where $H(n) = \log(2\pi e N)^{\frac{1}{2}}$ from above. Now $H(y) = \log(2\pi e \{P + N\})^{\frac{1}{2}}$

since the output power is $(P + N)$. The capacity C is therefore $H(v) - H(n) = \log((P + N)/N)^{\frac{1}{2}}$. Assuming that we take $2W$ samples/s as before, the capacity (expressed as information/s) is given by

$$C = W \log \left(1 + \frac{P}{N}\right) \text{ bits/s} \tag{11.5}$$

Note that this is almost identical with the result obtained by our sample intuitive approach in section 11.1; in fact, we could have obtained an identical result by taking the number of levels to be $((S/\sigma_n) + 1)$.

This is a very important and significant expression. It refers to a very general signal, yet tells us the information per second in terms of only the bandwidth W and the signal-power-to-noise ratio P/N.

Although it may not be apparent from the above derivation, it has a further significance. Not only is it the maximum information transfer — it is also the maximum error-free communication rate! Equation (11.5) is known as the ideal communication theorem and the capacity as the ideal communication rate. Information can be transmitted at any rate up to and including C with no net errors at all.

This is because the expression represents a capacity. We saw previously for discrete signals that by selecting only a fraction of the possible code groups as messages we could make the error rate vanishingly small provided that we kept the rate R less than or equal to the capacity C. Since a continuous signal can be sampled into discrete values, the two situations become the same and we have the same result. It is, however, possible to prove the result in a number of ways; a formal proof will not be given, but we will outline a method given by Shannon, since it is very instructive and gives another insight into the situation.

Suppose we have a signal lasting for a time T so that the information carried is $C \times T$ or $WT \log(1 + P/N)$ bits, and that the signal is sampled at the Nyquist rate giving $2WT$ samples. We can (attempt to) imagine our signal (of $2WT$ values) to be represented by a single point in a multi-dimensional space of $2WT$ dimensions! Another signal, of the same characteristics and duration, would be represented by another point in the same space. The signal will be perturbed by noise, whose effect will be to 'blur' the signal so that instead of being represented by a point it becomes a small 'sphere' centred on the point. The number of distinguishable signals is just the number of such 'spheres' that can be packed into the space. The properties of multi-dimensional spaces provide the required result, and it is found that if the number of samples tends to infinity the above expression for C is indeed the maximum error-free rate! The actual derivation is somewhat lengthy (see Rosie, 1973, pp. 96–103).

Of course, the objection can again be raised that the expression or its derivation does not tell us how to go about setting up a system to communicate at or near this rate. However, at least we know that we must use gaussian-distributed waveforms of long duration, and schemes similar to that of figure 11.4 have been suggested (Rice, 1950).

Many noise-like signals

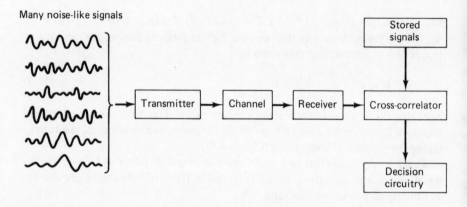

Figure 11.4   Hypothetical 'ideal' communication system

A large number of different signals represent the messages to be transmitted. They are all bursts of random noise of the same duration. The same signals are also stored at the receiver and when a particular signal (blurred by noise) is received it is cross-correlated with each of the stored signals in turn, and identified by the largest output. The system suffers from the same problems as found previously in the discrete case; it is necessary to use an impossibly large number of signals, to select them to be as different from one another as possible, and very long time delays occur in the decision process.

It is instructive to compare the capacity and error rate of a simple binary system with that given by the ideal theorem. In chapter 7 we calculated the error rate of a system in which a binary pulse train is perturbed by random noise of mean power 0.1 V^2 in bandwidth 1 kHz. We found that the error rate was 8×10^{-4}. The signal-power-to-noise ratio is 10. We have

$$I(xy) = 1 - H(p) = 0.99 \text{ bits}$$

Assuming that we signal at the Nyquist rate (that is, $2W$ pulses/s), the information rate is 1981 bits/s with an error rate of 8×10^{-4}.

Ideally, $C = W \log (1 + P/N) = 3459$ bits/s and there are no net errors at all. The binary system is surprisingly good, considering that it is not much like a burst of random noise (though a good approximation to random noise can be generated from a pseudo-random train, as shown above).

11.4   Deductions from the Ideal Theorem

Although we cannot at present approach very close to the ideal communication rate predicted by equation (11.5), it serves as a useful standard against which to compare practical systems. In addition, several important deductions can be made which do have useful practical applications.

The information transmitted in a time T is

$I = WT \log (1 + P/N)$

as above. It is clear that a given amount of information I can be transmitted by many different combinations of bandwidth W, duration T and signal-power-to-noise ratio P/N. For example, keeping the bandwidth constant we can exchange P/N and T; a trivial example of this is simply repeating a message. Similarly, W and T may be exchanged; for example one could record a message on tape at high speed (large W, small T) and play back slowly (small W, large T) down say a telephone channel. These two exchanges are obvious of course, and do not owe much to the ideal theorem; however, the exchange between W and P/N is much less obvious, yet very important.

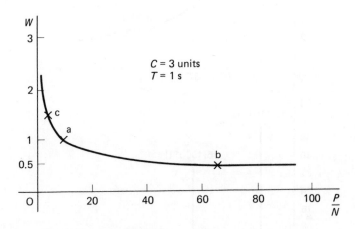

Figure 11.5   Exchange of bandwidth and power-to-noise ratio

We will use numerical values to illustrate the possibilities, and let the information I have a value of 3 bits. Figure 11.5 is the locus of values of W and P/N for constant I (= 3 bits) and T (= 1 second).

We could try to save on W by increasing P/N, or to save on P/N by increasing W. Such possibilities are very important in practice. There is great pressure on bandwidth in broadcast systems whereas signal power is less critical, so a saving in bandwidth could be very valuable. However, the opposite requirements apply in communications with a space probe; the power on the probe is strictly limited but there may be adequate bandwidth allocated.

We will take the point a in figure 11.5, where $W = 1$ and $P/N = 7$, as a reference. If we halve the bandwidth the corresponding P/N must be 63 (point b), whereas if we halve P/N the corresponding bandwidth becomes about 1.5 units (point c). The first possibility, reducing bandwidth by increasing power, is simply not on; it requires a vast increase in power of nine times in this case to halve the bandwidth. However, the second possibility is very much on; the power can be halved at the cost of only a 50 per cent increase in bandwidth!

The question now arises, of course, as to how the exchanges could be carried out. Considering the impractical one first, two successive samples of a waveform could be combined into one larger value which could be transmitted in a narrower bandwidth (that is, at half the sampling rate). This is illustrated in figure 11.6,

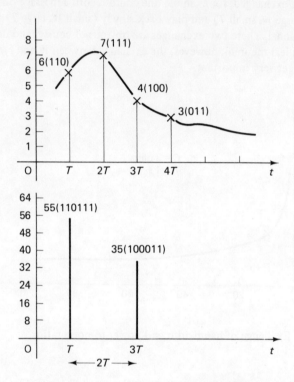

Figure 11.6   Reduction of bandwidth by combining samples

where the input waveform is quantised to one of eight possible levels. The binary codes for two successive samples of 6 units (110) and 7 units (111) are combined into the code 110111 (= 55), and a single pulse of 55 units transmitted (in a 64 level system). The power is increased from $(6^2 + 7^2)$ to $(55)^2$, or by a factor of about 35, though the required bandwidth is halved.

The second possibility arises naturally in several typical communication systems, such as frequency modulation (FM) and pulse-code modulation (PCM). In these systems the signal spectrum is modified such that the transmission band-width on the channel is much larger than the original signal bandwidth, and the result is that much less transmitter power is required. The technique of PCM is rather similar to that shown in figure 11.6. The signal is quantised into one of a given number of levels, but instead of two samples being combined into one large pulse a train of binary pulses is transmitted which represents the samples in binary (for example, 110111 for the first two samples in figure 11.6). The bandwidth is increased by a factor of 3 (in this case), and the required power considerably reduced. PCM and FM will be described in more detail in the next chapter.

Another interesting deduction is of the minimum power required to transmit one bit of information. The total noise power N can be written as $G_n \times W$, where G_n is the power spectral density of the noise. The maximum value of C occurs for W tending to infinity and P/N tending to zero; that is

$$C_{max} = \lim_{\substack{W \to \infty \\ P/N \to 0}} W \log \left(1 + \frac{P}{G_n W}\right) \text{ bits}$$

Working in natural units, since $\lim_{x \to 0} \log_e(1 + x) = x$, we have

$$C_{max} = W . \frac{P}{G_n W} = \frac{P}{G_n} \text{ nats}$$

The value of G_n for Johnson noise is kT, so we have the surprising result that the minimum amount of power required to transmit one natural unit of information is kT watts (about 4×10^{-21} W). Usually one works in bits of course (small ones where students are concerned), but it could be said that the nat is a bit more natural!

11.5 Exercises on Chapter 11

11.5.1. Find the relative entropy of the waveform of figure 11.7 and compare with that of gaussian noise, normalising to unity mean power in each case.

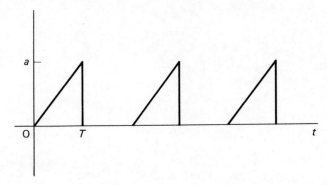

Figure 11.7 Sawtooth waveform

11.5.2. A telephone channel has a bandwidth of 3 kHz and a power-to-noise ratio of 100. Compare the rate of transmission of information when binary pulses are transmitted with that for an ideal communication system of the same parameters.

Note. Assume that the error rate for the binary pulses is zero.

12 Communication Systems

12.1 Modulation

Communication Theory is an essential part of Information Technology. It is an important subject in its own right, and is closely connected with Information Theory; indeed it is difficult to decide where one begins and the other ends. In this chapter we will review some of the important topics in Communication Theory in the light of the results of the previous few chapters, and in preparation for their use in the next chapter.

We noted right at the beginning of this book that information is rarely produced in a form that is suitable for immediate communication, and that it must be modified before transmission. We referred to this as coding, in a general sense, and to the reverse process at the receiver as decoding. It is usually called modulation in Communication Theory, where it involves impressing the information to be transmitted on to some form of 'carrier' waveform. For example, if we wish to transmit a speech waveform by radio, the speech cannot be broadcast directly because radio aerials transmit efficiently only at relatively high frequencies (when the aerial length is of the order of half a wavelength). The (low-frequency) speech waveform is therefore impressed on to a high-frequency sinusoidal carrier (which *can* be broadcast efficiently), which is said to be 'modulated' by the speech signal.

There are two basic types of modulation, analogue modulation and pulse modulation. In the former the carrier is a sinusoid and in the latter a stream of pulses. Even in the latter case, however, the final transmission is usually via a modulated sinusoid (for example, by switching a sinusoid between two levels), the pulse modulation being used only at an intermediate stage.

12.2 Analogue Modulation

A sinusoidal waveform of amplitude a_c, angular frequency ω_c and phase ϕ can be described by $v_c(t) = a_c \cos(\omega_c t + \phi)$. We have seen that a pure sine wave does not carry information, since it is totally predictable. However, we can impress information on to it by modifying a_c, ω_c or ϕ in sympathy with the signal to be transmitted. Methods for modifying a_c are known as *envelope modulation*; those in which the instantaneous phase $(\omega_c t + \phi)$ of the sine wave is modified are known as *angle modulation*.

149

12.2.1 Amplitude modulation

The most familiar and widely used form of envelope modulation is known as
amplitude modulation (AM). When a carrier $v_c = a_c \cos \omega_c t$ is amplitude modulated by a signal $v_s = a_s \cos \omega_s t$, the resulting waveform is given by

$$v_m = a_c(1 + m \cos \omega_s t) \cos \omega_c t \qquad (12.1)$$

where m is known as the modulation index.

The three waveforms are sketched in figure 12.1(a). It can be seen that the signal
v_s determines the envelope of the modulated waveform; v_m can range in amplitude from $a_c(1 + m)$ to $a_c(1 - m)$ and clearly cannot be allowed to become
negative (or the correct waveform would not be recovered from the envelope)
so we have the restriction that $|m| < 1$.

Equation (12.1) can be rewritten in the form

$$v_m = a_c \cos \omega_c t + \frac{ma_c}{2} \cos (\omega_c + \omega_s)t + \frac{ma_c}{2} \cos (\omega_c - \omega_s)t$$

showing that it consists of three terms, the carrier and two sidebands, which
constitute the spectrum of the modulated waveform for the case of modulation
by a sinusoidal signal. The form of the spectrum for a more general signal $f(t)$,
such as a speech waveform, is easily seen by convolution. Equation (12.1)
becomes

$$v_m = a_c(1 + m f(t)) \cos \omega_c t$$

$$= a_c.m.f(t).\cos \omega_c t + a_c \cos \omega_c t$$

The first term is a product between $f(t)$ and $\cos \omega_c t$ and the spectrum is therefore the convolution between the spectrum of $f(t)$ and impulses at $\pm f_c$; the
second term (the unchanged carrier) simply produces impulses at $\pm f_c$. This is
illustrated in figure 12.1(b). The spectrum $F(f)$ of the speech waveform $f(t)$ is
simply reproduced (scaled by m) centred on the carrier frequency, together with
the unchanged carrier. The effect of AM is thus simply to shift the spectrum by
an amount equal to the carrier frequency, placing it at a suitable frequency for
transmission. The appearance of the two sidebands is a direct consequence (and
an instructive illustration) of Fourier Theory; if one insists on representing spectra
in terms of only positive frequencies, one finds nevertheless that a second (mirror-
imaged) sideband miraculously appears, whereas using Fourier representation the
complete two-sided spectrum is simply shifted up to f_c (and down to $-f_c$).

The fact that an unchanged carrier is present in the modulated waveform is
wasteful in terms of transmitter power, but makes detection easier. It is possible
to suppress the carrier (suppressed carrier AM, SCAM) or to generate only a
single sideband (single sideband AM, SSAM) but detection is much more difficult
and such systems are not economic for broadcast purposes. The efficiency of
AM, in comparison with the ideal communication system, is still very low. AM

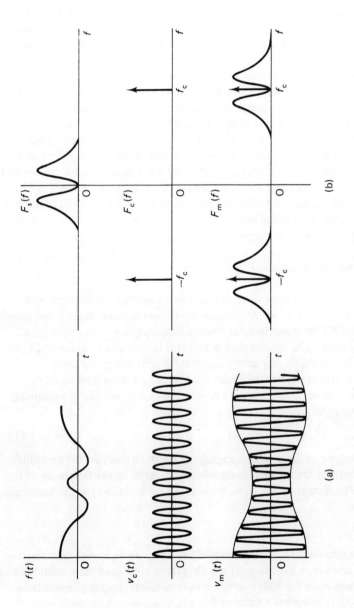

Figure 12.1 (a) Amplitude modulation, (b) spectrum of amplitude-modulated waveform

is inherently a simple frequency translation system making the bandwidth on the channel the same as that of the signal, whereas ideally one wants the channel bandwidth to be much greater.

There are many methods for the production and detection of AM. However, the essential point is that modulation and demodulation involve multiplication and are therefore non-linear processes. We saw above that a characteristic of a linear system is that no frequencies are produced at the output that were not present at the input (only amplitude and phase changes occur), whereas the spectrum is actually shifted in frequency in AM. AM can easily be produced by multiplying a carrier by the signal, and adding in some unchanged carrier. (If the carrier is omitted one obtains product modulation or SCAM.) Demodulation involves a further multiplication by the carrier; in figure 12.1(b) the original spectrum can be recovered by convolving the spectrum of the modulated waveform by impulses at the carrier frequency, that is, by a multiplication by the carrier in the time domain. In practice a simple method of envelope detection using a diode is employed; the diode is actually switched on and off by the carrier (a non-linear process equivalent to multiplication) and a smoothing filter recovers the signal from the resulting half-sine waves.

12.2.2 Frequency modulation

There are two forms of angle modulation, known as phase modulation and frequency modulation. Phase modulation modifies the phase angle ϕ and frequency modulation (FM) the instantaneous angular frequency ω_c. One might expect phase modulation to be simpler, but in fact it is less easy to produce and turns out to have less desirable properties than FM, so that it is rarely used.

Figure 12.2(a) illustrates frequency modulation. A sinusoidal signal $v_s = a_s \cos \omega_s t$ modulates the carrier $v_c = a_c \cos \omega_c t$ to produce a modulated waveform v_m given by

$$v_m = a_c \cos (\omega_c t + D \sin \omega_s t) \tag{12.2}$$

where D is known as the modulation index for FM. In this case the amplitude of v_m is constant and the information is entirely in terms of the frequency of the waveform. The instantaneous phase angle is $(\omega_c t + D \sin \omega_s t)$ so the instantaneous frequency is

$$f_{inst} = f_c + D f_s \cos \omega_s t$$

f_{inst} deviates sinusoidally from the carrier frequency to an extent dependent on $D \times f_s$. The maximum deviation Δf is $\pm D f_s$; there is no need for a restriction on D (as there was on m for AM) since f_c is usually several orders of magnitude higher than f_s. D often has a value of 5 in practice.

At this point it is necessary to make an admission that brings tears to the author's eyes — it is not possible to obtain the spectrum of FM by convolution! This is because we require a cosine of a sine, as in equation (12.2), or more

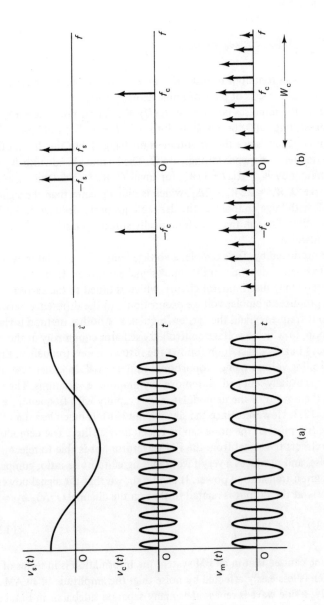

Figure 12.2 (a) Frequency modulation, (b) spectrum of frequency-modulated waveform

generally a cosine of some function $f(t)$. Such requirements always produce rather unpleasant mathematical entities known as Bessel functions, which are tabulated functions of an oscillatory form. It can be shown that the modulated waveform v_m can be written as

$$v_m = \sum_{n=-\infty}^{+\infty} a_c J_n(D) \cos(\omega_c + n\omega_s)\, t$$

where $J_n(D)$ are Bessel functions of order n. The form of the spectrum is sketched in figure 12.2(b) and consists of pairs of impulses at $f_c \pm nf_s$.

The strength of the impulses depends on $J_n(D)$, the carrier not necessarily being the strongest, but $J_n(D)$ becomes small for $n > D + 1$. The total power in the waveform is constant, since the amplitude is unchanged, but the distribution of power with frequency depends strongly on D. The channel bandwidth W_c is given approximately by $W_c = 2(D + 1)W_s$; for small D, $W_c \approx 2W_s$ (that is, as for AM) but, for large D, $W_c \approx 2DW_s = 2\Delta f$, which is much greater than the signal bandwidth. FM, with large D, thus has the desirable property deduced from the ideal communication theorem that it automatically spreads the signal energy over a wide bandwidth.

FM is easily produced by, for example, a voltage-controlled oscillator, whose instantaneous frequency depends on the input signal amplitude. It can be detected by a frequency discriminator circuit, which is tuned to the carrier frequency and produces a bipolar voltage proportional to the difference between the instantaneous frequency and the carrier frequency. Another method is via a phase-locked loop, in which a voltage-controlled oscillator (nominally at the carrier frequency) in a feedback loop follows the instantaneous frequency, the necessary controlling voltage being proportional to the signal. In either case the input waveform is usually 'clipped' to remove any amplitude variations. The noise power at the output of the demodulator rises rapidly with frequency, as shown in figure 12.3. However, since the signal bandwidth is much less than the channel bandwidth, most of the noise can be rejected by a filter. The demodulator thus fully extracts the signal from the FM waveform but is able to reject most of the noise, and produces a very favourable signal-to-noise ratio, compared with AM, for a given transmitted power. It can be shown that the signal-power-to-noise ratio $(P/N)_0$ at the output is related to that on the channel $(P/N)_c$ by

$$\left(\frac{P}{N}\right)_0 = 3D^2 (D + 1)\left(\frac{P}{N}\right)_c \tag{12.3}$$

Intuitively one can see that in an FM system the information is in terms of frequency, which is less easily affected by noise than the amplitude in an AM system; similarly, a sine wave is repeated as many separate sidebands in FM, but only as two in AM.

An improvement in FM in practice can be obtained by a technique known as pre-emphasis, in which the higher-frequency components of the signal are

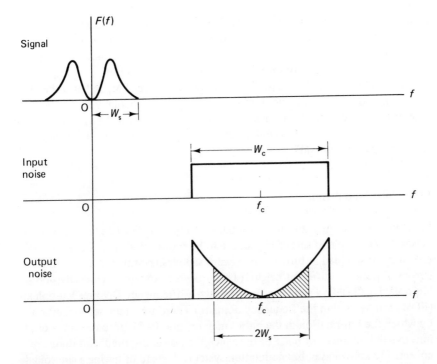

Figure 12.3   Rejection of noise in frequency-modulated system

boosted before transmission, with the reverse operation (de-emphasis) applied at the receiver. The higher-frequency noise components are thus further reduced, so $(P/N)_0$ is improved.

A threshold effect occurs in all practical systems that exchange bandwidth for power-to-noise ratio. In the case of FM, if we try to make W_c too large this makes $(P/N)_c$ so low that noise causes unwanted zero crossings to occur. This causes a dramatic fall in $(P/N)_0$ so in practice a minimum $(P/N)_c$ has to be maintained.

EXAMPLE 12.1

AM and FM can be compared for a radio broadcast system.
The comparison is a little artificial because AM is used for relatively low-quality applications (speech etc.) and the bandwidth limited to only about 5 kHz, whereas FM is preferred for higher quality (music etc.) and a bandwidth of about 15 kHz used. We will use a bandwidth of 15 kHz in each case, with modulation indices $m = 1$ and $D = 5$.

For AM the channel bandwidth will be 30 kHz and the $(P/N)_0$ will be just twice $(P/N)_c$ because of the factor of two. The bandwidth occupied by FM will be $2(D + 1)W_s$ = 180 kHz. If the transmitted powers are the same in each case then $(P/N)_c$ for FM will be six times lower than for AM (the bandwidth ratio) but the factor of $3D^2(D + 1)$ in equation (12.3) has a value of 450 and greatly outweighs this. The ratio of output-power-to-noise-ratio is thus $\frac{1}{2} \times (450/6)$ or about 37. This ignores the possibility of pre-emphasis for FM, and also the fact that even with $m = 1$ only one-third of the AM power is actually in the sidebands (the rest is in the unchanged carrier, which carries no information). Alternatively, for the same output-power-to-noise ratio FM requires only 1/37 times the transmitter power of AM!

12.3 Pulse Modulation

In many practical situations the information to be transmitted is in the form of pulses. For example, if several signals are to be transmitted via a single channel they may be sampled in turn and successive samples transmitted, producing a stream of pulses of different height. (This process is known as Time Division Multiplexing (TDM); a similar process known as Frequency Division Multiplexing (FDM) can be used in the frequency domain.) There are a number of methods by which the information in the pulses may be modified before transmission, to improve the tolerance of noise or to reduce the power required, and these are collectively known as pulse modulation systems. Instead of having a sinusoidal carrier as in analogue modulation, the carrier is replaced by a stream of pulses and there are several ways in which information can be impressed on to them.

12.3.1 PAM, PWM and PPM

The principal methods are illustrated in figure 12.4, in which the signal is a triangle wave.

In pulse amplitude modulation (PAM) the signal is simply sampled directly at a suitable rate, that is, greater than $2W/s$ where W is the signal bandwidth, producing a stream of pulses of height proportional to the signal. The pulse width is usually made small compared with the time between samples (so that samples from other signals can be interleaved if required). We have seen that the spectrum of the sampled waveform consists of repetitions of the signal spectrum spaced at the sampling frequency $1/T_s$. PAM is similar to AM in that the channel bandwidth is the same as the signal bandwidth and it is therefore inefficient in terms of power required for a given output-power-to-noise-ratio.

The information in a pulse-width modulation system (PWM, or PDM for pulse duration modulation) is in terms of the width of the pulses, a standard width for zero signal being increased or decreased dependent on signal polarity. Similarly, in pulse-position modulation (PPM) the information is in the position of the pulse with reference to a standard position corresponding to zero signal. In both these cases the shape of the pulse is important as the leading or trailing edges

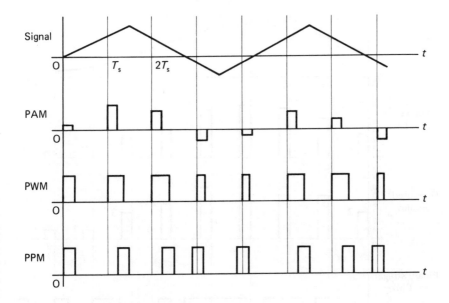

Figure 12.4   Pulse modulation systems

have to be located accurately. A trapezoidal pulse with rise time τ_r is often used
and the required channel bandwidth taken as $1/2\tau_r$. An infinite bandwidth is
needed for perfect transmission, so any practical value is a compromise. PWM
and PPM are a little like FM in that the channel bandwidth is greater than the
signal bandwidth, and are therefore more efficient than PAM. However, they
have been largely replaced by pulse code modulation (PCM) in recent years.

12.3.2 Pulse Code Modulation

In PCM the signal is first sampled as in PAM and the samples then quantised to
the nearest of a preset number of levels. The quantised values are then converted
to binary numbers and a stream of corresponding binary digits representing the
successive samples transmitted. The information is neither in the pulse height
nor its position, but in the actual sequence of 0s and 1s (a similar quantising
process occurs when digital information is read into a computer via an ADC).
Figure 12.5 illustrates the process for a simple system with eight levels.

In general, if we have a signal bandwidth W_s then we must sample at $> 2W_s/s$.
In a binary system the total number of levels M is given by $M = 2^m$, where m is
the number of pulses required to represent each sample (in figure 12.7, $M = 8$
and $m = 3$). Using the general rule that a channel of bandwidth W_c can accept
$2W_c$ binary pulses/s, the channel bandwidth required is $2W_s \times m \times \frac{1}{2} = mW_s$
(sampling at exactly $2W_s$). It is therefore much greater than the signal bandwidth, so that the efficiency will be high.

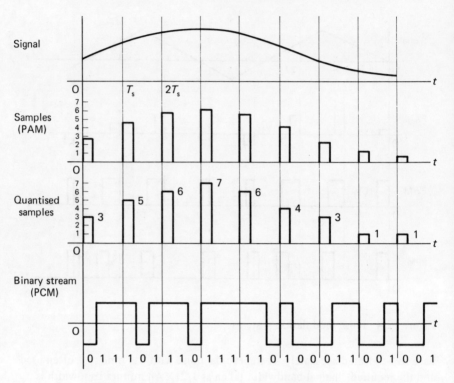

Figure 12.5   Pulse code modulation

EXAMPLE 12.2

Compare the channel bandwidths required for PAM and PCM in a system comprising 24 3 kHz telephone channels each sampled at 8 kHz.

The PAM system simply requires 24 × 4 kHz = 96 kHz, allowing for the (desirable) separation between spectra. A typical PCM system may use $M = 128$ levels plus an additional synchronising bit, giving $m = 7 + 1 = 8$. The bandwidth required is therefore $\frac{1}{2}.24.8000 \times 8 \approx 800$ kHz.

The particular advantages of PCM are that it is very tolerant of noise and very efficient in terms of power required for transmission. It is only necessary to determine at the receiver whether the received digit is a '0' or a '1', and provided that binary errors do not occur the system is noiseless! In fact, binary errors must not be allowed to occur, since their effect would clearly be disastrous, so the digits must be transmitted at a sufficiently high power-to-noise ratio to make the probability of an error negligibly low. This is another example of the threshold effect mentioned above; if one reduces the power too much the system rapidly becomes useless. Fortunately the power-to-noise ratio required for an acceptable error rate is surprisingly low. Using the method described earlier for finding the error rate of a binary signal perturbed by gaussian noise, the critical value is found to be about 20 (corresponding to a root mean square signal-to-noise ratio of 4.6) for an error probability of 10^{-5}; increasing the signal above this value produces a rapid decrease in errors.

Although PCM is noise free in the sense described above, things are rarely ideal in theory, let alone in practice. The effect of random noise is indeed negligible, but the quantising process produces a new form of noise; when PCM is decoded it exactly reproduces the quantised values, not the original samples, and the difference between the two is known as quantising noise. It is fairly simple to work out its magnitude. Consider a system as in figure 12.6(a) with a

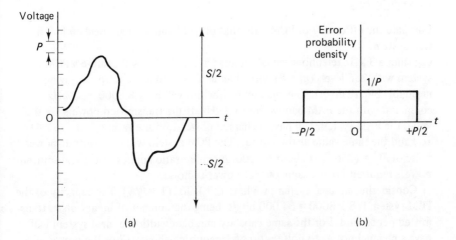

Figure 12.6   Quantising errors (a) and their probability distribution (b)

maximum signal range S which is quantised into M levels, so the spacing between levels is $P = S/M$. Assuming that quantising errors may have any value between $+P/2$ and $-P/2$ with equal probability, the probability density distribution for errors is uniform as in figure 12.6(b) and the mean square error ($\overline{q}^2$) is

$$\overline{q}^2 = \int_{-P/2}^{P/2} \frac{1}{P} v^2 \, dv = \frac{P^2}{12}$$

The mean square signal may be found in a similar manner. Assuming that the signal ranges from $S/2$ to $-S/2$ and that all quantised levels are equiprobable, the probability density distribution has a value of $1/((M-1)P)$ and extends from $-(M-1)P/2$ to $+(M-1)P/2$ (because of the zero level), and we find that $\overline{S}^2 = (M-1)^2 P^2/12$.

Since $M \gg 1$ in practice we have the simple result that the output power-to-noise ratio is $(P/N)_0 \approx M^2$.

A further advantage of PCM is that binary pulses can be processed much more easily than in systems where pulse height or position is important. In many communication systems it is necessary to place 'repeaters' at suitable intervals to reshape the signal before unacceptable attenuation or distortion occurs. In PCM one simply has to produce clear ones and zeros again, so the process is very straightforward. Moreover, no information is lost in the process (unlike PAM etc.) since the original data are exactly restored (assuming no binary errors again). This, of course, is the desirable characteristic of digital systems, and the same advantages apply for example to digital audio discs as opposed to conventional analogue discs.

EXAMPLE 12.3

Compare the efficiency of PCM with that of PAM and with an ideal communication system.

Consider a 3 kHz telephone signal sampled at 8 kHz. We will assume a PCM system with 256 levels (m = 8) with channel power-to-noise ratio 20 (giving negligible binary error). The channel bandwidth will be $\frac{1}{2}$.8.8000 = 32 kHz compared with the PAM bandwidth of 4 kHz. If the transmitted powers are the same, the PAM system will have a channel power-to-noise ratio of 20 × (32/4) = 160 and the same value at the output. The PCM system will have output-power-to-noise of M^2 = $(256)^2$ or about 65,000. A similar ratio applies to the transmitted powers required for the same output-power-to-noise.

Considering an ideal system, we have $C = W \log(1 + P/N)$. The capacity of the PCM system is 8 × 8000 = 64,000 bits/s, being the number of binary digits transmitted per second. For the same capacity and bandwidth the ideal system will have a channel power-to-noise ratio of 3, requiring about 1/7 of the power of PCM.

12.4 Binary Communication Systems

PCM is a remarkably effective technique, comprising easily processed binary pulses yet providing good protection against noise, and comparing reasonably in efficiency with an ideal system. Although it is possible to transmit a binary train of pulses directly in some systems, it is usually necessary to impress them on to some form of sinusoidal carrier.

The simplest method is to switch a sinusoidal carrier between two levels, one of which is usually zero, the method then being known as on–off keying (OOK). Its properties are similar to AM, involving essentially a multiplication of the carrier by the modulating signal. In phase shift keying (PSK) the phase of the carrier is reversed when say a '0' is to be transmitted compared to the phase for a '1'; the system is much more tolerant of noise than OOK, because the amplitude remains constant, but it is more difficult to implement since an accurate reference is needed. Frequency shift keying (FSK) involves representing '0' and

'1' by two different frequencies, and provides better performance than OOK (but worse than PSK). However, it is easy to implement and is used, for example, in cassette-loaded home computers. The three techniques are shown in figure 12.7.

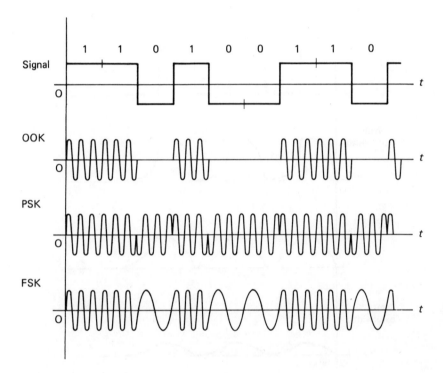

Figure 12.7   Binary communication systems

12.4.1 Capacity of a binary channel

We have already assumed several times that the maximum number of binary pulses that can be transmitted per second down a channel of bandwidth W_c is $2W_c$. This is the same 'magic number' as in the Sampling Theorem, though the two problems are not related. There is an exact answer to the sampling requirement; one must sample at $2W_c$/s or more. However, there is no exact answer here; it depends on what one considers acceptable and also on the exact characteristics of the channel bandwidth.

We will assume that we are transmitting a pseudo-random train of pulses down a channel of limited bandwidth, but we will take the 'worst case' of a square wave (that is, successive 0s and 1s). We need consider only a single rectangular pulse (a '1') and must determine the extent to which the response to it overlaps the next pulse (a '0'). Figure 12.8 illustrates the situation for channels of different bandwidths. An acceptable criterion could be that the overlap of the '1' at the centre of the '0' should not be more than 50 per cent of the value at the centre of the '1'.

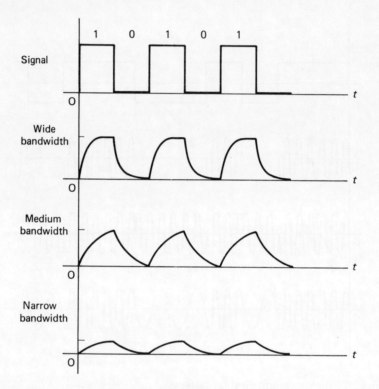

Figure 12.8   Capacity of a binary channel

Consider a hypothetical case where the bandwidth W_c is rectangular, falling to zero at W_c Hz. This is equivalent to feeding the signal to a filter of transfer function $H(f) = 1$ for $f \leqslant W_c$ and $H(f) = 0$ for $f > W_c$. Such a filter cannot be realised physically; practical filters must have a non-zero phase response and cannot cut off indefinitely sharply. We know that a rectangular pulse of height A and width θ has a spectrum $F(f) = A\theta \, \mathrm{sinc} \, f\theta$. The output spectrum of the filter is $G(f) = H(f) \times F(f)$ so the output time response is $h(t) * f(t)$. The impulse response $h(t)$ is just a sinc function $h(t) = 2W_c \, \mathrm{sinc} \, 2tW_c$, and the functions are sketched in figure 12.9.

The larger W_c the narrower the impulse response $h(t)$ and the more faithfully the pulse is transmitted. For the case $2W_c = 1/\theta$ (shown in the figure) the output at time θ will be rather more than half that at time zero, since the convolution area is half the first lobe of the sinc function. This corresponds to the centre of

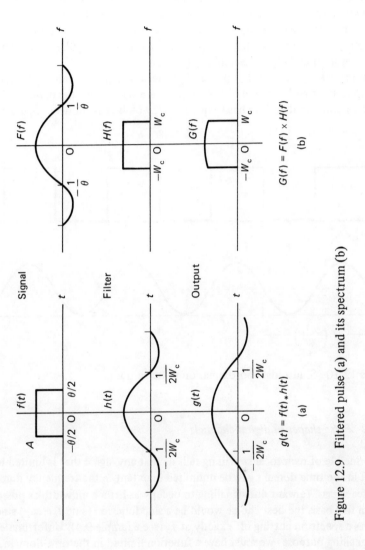

Figure 12.9 Filtered pulse (a) and its spectrum (b)

the 'zero' following the 'one' represented by the rectangular pulse. The number of pulses per second is $1/\theta$, so our criterion gives $2W_c$ as the maximum number of pulses/s.

Strictly we should consider a physically realisable filter. For example, a first-order low-pass filter has a transfer function $W_c/(W_c + jf)$, though most channel bandwidths would be limited much more sharply. Schwartz (1970) considers a filter cutting off ideally at W_c but with a linear phase response (that is, $\Phi(f)$ proportional to f) and calculates responses as a function of pulse width. The result is again that $2W_c$ per second is a good choice.

It is interesting to note that the result corresponds to transmitting frequencies only up to the first harmonic of the input square wave, since the period is 2θ and the first harmonic therefore has frequency $1/2\theta$ ($= W_c$) as shown in figure 12.10.

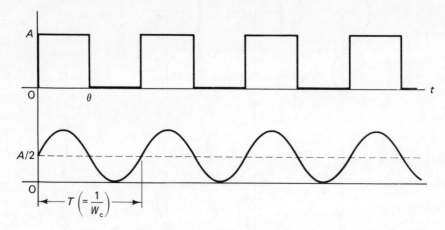

Figure 12.10 Sinusoidal approximation to pulse train

12.4.2 Pulse shapes in digital channels

The principle of reciprocal spreading tells us that any signal that is limited in extent in the time domain will be unlimited in extent in the frequency domain, and vice versa. We want our signalling to occupy as little bandwidth as possible, and on this basis the best choice would be a sinc function (sinc $f_c t$, say) since this has a spectrum cutting off exactly at f_c (see example 9.4). Unfortunately, for signalling purposes we must have a function limited in the time domain, so the sinc function is no good, and we need to compromise as to what amount of spreading in the frequency domain is acceptable.

Some of the possible pulses and their spectra are shown in figure 12.11. The rectangular pulse requires a wide bandwidth for faithful transmission since the energy falls off as $1/f$, whereas the triangle and half-cosine are much better, with

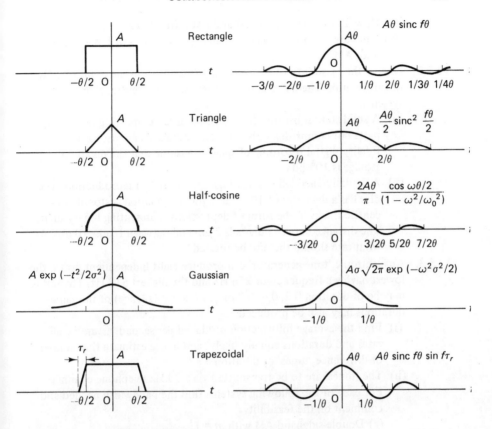

Figure 12.11 Various pulses and their spectra

energy falling off as $1/f^2$. The trapezoidal pulse is also a reasonable choice and is similar to the square wave and is easy to generate; in contrast, the gaussian pulse, though having the interesting property of the same shape in each domain, is inconvenient in practice since it is unlimited in extent. In binary systems one usually uses rectangular pulses, accepting the resultant degradation as explained in section 12.4.1, whereas in PPM and PWM trapezoidal pulses are preferred.

12.5 Exercises on Chapter 12

12.5.1. (i) How does the power in an AM wave depend on the modulation index?

(ii) Is any information lost if only one AM sideband is transmitted? Why are both sidebands usually transmitted?

(iii) How does the power in an FM wave depend on the modulation index?

(iv) How do the spectra for AM and FM differ if D is very small?

(v) What are the main advantages and disadvantages of FM compared with AM?

12.5.2. Discuss the feasibility of the following systems from the point of view of Information Theory, comparing them with conventional analogue systems.

(i) A solid state substitute for a tape recorder, employing no moving parts but comprising only logic and storage elements, for low-fidelity digital recording of speech. Assume that the maximum storage is 10^6 bits.

(ii) A digitally-encoded disc for high-quality sound reproduction. The disc has a diameter of 10 cm and the information is stored in concentric tracks in the form of depressions representing binary digits. The distance between digits is 2 μm and between tracks 10 μm. At what rate should the disc be rotated?

12.5.3. An electronic 'tune generator' can produce eight independent notes, the lowest having a frequency of 256 Hz and the highest 512 Hz. The notes may be of duration 0.2, 0.4, 0.8 or 1.6 s; a rest (silence) of the same durations may also be produced.

(i) Find the average information produced per second, assuming all rates and durations equally likely, and hence estimate the number of difference 'tunes' of duration 5 s.

(ii) The 'tunes' are to be transmitted via a 3 kHz telephone channel. For each of the following systems find the bandwidth needed and comment on the feasibility:

(a) Double-sideband AM with $m = 1$;

(b) FM with $D = 5$;

(c) PCM with 256 levels;

(d) A tone-coding method in which a binary code is assigned to each tone or rest specifying its frequency and duration.

13 Applications of Information Theory

The developments in technology over the last few years and the emergence of Information Technology as a new scientific discipline have greatly increased the practical applications of Information Theory. However, technological progress has been so rapid that many would-be information technologists have been unable to develop the necessary theoretical background on which real understanding and progress depends. Information Theory is the basic theory behind Information Technology and an understanding of its principles is essential in order to exploit the great potential offered by Information Technology.

We will not attempt a survey of the applications of Information Theory. Such 'overviews' tend to become simply a list of words; they are easy reading and may enable one to follow some of the current technological jargon but add little to one's real knowledge of the subject. Instead we will first consider the properties and applications of some important practical information channels, such as video and telephone channels, and then discuss some of the interesting recent developments such as speech synthesis, optical character recognition and music synthesis.

13.1 Typical Information Channels

The main means of telecommunication nowadays are of course via radio or cable. Radio communication systems include television and sound broadcasts, navigation systems, time broadcasts, microwave links, wireless telegraphy etc. and many special-purpose systems (spacecraft communications, emergency services etc.). Cable systems involve coaxial cables and 'twisted pairs'. The former provide channels of wide bandwidth suitable for television, radio or many multiplexed telephone channels, whereas the latter are low bandwidth channels for data or telephones. Optical fibres are now replacing coaxial cables for some applications on account of their greater bandwidth, smaller diameter and freedom from electrical interference.

Television and telephone channels are the most interesting, partly because they can be quantitatively analysed but mainly because of the important recent developments in information services via the teletext (Ceefax and Oracle) and viewdata (Prestel) systems. The feasibility of these systems depended very much on the fact that almost everyone has ready access to television and telephone receivers, and also on the availability of cheap yet powerful processing equipment. There is no doubt that such systems will be rapidly expanded in the next few years. Although some people do not like the idea of direct access to and

167

from their homes via telephone/television/computer they would be better advised to spend their energies on understanding the systems than on arguing against them. We will discuss television and telephone channels in some detail, and the information services now available using them.

13.1.1 Television channels

A black and white television picture is composed of 625 horizontal 'lines' containing the brightness information, one complete picture (one frame) being transmitted 25 times per second. The form of the signal is shown in figure 13.1(a). A technique known as 'interlaced scanning' is used, whereby every other line is sent 50 times/s; this avoids the flickering that would be apparent if all the lines were sent together 25 times/s, and uses only half the bandwidth required by a flicker-free 50 frame/s system.

Suppose the picture has height h and width w, as in figure 13.2. The vertical resolution is $h/625$ and it is reasonable to assume a similar horizontal resolution, dividing the picture into many small square elements (picture elements or 'pixels'). The bandwidth used is actually chosen to make this approximation valid.

A typical ratio of w to h is 4/3 so the total number of pixels is $625 \times 625 \times \frac{4}{3}$ and the number transmitted per second about 1.3×10^7. Using the usual rule this requires a bandwidth of 6.5 MHz. In practice, time has to be allowed between lines and frames for synchronisation, only 575 being used for the picture (some of the remainder are used for teletext) and the overall bandwidth allowed per channel is 8 MHz. Colour information can also be accommodated within this bandwidth, since the colour in a picture changes only slowly compared with the brightness. The transmission method used is known as vestigial sideband AM; one of the two sidebands is severely attenuated to reduce the (very high) bandwidth requirement. The spectrum is shown in figure 13.1(a).

The total information in one frame is equal to the number of pixels times the information per pixel. The latter depends on the number of distinguishable shades, which in turn depends on the signal-power-to-noise ratio. If we assume that 32 shades can be distinguished, the information per frame becomes $625 \times 625 \times \frac{4}{3} \times \log(32) \approx 2.6 \times 10^6$ bits equivalent to 6.5×10^7 bits/s. (The terms 'baud' or 'baud rate' are often used, meaning 'binary digits per second'.) This is quite a lot of bits! A typical microcomputer 'high-resolution' screen (say 256×256) occupies about 8K bytes (6.5×10^4 bits) of memory, and has much lower resolution.

The theoretical capacity depends on the power-to-noise ratio. Assuming a value of 1000 we obtain $C = 8 \times 10^6 \log(1000) \approx 8 \times 10^7$ bits/s, in close agreement with the above value. However this excellent result is because we have cheated in making the various assumptions, though it was done somewhat subtly. We saw above that the ideal communication theorem can be derived approximately by assuming that the number of distinguishable levels is equal to the root mean square signal-to-noise ratio, and our chosen number of levels (32) is very

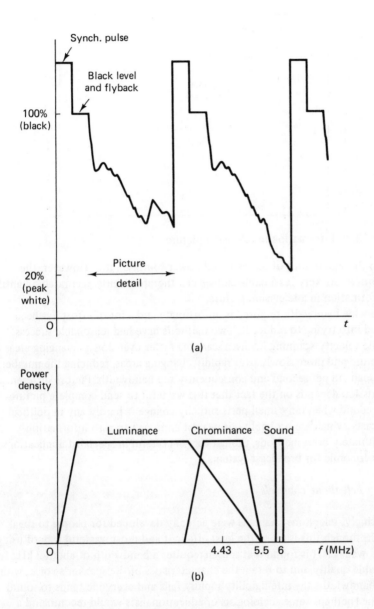

Figure 13.1   Television signal (a) and its spectrum (b)

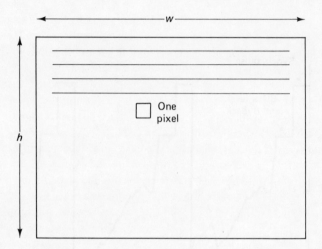

Figure 13.2   Information in television picture

near to the square root of our assumed power-to-noise ratio. However, the assumptions are very reasonable and we can therefore fairly accurately quantify the information in a television picture.

The wide bandwidth required is unfortunate and a lot of effort has been directed into trying to reduce it. Two methods have had reasonable success. Variable velocity scanning involves scanning faster over slowly changing areas of the picture and more slowly over rapidly changing areas, reducing the number of pixels scanned per second and consequently the bandwidth. Picture difference transmission depends on the fact that it is wasteful to send complete pictures every second when only small parts actually change — hardly any in political broadcasts, which are probably our nearest approach to zero information. Unfortunately both methods, though very successful in specialist applications, are uneconomic for broadcast systems.

13.1.2   Telephone channels

Surprisingly, telephone channels were actually developed for people to speak through, though this is much the least efficient and most wasteful way of using them nowadays. It is found that speech requires a bandwidth of about 3 kHz for reasonable quality and to retain the characteristics of the speaker's voice; with lower bandwidths the intelligibility rapidly falls and everyone tends to sound the same (perhaps some sociologists or educationalists would recommend a reduction). The actual bandwidth is taken as 300–3400 Hz; 4 kHz is usually allowed per channel, to allow some separation, and sampling is typically at 8000/s as previously assumed.

Assuming a power-to-noise ratio of 100 (not cheating this time) the ideal capacity is $3000 \log(100) \approx 20{,}000$ bits/s. Speaking at a rate of two five-letter words per second provides about 10 bits/s (50 bits/s, ignoring redundancy) which does not compare too well. Speaking is clearly the world's worst way of conveying information; it can be calculated that if the author had been able to use the bandwidth of his voice efficiently the information in his lecture course on Information Theory could have been given in only 30 seconds! The problem lies in the way in which the speech information is carried and the relatively large bandwidth required to communicate it; we will discuss the matter in some detail later, when dealing with speech synthesis.

The transmission of data by telephone is a much more efficient process. The bandwidth of 3 kHz can accommodate up to 6000 binary pulses per second, giving a maximum of 6000 bits per second, which compares reasonably with the ideal figure of 20,000 bits/s. Data links via telephone line (and higher bandwidth systems with correspondingly higher baud rates) are very widely used for information exchange in computer systems via modems (modulator–demodulators). It is possible to attain even higher rates than the basic 6000 bits/s by using special techniques (such as digital FM), which approach nearer to an ideal system.

An interesting application of a telephone data channel is a facsimile system (FAX) for pictorial data. A document or photograph is scanned optically, in much the same way as a television picture is produced. A scanning rate of 3 lines/s with a vertical resolution of 4 lines/mm produces about 2500 pixels/s for a 210 mm wide page, assuming 'square' pixels of side 1/4 mm. This requires a bandwidth of 1250 Hz so double-sideband AM can be used for transmission via a standard telephone channel. The time taken for a page of A4 size (approximately 210 mm × 300 mm) is about 5 minutes, so the method is somewhat limited in its application. There are various ways of improving it for specific requirements, such as decreasing the resolution or scanning only selected areas (see exercise 13.5.1).

13.1.3 Teletext and Viewdata

The U.K. has always been at the forefront in Information Technology, and was the first country to provide public information services in teletext and viewdata. Teletext transmissions (the BBC's Ceefax and IBA's Oracle) began in 1976 and Viewdata (British Telecom's Prestel) started in 1979. Both systems provide a wide variety of information to the user for display on a television screen; in teletext the information is transmitted with the normal TV picture, but in viewdata the TV set is linked to a telephone. The systems were developed together and use the same screen format, one page comprising 24 rows of 40 characters. Some graphics characters are included, employing a 2 × 3 matrix as shown in figure 13.3, so that the screen resolution for graphics is 80 × 72. This is fairly coarse, though seven colours are available, but has the particular advantage that the screen data can be stored in only 1K byte of RAM, since an ASCII-type code is used (that is, 40 × 24 × 1 byte ≈ 1K byte).

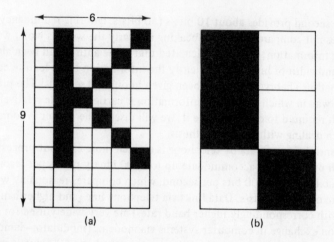

Figure 13.3   Teletext/viewdata character (a) and graphics shape (b)

The teletext system uses four otherwise-unused lines per frame, two in each interlaced scan. The data are digitally encoded and transmitted at a rate of 6.9375×10^6 baud. Each line carries the data for one 40-character row so about four pages are transmitted per second. The data rate can be seen to agree with this, since

$$\frac{4}{625} \times 6.9375 \times 10^6 \times \tfrac{1}{8} \approx 4\text{K bytes (allowing for some synchronisation)}$$

The system library comprises 800 pages, divided into 100-page 'magazines' so the cycle time is 3 minutes and 20 seconds. However, some of the more popular pages are included more than once per cycle so the access time is reduced. In addition, each page may have up to 3200 sub-pages (making about 2.5 million in all) but the access times become very long since only one sub-page step would be available per 800-page cycle. Page buffers are often available, so several pages may be stored by the user.

The alphanumerics, graphics and control characters are all represented by a 7-bit code plus one parity bit. Single errors are detected and the character ignored, so that some gaps are left in the received page on its first reception. However, double errors can be very serious, especially if they occur in a control character, so that a whole line of text could be changed in colour or into graphic characters. This possibility is reduced in headings, magazine and row addresses, by employing Hamming codes to provide single-error correction and double-error detection, characters with detected double errors being ignored.

The viewdata method has the advantage that it is a two-way interactive system so that the library is not essentially limited to the 800 pages of teletext, but only by the size of the controlling host computer. About 200,000 pages are usually available, the system capacity being 250,000. Data are transmitted both to and from the host computer by FSK, switching between 390 and 470 Hz at 75 baud from user to host and between 1300 and 2100 Hz at 1200 baud in the other direction. The same 7-bit code plus a parity bit is used, but start and stop bits are added. The transmission of one page (960 ten-bit characters) takes 8 seconds; the lines are displayed as soon as they are received, so this is faster than they can actually be read. This is much better than the average access time for teletext; in fact a higher graphics resolution could have been obtained in viewdata had not the systems been required to be compatible, the problem being the critical access time for teletext. Page buffers are usually available.

The error rates in viewdata systems are usually low, because of the small data rates involved. Characters from the user's terminal are actually checked for validity by the host computer before display. Hamming and parity check methods are also used on data being transmitted to the user, and errors are rare.

13.2   Speech Processing, Synthesis and Recognition

13.2.1   Bandwidth compression systems

We saw above that there is a serious discrepancy between the ideal capacity of a telephone channel (20,000 bits/s) and the information rate when the same channel is used for speech (10 bits/s). Expressed in another way, the bandwidth required to transmit speech (3 kHz) is much greater than implied by its information content. This was realised many years ago, and many attempts have been made to improve the situation. It appears that the information in speech is carried more by the low-frequency modulation of various 'carrier frequencies' in the waveform than by the 'carriers' themselves. When a particular sound is spoken a particular set of harmonics is produced, but it is the modulation of the individual harmonics that is most important. Figure 13.4 shows a typical speech waveform and the corresponding 'spectrogram', showing how the frequency components vary with time. Since one usually has to transmit most of the harmonics a large bandwidth is required, whereas if one could extract the modulation itself a considerable saving would result.

This is a simplification, of course, but a system based on this idea was demonstrated as long ago as 1936 by Dudley in the vocoder (Dudley, 1936) and is shown in figure 13.5.

The speech was divided into a number of bands, mostly 300 Hz wide, and the low-frequency modulations in each band extracted by envelope demodulation using diodes followed by 25 Hz low-pass filters, as in AM. One of the channels was used to detect whether the sound was predominantly a 'buzz' or a 'hiss' and transmitted its frequency in the former case. The overall bandwidth was thus reduced to 250 Hz from the original 3 kHz. The ten channels could be multiplexed together and transmitted to the receiver, using SSAM or other methods,

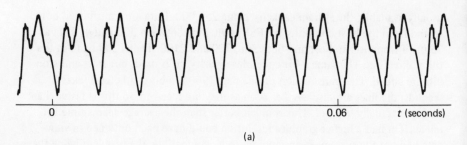

(a)

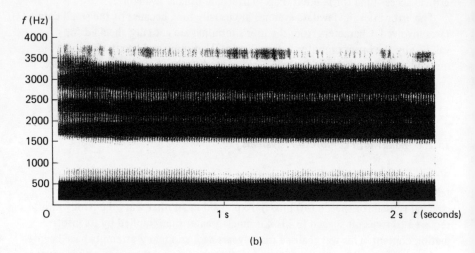

(b)

Figure 13.4   Speech signal for the sound 'EEEE' (a) and its spectrogram (b)

and using a bandwidth still of the order of only about 300 Hz. The receiver comprised a similar set of band-pass filters, the inputs being controlled by the 'buzz/hiss' channel. A noise generator was switched in for a 'hiss' and a square wave of appropriate frequency for a 'buzz', the 25 Hz modulation signals being used to modulate the appropriate frequency band.

Dudley's vocoder produced intelligible speech, though all speakers sounded much the same. It was a remarkable achievement at the time, and even with the technological developments now available it is difficult to obtain a bandwidth reduction of better than a factor of ten.

The distribution and characteristics of the harmonics present in speech clearly have a critical effect on the sound produced. The author has an interesting theory on the subject. It is not yet widely accepted; in fact he is unaware of anyone else who admits to believing it, there being a certain lack of quantitative evidence in its support. It is that specific groups of harmonics in a speaker's voice produce specific emotional effects. The theory developed from the author's critical observations of his children. It is well known that small children are binary

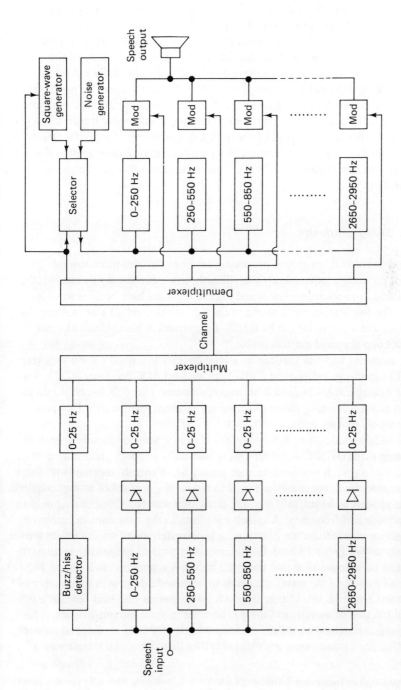

Figure 13.5 Bandwidth compression system (Vocoder)

creatures – they are either sleeping or crying. In the former case they are only mildly unpleasant but in the latter they are particularly nasty and require either feeding or changing. The author noted that his older child's crying was quite soothing and could easily be slept through. However, at the first cry of the younger child he was instantly awakened and had to be physically restrained from attacking it (he did not attempt to feed or change it). Clearly a particular set of harmonics were inducing an uncontrolled emotional response. Even more convincing is the author's observations on students attending his lectures. It is clear that the harmonic content of his voice has a pronounced soporific effect on students! They fall asleep within a few minutes but awaken as soon as the lecture is over. There appears to be no other explanation than the harmonic–emotional one*.

13.2.2 Speech synthesis

In recent years work on speech processing has been directed more towards reducing its storage requirements than directly towards reducing its bandwidth, particularly since microprocessors and microcomputers have become so wide-spread. The two approaches amount to the same in the end, of course, since the speech data in a computer can be readily transmitted in binary form at a rate dependent on the bandwidth available.

The amount of speech that can be stored directly in a small computer is very small. For example, sampling at 8 kHz with an 8-bit ADC produces 8000 bytes/s and the available RAM in most 8-bit microcomputers (say 32K bytes) would be filled in about 4 seconds, giving a vocabulary of about eight words! However, the quality would be very good ($(P/N)_0 \approx M^2 = 65,000$).

One widely used system is based on the National Semiconductors' speech processing chip (DT SPC – 1050). This is essentially a speech-processing method as opposed to speech synthesis; various properties of speech, together with some modern processing techniques, are used to reduce the amount of storage required. The ear appears to be insensitive to the phase of a waveform, responding only to its amplitude and frequency. A speech waveform in the time domain consists of a succession of repetitive waveforms of approximately fixed waveshape, as shown schematically in figure 13.6(a). Considering one cycle of a repetitive section, the phase can be changed such that the cycle becomes symmetric, as in figure 13.6(b). Only half a cycle of the waveform needs to be stored, along with the number of repetitions required. In addition, a speech waveform may be near zero for a sub-stantial fraction of a cycle, and there is no need to store the small values. A further saving is obtained by using a technique known as delta modulation, whereby the difference between samples is stored rather than the actual sample values

---

*This has led to an interesting definition of a lecturer as 'someone who talks in other people's sleep'.

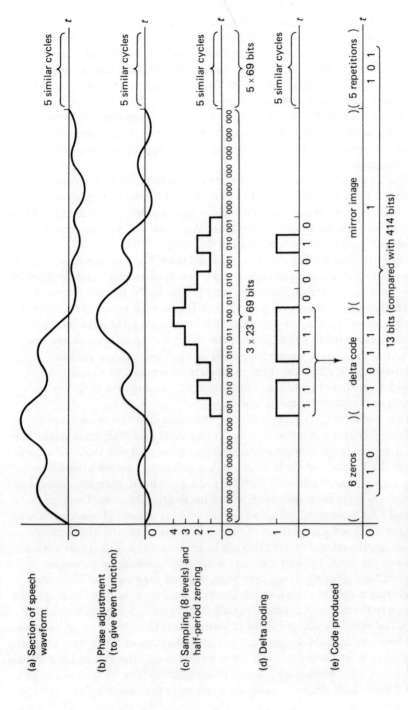

Figure 13.6 Speech waveform (a) and its compression (b, c, d and e) (schematic)

(similar to picture difference transmission). These three factors permit a saving by a factor of about 30, making the system feasible for small computers.

A typical system has a vocabulary of 50–100 words in each of a set of up to eight 64K bit ROMs, the ROMs being switchable by software. The programmer simply selects the ROM number and word number required and can therefore store desired phrases or sentences in RAM as short character strings, for example, requiring little memory. The quality produced is very good, retaining the original speaker's characteristics, and ROMs can be supplied containing one's very own words by sending a tape to the manufacturer. However, a fixed vocabulary of even a few hundred words is very limiting in some applications, especially amorous ones.

Most of the other systems available are known as 'vocal-tract' models. Instead of using the characteristics of speech to achieve data compression, the systems are said to be based on electronic models of the vocal tract. They are so based to some extent, but the approximation is not very close and it is just possible that salesmanship may have been involved in the choice of title.

Figure 13.7(a) shows a sketch of the vocal tract. The basic sound is produced by air rushing into the larynx; this sound is rich in harmonics and is modified by the various cavities (nasal, throat etc.) and further by the lips and tongue. An electronic model is shown in figure 13.7(b). It comprises two sound sources, a 'voicing source' for the vowel sounds and a 'noise source' for some consonants. The sources are fed to sets of filters, determining the amplitude and frequency of the vowel sounds or the characteristics of nasal sounds (m, n etc.) and fricatives (s, z, th etc.). About ten parameters are required to include most of the characteristics of speech, and these must be varied in time in the correct manner to produce continuous 'speech'.

Two 'vocal-tract' systems are popular at present. The first is known as a 'phoneme' system and is based on the Votrax SC01 chip. Phonemes are the basic speech sounds (such as in the initial teaching alphabet), being about 40 in number. In the Votrax chip the filter-controlling parameters are not available to the user. Instead, a six-bit input is provided and a given input internally decoded so as to produce the filter characteristics for the desired phoneme. There are therefore 64 (2^6) 'phonemes', including various versions of some phonemes (different duration etc.) and some periods of silence. There is no control of individual phonemes, though the overall pitch can be changed and a further two bits are available for stress. The user therefore selects the succession of phonemes required for a given word, one byte being required per phoneme. The storage requirements and data rate are very low. One word requires about four bytes on average so the rate is of the order of only 8 bytes/s which compares well with the actual rate for speech of about 10 bits/s. A large number of words can therefore be stored in RAM if required. The other advantage of this system is that the vocabulary is 'unlimited' (it has a North American accent which makes it difficult to produce some words with 'correct' pronunciation). The main disadvantage is that it does sound distinctly more like a computer than a human. One rapidly

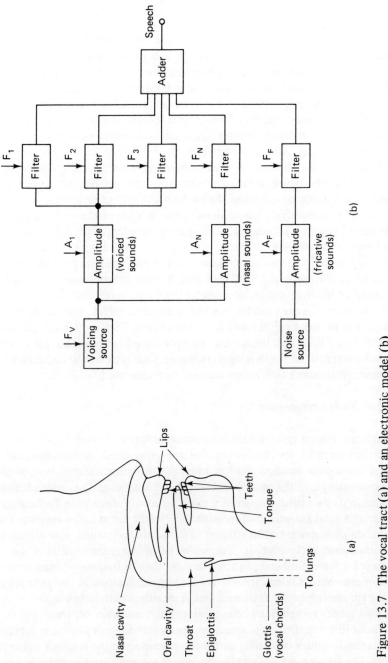

Figure 13.7 The vocal tract (a) and an electronic model (b)

becomes used to its accent, however, and is then considerably put out when some poor unfortunate who is unfamiliar with the system is unable to understand one's brilliant phrase.

A more flexible system is available using the Texas TMS-5100 chip. This is again based on a 'vocal-tract' model but the user has access to the controlling parameters. A vocabulary of several hundred words is available in ROM, typically 200 in 16K bytes. Each word is represented by the filter parameters required to produce it, these being derived by the manufacturer using a large computer to carry out a frequency analysis of the original speech. The system uses a technique known as 'linear predictive filtering', in which each output sample is dependent on previous samples. About 100 bytes are required per word, roughly ten times more than with the phoneme synthesis system. However, the 'speech' produced is of good quality, owing to the predictive technique, and is comparable with that of the National SPC system. Moreover, the user does have the possibility of constructing or modifying words himself. The data have to be sent as a pre-determined sequence of values governing the parameters of the filters, but these can be modified at will so that a desired word can be built up by trial and error. Another possibility is that sets of parameters to produce a range of phonemes could be stored, and a trial word then rapidly built up from them. It could then be modified relatively easily, by changing the durations etc. as required.

Systems are already available in which acceptable speech is produced in response to normal English typed from a keyboard. They involve complicated algorithms (in ROM) for breaking down words into phonemes, and are therefore very characteristic of the developer. However, such systems will undoubtedly become rapidly more satisfactory and will be widely used.

13.2.3 Speech recognition

Speech recognition systems have been available for small computers for several years, but are much less satisfactory than speech synthesis systems and have found less application. Speech recognition is much more difficult. It is, of course, just one example of the general problem of pattern recognition, which is a large subject in its own right, though very much a part of Information Technology and requiring a good knowledge of Information Theory for its understanding. The two main problems are often referred to as 'feature extraction' and 'classification'. Feature extraction involves deciding which particular characteristics of the pattern are the critical ones, and may involve time or frequency domain properties, or even both. Classification refers to the methods used to decide to which of the (predetermined) classes a particular measured pattern belongs.

Most speech recognition systems follow the 'vocal-tract' approach and use bandpass filters to divide the speech spectrum for each word into a number of ranges (two or three in small systems) corresponding to the known vocal resonances. The frequencies and amplitudes in each range are then sampled as rapidly as feasible, say 100 times per second. A serious problem is that of finding the

beginning and ending of words. The characteristics of the beginning of a word
vary considerably, depending on whether it begins with a vowel or consonant,
so one or more of several parameters must be satisfied for a predetermined time
before the start of a word is recognised by the computer (for example, large and
increasing amplitude for a vowel start or low amplitude but high and increasing
frequency content for a consonant start). The end of a word is sought in a
similar manner, and must be distinguished from a pause in the middle of a word
by setting appropriate thresholds for duration etc. When the beginning and end
have been found the data are normalised to remove the effect of speed of speaking by dividing the input data into a given number of equally spaced regions, say
16 or 32, and storing these averaged values as the representation of the word.
One word may thus require $16 \times 3 \times 2 \approx 100$ bytes (one byte for the amplitude
and frequency of each range), a similar order to the storage requirements in the
speech synthesis systems described above.

The problem of classification is relatively difficult in a small computer
system, because of the limited processing power available. The computer is first
'taught' the set of words to be used (typically 32 or 64 in small systems) by the
speaker repeating them several times, until a satisfactory average is obtained. It
is not usually possible to carry out a proper cross-correlation between the
received word and all the stored words, and a simple byte-by-byte comparison
is often used to find the best match. This is accepted if the sum of the differences
(ignoring signs) is less than a preset threshold; otherwise an error message is given.

Small microcomputer systems can store several vocabularies, each of 32 or 64
words, and can find the nearest match in a given vocabulary within about one
second, though switching between vocabularies (to find a match) is not usually
feasible. Unfortunately, however, it does not take much to mislead the system;
for example, a student rattling his coffee cup may easily be taken as a response
by the computer, even if that was the last thing he intended. The brain has the
remarkable ability of extracting one desired sound from a high level of background noise, as at a party for example, and it may be several years before this
can be matched by computers.

13.3 Optical Character Recognition

Optical character recognition has many features similar to speech recognition. It
is usually easy to find the start or end of a letter, except when dealing with hand-
writing, but the complexity of the system depends very much on its versatility.
Systems capable of reading several different fonts or hand-written symbols
require powerful computers, whereas those dealing with only one fixed size and
style can be implemented successfully on microcomputer systems.

The main problem is that of feature extraction, which is inherently less
obvious than in speech recognition, where vocal-tract resonances are an obvious
approach. The character is usually magnified optically and scanned by photocells,

and a size-normalisation procedure applied. A code is then produced which may simply contain information regarding the regions occupied by the character, or may include data on symmetry, corners, lines etc. The problem of feature extraction is of course closely related to that of classification, and a compromise between the feature data and their presentation in relation to the classification method and time allowed for a decision is necessary. The efficiency of the classification algorithm is critical, and 'tree-structured' dictionaries are considered preferable. 'Learning' methods are usually employed, whereby the computer is 'taught' the various character sets or the hand-writing styles of various individuals.

In a small microcomputer system an important requirement is to reduce the amount of information required to represent each character. Considering a single character set the actual information per character is only about six bits, allowing for upper/lower case and punctuation (the ASCII set uses seven bits). However, the characters usually produced by a computer, for example, are via a rectangular or square matrix of dots (for example, 7×9 or 8×8) so the actual information per character is about 64 bits, or an order of magnitude greater than that really required. It is more convenient to scan the text using a hand-held probe; this may be a single optical fibre of suitably large diameter, the character being magnified and scanned remotely, or may be a matrix of small fibres with photocells at the other end. In either case one can use only about eight detectors, for economic reasons, so the complete character is read in as a series of, say, eight successive bytes. It is necessary to read in the character at this resolution (at least), since lower resolution is inherently insufficient to distinguish between characters in their normal representation, but one can then try to reduce the data to be stored to improve both storage requirements and speed of classification. Figure 13.8 shows one possibility in which data on the characters 'weight' and 'line-length' in two perpendicular directions are extracted.

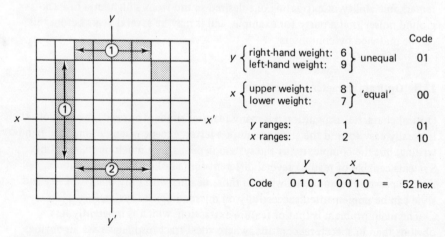

Figure 13.8   Information reduction in an optical character

In this example the data are reduced to one byte per character, but this is somewhat optimistic in practice. However, a significant reduction on the raw eight bytes is feasible. Much of this initial processing can be done as the character is being read in, so that as much time as possible can be spent on the classification procedure.

Small computer systems capable of dealing with a single font, or with other fonts by changing probes or internal scaling factors, have recently become available. They offer low error rates and impressive speeds, but are about an order of magnitude more expensive than speech synthesis or recognition systems because of the optics and detectors involved.

13.4 Music Synthesis

The words 'music synthesis' are an anathema to some people, but the subject is evolving rapidly and the day is fast approaching when even professional musicians will have difficulty in determining whether a piece of music is real or synthesised. That day has already arrived for many of us. We will concentrate in this section on the information theory aspects of the production of sounds, musical or otherwise, by small computer systems.

Most small computers contain a loudspeaker of sorts, even if it is only an on/off 'bleeping' type. The simplest way of producing a tone is to 'bleep' it at a suitable rate by means of a short machine-code loop. The resulting spectrum is that of a rectangular pulse train and is therefore very rich in harmonics, but the sound is better than that of a square wave and not very unpleasant. However, although such systems can produce 'tunes' they are very limited and have no facility for controlling loudness or sound quality.

Far more flexibility is provided if one of the currently available sound generator chips is added. These are digital programmable devices, usually having three tone channels and a noise channel. The tone channels are programmable in pitch over several octaves and also in amplitude, and there is usually some overall envelope control. These devices essentially produce square waves, and substantial processing of the waveforms is necessary to make the sounds acceptable musically This is known as 'subtractive synthesis', that is, removing unwanted harmonics by filtering in order to obtain the desired spectrum. The characteristic sound of a musical instrument is governed partly by its spectrum but very much by the envelope of the waveform, which is usually divided into sections known as attack, sustain, decay and rest or release (A, S, D, R). Control of both amplitude and frequency (to a lesser extent) in these regions is essential in simulating a sound, but sound generator chips are somewhat limited in these respects and the music produced tends to be rather disappointing. However, they are excellent for computer games!

A much more satisfactory result is obtained by fully digital systems employing 'additive synthesis', in which the required spectrum is built up by adding in the harmonics required in the usual Fourier synthesis manner. In order to simulate the sound of a given instrument the values of one cycle of the corresponding waveform are stored in RAM in the form of a 'waveform table' of say 256 successive bytes (that is, one 'page'). This amplitude resolution is sufficient for most purposes, giving adequate signal-to-quantising noise ratio. In order to change the frequency of the output waveform one simply steps through the waveform table at the appropriate rate, up to a maximum step size of 128 (so as to give two samples per cycle). To achieve sufficient frequency resolution it is necessary to use two bytes for the stepping size, but one can then cover some seven octaves with a frequency error of only about 0.5 Hz. The sound is produced by feeding the stored values to a DAC and then to an amplifier and loudspeaker. The necessary envelope control can be applied before the DAC or by the DAC itself, and the overall volume is controlled in a similar manner, usually in 256 steps. The higher-order spectral frequencies must be filtered out, of course.

Several waveform tables can be sampled successively and one of the most versatile systems comprises 16 'voices', having 16 independent DACs. In order to simulate an instrument one requires detailed knowledge of its spectral components and envelope characteristics, but these are available or can be measured. An instrument definition is then built up by adding in the appropriate harmonics, often up to 20 in number, and then by putting in the necessary envelope data. It is sometimes necessary to use several waveform tables for a single instrument since the spectrum may contain additional lines at non-integral values of the fundamental, so that even with 16 DACs one may be able to produce music with only four or five parts.

The amount of information in a system such as this can be a problem. In order to cover a frequency range of, say 30 Hz–15 kHz (to produce reasonable music) one has to sample at 30 kHz or more, and with 16 separate waveform tables this leaves only about 2 μs per table. This cannot be done directly via the microprocessor but is possible using direct memory access (DMA) in which the memory contents are read out directly into the DACs. In addition, it is clear that a compiling procedure must be carried out on the actual raw data input, to convert it into a suitable form for direct readout from RAM. This usually means that immediate feedback of the notes entered is not possible and that the length of a composition is limited to a few minutes. Further problems are that the spectrum and envelope characteristics of most instruments change significantly with pitch, so that a good simulation at one pitch may become unacceptable in the next octave, and that some musical effects are difficult to simulate at all.

One of the disadvantages of present systems is that the process of entering the music, usually via the computer keyboard in fairly standard notation, is a slow process. The author has found that the ratio between entering time and playing time may be as much as 100:1 for pieces in four or five parts. Unfortunately he did this at Christmas, choosing some carols, and discovered afterwards that such compositions are somewhat inappropriate except for about one week each year.

However, systems of the type described can produce surprisingly convincing and pleasantly satisfying music. It is sometimes asked if there is really any point in producing music this way, since it is technically somewhat difficult. The case of the old lady who went to her doctor complaining that she found it difficult to touch her toes has been quoted in illustration; he replied 'Well don't do it, then'. However, such pursuits can be very enjoyable and educational, the latter particularly in schools where the sound of a given instrument at a chosen pitch can be instantly produced, and its characteristics varied. Some (modern) professional musicians already use these techniques in developing compositions, and can of course create their own 'instruments' to suit a particular requirement, and amateurs can produce compositions or variations of existing pieces played by several instruments which would be totally impossible to them otherwise. However, it is unlikely that these developments will replace or even diminish the playing of or learning to play conventional instruments; it is more likely that they will complement and encourage such pursuits, which provide a particularly high degree of satisfaction and enjoyment to the performer, even at the beginner level (although not always to the listener)*.

13.5 Exercises on Chapter 13

13.5.1. A system is required for transmitting hand-written diagrams down a standard 3 kHz telephone channel in real time. A proposed system employs an arrangement whereby the position of a pen, moving over a square pad of paper, is monitored in two perpendicular directions by analogue displacement transducers attached to the pen. The outputs of the transducers are digitised and transmitted down the channel as a sequence of binary pulses.

Discuss the feasibility of the system from the standpoint of Information Theory. Pay particular attention to the resolution of the transmitted diagrams and the speed at which they may be drawn, giving examples of possible resolutions and speeds.

Compare the applications and advantages of this system with a standard facsimile system.

13.5.2. Compare the systems (i), (ii) and (iii) below in terms of the time taken for the transmission of one page of English text along a standard 3 kHz telephone line. Assume that the page measures 30 cm × 20 cm and contains about 300 words.

(i) A facsimile system employing double-sideband amplitude-modulation of a 1.5 kHz carrier, with vertical resolution of 0.5 line/mm.

(ii) An automatic text reader, which identifies each letter in the text and converts it to a five-digit binary code suitable for double-sideband amplitude-modulation as above. (The reader/coder may be assumed to operate instantaneously.)

*These heartfelt words were added by the author's family.

(iii) A person reading the page into the telephone at a normal rate.

Comment on the advantages and disadvantages of the three systems. Compare each of these systems with a hypothetical ideal channel of the same bandwidth and signal-power-to-noise ratio of 30 dB.

13.5.3. 'A picture is worth a thousand words'. Discuss this statement from the standpoint of Information Theory, paying attention to the logical premises assumed, and to the derivation from them of a measure of quantity of information. Give a quantitative comparison between the information capacities of typical pictorial displays (such as television and newspapers) and typical text (such as books and newspapers). Include a comparison of the transmission rates and bandwidths involved.

13.5.4. Video information can be stored in terms of the position of small depressions arranged spirally on a standard-size long-playing disc, and monitored optically; the disc rotates at 25 rev./s and one frame is stored per revolution.

Estimate the information in one frame of a black and white 625-line TV picture. Calculate the minimum spacing of the depressions and hence the playing time of one side of the disc, assuming that each depression represents one 'bit' of information and that the spacing is the same in the radial and tangential directions. Discuss the ways in which the digital information can be used to carry the brightness and sound information in a typical TV picture.

13.5.5. The high cost of the postal service suggests the use of alternative methods of transmission of printed information. One possible method is to modify a typewriter so that the depression of a key causes a suitable binary code to be recorded at a slow speed on magnetic tape. The tape is then replayed at high speed with the loudspeaker close to an ordinary telephone receiver so that the information is transmitted down a standard 3 kHz telephone line.

Discuss the feasibility of such a system and the coding, recording and playback requirements. Compare the cost of sending a typical letter by this method with the cost by First Class Mail ($8\frac{1}{2}$p).

(Assume that the telephone call charge is 3p for 15 s.)

13.5.6. A speech signal may be assumed to occupy a bandwidth from 300 Hz to 3 kHz. It is sampled at a rate of 8000 samples/s and digitised using an 8-bit ADC. Find the amount of memory in bytes needed to store 10 s of continuous speech in computer memory, assuming that each 8-bit sample is stored as one byte.

Explain the principles of methods of reducing the computer storage requirements of speech waveforms usually described as:

(a) Bandwidth compression systems, in which the speech bandwidth is reduced prior to sampling.

(b) Data compression systems, in which the speech data are processed to reduce their storage requirements.

(c) Vocal-tract systems, in which the vocal tract is modelled electroni-
cally.

In each case estimate the storage requirements for 10 s of speech,
and comment on the quality of speech produced and the application of
the method.

Comment on the extent to which systems conventionally known by
these names are actually distinct.

14 Solutions to Exercises

14.1 Solutions to Exercises on Chapter 1

1.5.1. (i) The probability of any number is $1/6$, so $I = \log_2 6 = 2.58$ bits.
(ii) The probability of getting a six or a one is $1/6 + 1/6 = 1/3$, so $I = \log_2 3 = 1.58$ bits.
(iii) Since some number must occur, $p = 1$ and $I = \log_2 1 = 0$.

1.5.2. (i) If the three shades are equiprobable, $p = 1/3$ and $I = \log_2 3 = 1.58$ for each dot. Therefore, total information $= 20 \times 20 \times 1.58 = 632$ bits.
(ii) The average information per dot is given by

$$H = -(\tfrac{1}{8} \log \tfrac{1}{8} + \tfrac{1}{4} \log \tfrac{1}{4} + \tfrac{5}{8} \log \tfrac{5}{8}) = 1.30 \text{ bits}$$

Therefore, total information $= 400 \times 1.30 = 519$ bits.

This is, of course, equivalent to saying that there are $400/8$ dots providing $\log 8 (= 3)$ bits, $400/4$ providing $\log 4 (= 2)$ bits and $(5/8) \times 400$ providing $\log 8/5$ bits.
Note. If one cannot assume that the arrangement of the dots is known, the information per dot is much greater, each dot having probability $(1/3) \times (1/400)$ in case (i).

1.5.3. (i) The average information (per symbol) is

$$H = -(\tfrac{1}{4} \log \tfrac{1}{4} + \tfrac{3}{4} \log \tfrac{3}{4}) = 0.81 \text{ bits}$$

Since the symbols each take 1 s, the rate is 0.81 bits/s.
(ii) This part cannot be done in the same way. The method to use is to say that in a typical sample of four symbols of the sequence there will be one A and three B's, and this sample will take 7 s. Each A provides $\log (4) = 2$ bits and each B provides $\log (4/3) = 0.42$ bits. On average in 7 s, one receives $2.0 + 3 \times 0.42$ bits or 0.47 bits/s.
Note. (i) can be done in the same way, giving one A and three B's in 4 s.

14.2 Solutions to Exercises on Chapter 2

2.4.1. $p(M) = p(M, M) + p(S, M)$
$\quad\quad = p(M)\, p(M/M) + p(S)\, p(M/S)$
$\quad\quad = p(M) \tfrac{5}{6} + p(S) \tfrac{1}{3}$
Since $p(M) + p(S) = 1$, we have $p(M) = \tfrac{2}{3}, p(S) = \tfrac{1}{3}$

$$p(M, M) = p(M).p(M/M) = \tfrac{2}{3}.\tfrac{5}{6} = \tfrac{5}{9}$$

Similarly, $p(S, S) = \frac{2}{9}$, $p(S, M) = p(M, S) = \frac{1}{9}$

$$H(j/i) = -\underset{i \; j}{\Sigma\Sigma} \, p(i, j) \log p(j/i) \rightarrow 0.74 \text{ bits/symbol.}$$

Redundancy $= (1 - 0.74) = 26$ per cent.

2.4.2. $p(B/B) = \frac{1}{2}$, $p(A/B) = \frac{1}{4}$, $p(C/B) = \frac{1}{4}$

$p(A/A) = \frac{5}{8}$, $p(B/A) = \frac{1}{4}$, $p(C/A) = \frac{1}{8}$

$p(C/C) = \frac{5}{8}$, $p(B/C) = \frac{1}{4}$, $p(A/C) = \frac{1}{8}$

Clearly $p(A) = p(C)$ by symmetry

$p(A) = p(A, A) + p(B, A) + p(C, A)$

$\qquad = p(A)\, p(A/A) + p(B)\, p(A/B) + p(C)\, p(A/C)$

$\qquad = \frac{5}{8} p(A) + \frac{1}{4} p(B) + \frac{1}{8} p(C)$

Since $p(A) = p(C)$ and $p(A) + p(B) + p(C) = 1$, we have

$$p(A) = p(B) = p(C) = \frac{1}{3}$$

$$H(j/i) = -\Sigma\Sigma p(i, j) \log p(j/i) \rightarrow 1.37 \text{ bits/symbol}$$

Redundancy $= 13.8$ per cent (maximum entropy $= \log_2 3 = 1.58$ bits/symbol).

Note. This solution is very tedious if one does not use the fact that $p(A) = p(C)$. In this example it may be noticed that $p(A, B) = p(B, A)$ etc., but this is not generally true in sequences of more than two symbol types.

2.4.3. $H(i, j) = -\Sigma\Sigma \, p(i, j) \log p(i, j)$

$\qquad\qquad = -\Sigma\Sigma \, p(i, j) \log p(i).p(j/i)$

$\qquad\qquad = -\Sigma\Sigma \, p(i, j) \log p(i) - \Sigma\Sigma \, p(i, j) \log p(j/i)$

That is

$$H(i, j) = H(i) + H(j/i) \text{ (since } \underset{j}{\Sigma} \, p(i, j) = p(i))$$

From 2.4.1

$$H(i, j) = \Sigma\Sigma \, p(i, j) \log p(i, j)$$

$$= 1.66 \text{ bits}$$

$$H(i) = -(\tfrac{2}{3} \log \tfrac{2}{3} + \tfrac{1}{3} \log \tfrac{1}{3}) = 0.917 \text{ bits.}$$

2.4.4. Single-letter words: α

$\qquad\qquad\qquad$ Information per letter $= (\log 1)/1 = 0$ bits.

$\quad$ Two-letter words: $\alpha\alpha, \alpha\beta, \alpha\gamma, \beta\alpha, \gamma\alpha$

$\qquad\qquad\qquad$ Information per letter $= (\log 5)/2 = 1.16$ bits.

Three-letter words: $\beta\alpha\gamma$, $\gamma\alpha\beta$, $\beta\alpha\beta$, $\gamma\alpha\gamma$

Information per letter = $(\log 4)/3 = 0.67$ bits.

Average over all words: there are ten words in all

$$\text{Average information/letter} = 0 \times \frac{1}{10} + 1.16 \times \frac{5}{10} + 0.67 \times \frac{4}{10}$$

$$= 0.85 \text{ bits}$$

A non-redundant system would give $\log 3 = 1.58$ bits/letter

The redundancy is $(1.58 - 0.85)/1.58 = 46$ per cent.

Note. The average length of the ten words is 2.3 letters. However, evaluating $(\log 10)/2.3$ gives 1.44 bits/letter, which is not the correct information per letter. This is because an actual language comprising words of unequal length would require a separate space symbol (or an instantaneous coding arrangement).

2.4.5.   A A A B A B A A B B A A A A B A A B A A A

(a) $p(A) = \frac{14}{20}, p(B) = \frac{6}{20}$

$p(A, A) = \frac{9}{20}, p(A, B) = \frac{5}{20}, p(B, A) = \frac{5}{20}, p(B, B) = \frac{1}{20}$

$p(A/A) = \frac{9}{14}, p(A/B) = \frac{5}{6}, p(B/B) = \frac{1}{6}, p(B/A) = \frac{5}{14}$

(b) $H(j/i) = -\Sigma\Sigma\, p(i, j) \log p(j/i) \to 0.854$ bits

Redundancy = $1 - 0.854 = 14.6$ per cent.

(c) Evaluate $p(A/A, A), p(A/A, B), p(A/B, B)$ etc.

It should be found that $p(A/AA) \approx p(A/A)$ etc. if intersymbol effects are only over adjacent symbols (the sequence given is not long enough to verify this).

$$H(k/ij) = -\underset{i\ j\ k}{\Sigma\Sigma\Sigma}\ p(i, j, k) \log p(k/ij)$$

would have to be evaluated instead of $H(j/i)$.

(d) Certainly not spoken since the redundancy is low.

14.3 Solutions to Exercises on Chapter 3

3.7.1. Using $p_i = (\frac{1}{2})^{\ell_i}$, $\ell_i = 1, 2, 3, 4, 4$

s_1 0

s_2 1 0

s_3 1 1 0

s_4 1 1 1 0

s_5 1 1 1 1 (by inspection).

3.7.2. Use either Fano or Huffman.

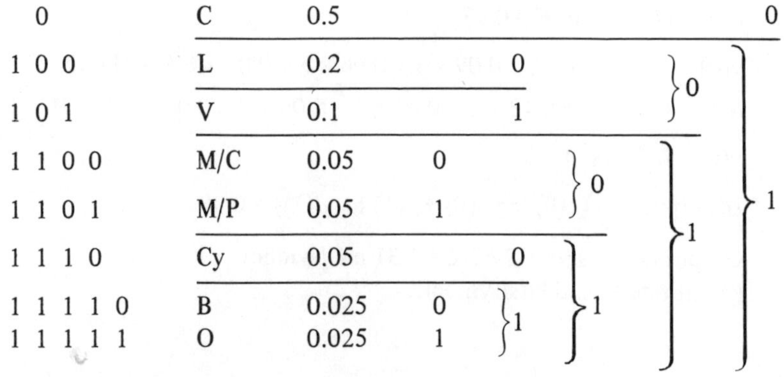

0 C 0.5 0
1 0 0 L 0.2 0
1 0 1 V 0.1 1
0
1 1 0 0 M/C 0.05 0
1 1 0 1 M/P 0.05 1
0
1 1 1 0 Cy 0.05 0
1 1 1 1 0 B 0.025 0
1 1 1 1 1 O 0.025 1
1
1
1
1

$L = 0.5 + 0.2 \times 3 + 0.1 \times 3 + 0.05 \times 12 + 0.025 \times 10 = 2.25$

$H = -\Sigma p_i \log p_i = 2.21$

$E = 0.98$

Simple binary code: 3 digits needed, $E = 2.21/3 = 0.74$.

Comment: The gain in storage is quite small and the extra complexity would not be worth while.

3.7.3. (i) Single.

0 A 0.6 0.6 0 1.0
10 B 0.3 0 0.4 1
11 C 0.1 1

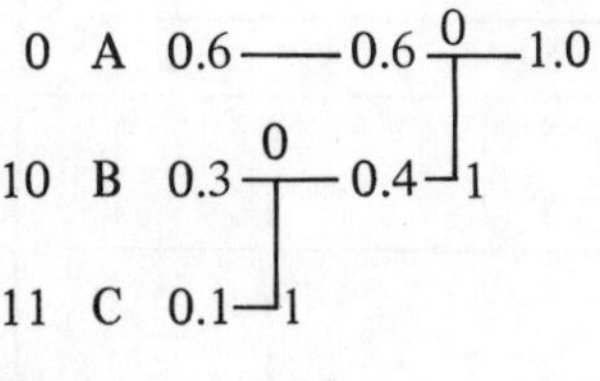

$H = -\Sigma p_i \log p_i = 1.30$
$L = 1.40$
$E = 0.93$

(ii) In pairs

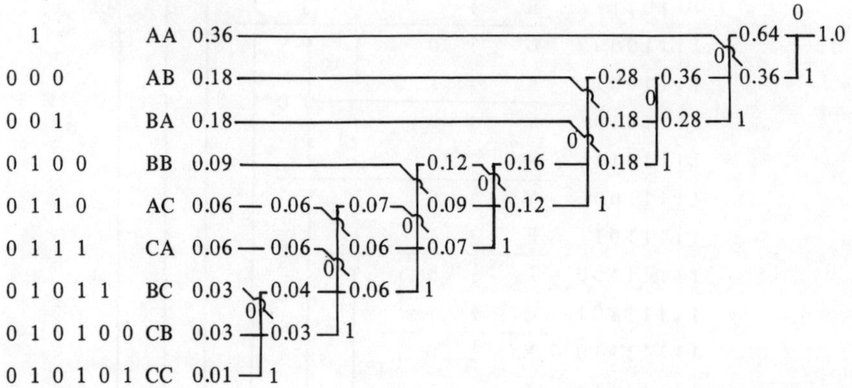

1 AA 0.36 0.64 0 1.0
0 0 0 AB 0.18 0.28 0.36 0.36 1
0 0 1 BA 0.18 0.18 0.28 1
0 1 0 0 BB 0.09 0.12 0.16 0.18 1
0 1 1 0 AC 0.06 — 0.06 0.07 0.09 0.12 1
0 1 1 1 CA 0.06 — 0.06 0.06 0.07 1
0 1 0 1 1 BC 0.03 0.04 0.06 1
0 1 0 1 0 0 CB 0.03 0.03 1
0 1 0 1 0 1 CC 0.01 1

$L = 2.67$ per pair, $E = 0.97$

$$\frac{p(0)}{p(1)} = \frac{0.18 \times 5 + 0.09 \times 3 + 0.06 \times 3 + 0.03 \times 6 + 0.01 \times 3}{0.36 \times 1 + 0.18 \times 1 + 0.09 \times 1 + 0.06 \times 5 + 0.03 \times 5 + 0.01 \times 3} = 1.41$$

$p(0) = 0.58, p(1) = 0.42$

$H(\text{output}) = -(p(0) \log p(0) + p(1) \log p(1)) = 0.98$

Output rate = $0.98 \times 2.67/2 = 1.31$ bits/symbol
(input rate = 1.30 bits/symbol).

3.7.4.

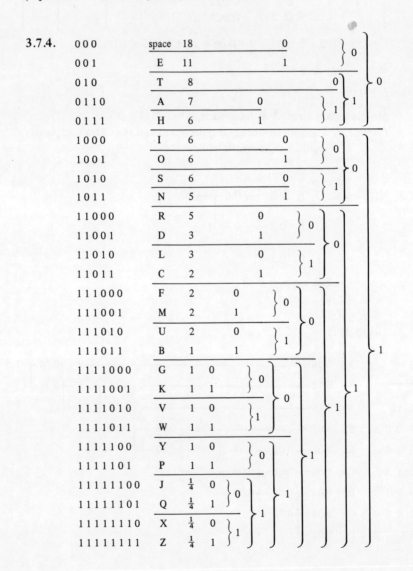

code	symbol	freq
0 0 0	space	18
0 0 1	E	11
0 1 0	T	8
0 1 1 0	A	7
0 1 1 1	H	6
1 0 0 0	I	6
1 0 0 1	O	6
1 0 1 0	S	6
1 0 1 1	N	5
1 1 0 0 0	R	5
1 1 0 0 1	D	3
1 1 0 1 0	L	3
1 1 0 1 1	C	2
1 1 1 0 0 0	F	2
1 1 1 0 0 1	M	2
1 1 1 0 1 0	U	2
1 1 1 0 1 1	B	1
1 1 1 1 0 0 0	G	1
1 1 1 1 0 0 1	K	1
1 1 1 1 0 1 0	V	1
1 1 1 1 0 1 1	W	1
1 1 1 1 1 0 0	Y	1
1 1 1 1 1 0 1	P	1
1 1 1 1 1 1 0 0	J	$\frac{1}{4}$
1 1 1 1 1 1 0 1	Q	$\frac{1}{4}$
1 1 1 1 1 1 1 0	X	$\frac{1}{4}$
1 1 1 1 1 1 1 1	Z	$\frac{1}{4}$

It should be noted that the procedure is quite easy and quick using the Fano–Shannon method, whereas Huffman's procedure would have required the wall of a large room!

Fortunately no code words are longer than eight digits.

$$L = 3 \times 0.37 + 4 \times 0.36 + 5 \times 0.13 + 6 \times 0.07 + 7 \times 0.06 + 8 \times 0.01 = 4.12$$

Saving in memory = 49 per cent (on 8-bits/character).
Actually the code is much better than ASCII but only about 20 per cent better than a simple equal-length 5-bit code (though this would lead to worse byte-packing problems).

14.4 Solutions to Exercises on Chapter 4

4.6.1.
x A A A A A A   B B B B B B   C C C C C C
y A A A A B C   B B B B B B   C C C C A B

x	A	A	A	B	C	C	C
y	A	B	C	B	C	A	B
$p(x)$	$\frac{1}{3}$	$\frac{1}{3}$	$\frac{1}{3}$	$\frac{1}{3}$	$\frac{1}{3}$	$\frac{1}{3}$	$\frac{1}{3}$
$p(y)$	$\frac{5}{18}$	$\frac{8}{18}$	$\frac{5}{18}$	$\frac{8}{18}$	$\frac{5}{18}$	$\frac{5}{18}$	$\frac{8}{18}$
$p(xy)$	$\frac{4}{18}$	$\frac{1}{18}$	$\frac{1}{18}$	$\frac{1}{3}$	$\frac{4}{18}$	$\frac{1}{18}$	$\frac{1}{18}$

$$I(xy) = 2.\tfrac{4}{18} \log \frac{\tfrac{4}{18}}{\tfrac{1}{3}\cdot\tfrac{5}{18}} + 2.\tfrac{1}{18} \log \frac{\tfrac{1}{18}}{\tfrac{1}{3}\cdot\tfrac{8}{18}} + 2.\tfrac{1}{18}\log \frac{\tfrac{1}{18}}{\tfrac{1}{3}\cdot\tfrac{5}{18}} + \tfrac{1}{3}.\log \frac{\tfrac{1}{3}}{\tfrac{1}{3}\cdot\tfrac{8}{18}}$$

$$= 0.712 \text{ bits.}$$

4.6.2. (a) $C = 1 - H(p) = 1 - 0.918 = 0.082$ bits.

(b) x A A A A A A A A A   B B B B B B B B B
y A A A A B X X X X   B B B B A X X X X

$$I(xy) = 2.\tfrac{4}{18} \log \frac{\tfrac{4}{18}}{\tfrac{1}{2}\cdot\tfrac{5}{18}} + 2.\tfrac{1}{18} \log \frac{\tfrac{1}{18}}{\tfrac{1}{2}\cdot\tfrac{5}{18}} + 2.\tfrac{4}{18} \log \frac{\tfrac{4}{18}}{\tfrac{1}{2}\cdot\tfrac{8}{18}}$$

    (AA and BB)   (AB and BA)   (AX and XA)

$$= 0.154.$$

Note that AX and BX lead to zero information.

(c) x A A A A A A A A A   B B B B B B B B B
y A A A A B X X X X   B B B B A X X X X
obs   A A A A B A A A A   B B B B A A A A A

$$I(xy) = \frac{8}{18} \log \frac{\frac{8}{18}}{\frac{1}{2} \cdot \frac{13}{18}} + \frac{4}{18} \log \frac{\frac{4}{18}}{\frac{1}{2} \cdot \frac{5}{18}} + \frac{1}{18} \log \frac{\frac{1}{18}}{\frac{1}{2} \cdot \frac{5}{18}} + \frac{5}{18} \log \frac{\frac{5}{18}}{\frac{1}{2} \cdot \frac{13}{18}}$$

$$= 0.106 \text{ bits.}$$

(d) x A A A A A A A A A   B B B B B B B B B

    y A A A A B X X X X   B B B B A X X X X

   obs   A A A A B A A B B   B B B B A A A B B

$$I(xy) = 2 \cdot \frac{6}{18} \log \frac{\frac{6}{18}}{\frac{1}{2} \cdot \frac{1}{2}} + 2 \cdot \frac{3}{18} \log \frac{\frac{3}{18}}{\frac{1}{2} \cdot \frac{1}{2}}$$

$$= 0.082 \text{ bits.}$$

It is rather surprising that guessing makes things worse, since one intuitively feels that one should be able to do better than chance (or at least as well). However, by comparing the relevant terms it can be seen that although the extra transmissions guessed correctly provide more information, this is more than cancelled by the negative information of those guessed wrongly. This will always be the case if the system has inherently a non-zero information transfer (guessing would not make matters worse only if no information was transmitted at all!).

4.6.3.   (a) $C_1 = 1 + (p \log p + \overline{p} \log \overline{p}) = 0.86$ bits.

       (b) $C_2 = 0.76$ bits.

       (c)

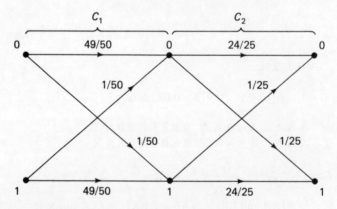

Figure 14.1   Cascaded binary symmetric channels

$$p(0/0) = \frac{49}{50} \cdot \frac{24}{25} + \frac{1}{50} \cdot \frac{1}{25} = 0.9416 = \overline{p}$$

$$p(0/1) = \frac{1}{50} \cdot \frac{24}{25} + \frac{49}{50} \cdot \frac{1}{25} = 0.0584 = p$$

$$C_3 = 1 - H(p) = 0.679 \text{ bits.}$$

The overall capacity is *always* reduced by cascading noisy channels (no form of 'noise-cancelling' ever occurs).

4.6.4. $p(A) = p(AA) + p(BA) + p(CA)$
$$= p(A)p(A/A) + p(B)p(A/B) + p(C)p(A/C)$$
$$= \tfrac{1}{4} \cdot \tfrac{2}{3} + 0 + 0$$
$$= \tfrac{1}{6}$$

Similarly $p(B) = \tfrac{1}{2}, p(C) = \tfrac{1}{3}$

$p(AA) = p(A)p(A/A) = \tfrac{1}{4} \cdot \tfrac{2}{3} = \tfrac{1}{6}$

$p(AB) = \tfrac{1}{12}, p(BB) = \tfrac{1}{4}, p(CB) = \tfrac{1}{6}, p(CC) = \tfrac{1}{3}$, others $= 0$

$$I(xy) = \tfrac{1}{6} \log \frac{\tfrac{1}{6}}{\tfrac{1}{4}\cdot\tfrac{1}{6}} + \tfrac{1}{12} \log \frac{\tfrac{1}{12}}{\tfrac{1}{4}\cdot\tfrac{1}{2}} + \tfrac{1}{4} \log \frac{\tfrac{1}{4}}{\tfrac{1}{4}\cdot\tfrac{1}{2}} + \tfrac{1}{6} \log \frac{\tfrac{1}{6}}{\tfrac{1}{2}\cdot\tfrac{1}{2}} + \tfrac{1}{3} \log \frac{\tfrac{1}{3}}{\tfrac{1}{2}\cdot\tfrac{1}{3}}$$

$$= 0.53 \text{ bits.}$$

4.6.5.

x	32 A's	16 B's	16 C's
y	$(9\times A, 3\times C, 3\times B, 1\times1!)\times2$	$(9\times B, 3\times11, 3\times A, 1\times C)$	$(9\times C, 3\times A, 3\times11, 1\times B)$
obs	$(9\times11, 3\times00, 3\times00, 1\times00)\times2$	$(9\times11, 7\times01)$	$(9\times11, 7\times10)$

number of 1s $= 36 + 25 + 25 = 86$ $\Big\}$ $p(1) = 0.672$

number of 0s $= 28 + \quad 7 + \quad 7 = 42$ $\Big\}$ $p(0) = 0.328$

Therefore

Information $= -(p(0) \log p(0) + p(1) \log p(1)) = 0.913$ bits.

Equivocation: The efficient observer simply sends say 1 for 'true' and 0 for 'false', but he works on *each bit* separately (that is, not on A, B, C). Therefore

Information $= -(\tfrac{1}{4} \log \tfrac{1}{4} + \tfrac{3}{4} \log \tfrac{3}{4}) = 0.811$ bits.

The other observer's strategy was not optimal; the complete two-digit code is repeated when incorrect, even if only one of the two digits is wrong. She provides more information than necessary.

14.5 Solutions to Exercises on Chapter 5

5.6.1. Consider a group of three digits

$$(\bar{p} + p)^3 = \bar{p}^3 + 3\bar{p}^2 p + 3\bar{p}p^2 + p^3$$
$$\quad\quad p(0) \quad\ p(1) \quad\ p(2) \quad p(3)$$

Single binary errors can be tolerated but two or more produce a symbol error. Therefore

$$p(\text{group error}) = p(2) + p(3)$$
$$p_g = 2.8 \times 10^{-2}$$

A symbol error will occur if either or both the two groups comprising a symbol are in error. Therefore

$$(\overline{p}_g + p_g)^2 = \overline{p}_g{}^2 + 2\overline{p}_g p_g + p_g{}^2$$
$$p(0) \quad p(1) \quad p(2)$$

$$p(\text{symbol error}) = p(1) + p(2)$$
$$= 0.055.$$

Note: It is incorrect to use terms of the expansion of $(\overline{p} + p)^6$, since the coding is specifically in threes, not sixes (although 6 digits are used per symbol).

5.6.2. (a) Since all combinations are used, one or more binary errors will produce a symbol error.

$$(\overline{p} + p)^5 = \overline{p}^5 + 5\overline{p}^4 p + 10\overline{p}^3 p^2 + \dots$$
$$p(0) \quad p(1) \qquad p(2)$$

$$p(e) = p(1) + p(2) + p(3) + p(4) + p(5)$$
$$= 1 - p(0)$$
$$= 0.226$$

Although English is very redundant, an error rate of 1 in 4 to 1 in 5 will produce barely understandable text.
(b) Adding a parity digit means that odd numbers of errors will be detectable, but symbol errors will occur for even numbers of errors.

$$(\overline{p} + p)^6 = \overline{p}^6 + 6\overline{p}^5 p + 15\overline{p}^4 p^2 + 20\overline{p}^3 p^3 + \dots$$
$$p(0) \quad p(1) \qquad p(2) \qquad p(3)$$

$$p\,(\text{parity error}) = p(1) + p(3) + p(5)$$
$$\approx p(1)$$
$$= 0.23$$

$$p\,(\text{symbol error}) = p(2) + p(4) + p(6)$$
$$\approx p(2)$$
$$= 0.03$$

Symbols may be repeated more than once, until the parity comes out even.

Probability of repetition $= 0.23 + (0.23)^2 + (0.23)^3 + \ldots$

$$= 0.30$$

Effective length per symbol $= 6 + 0.3 \times 6 \approx 8$ digits. Therefore

Effective symbol rate $= \frac{50}{8} = 6\frac{1}{4}$ symbols/s

An error rate of 0.03 would produce easily understandable text. It has been commented that this rate is similar to that in a certain well-known daily newspaper.

5.6.3. (a) There will be five information digits $(2^5 = 32)$ placed in positions 3, 5, 6, 7 and 9. We therefore require parity digits in positions 1, 2, 4 and 8. Position 10 will contain the overall parity digit.

	1	2	3	4	5	6	7	8	9	10
A	0	0	0	0	0	0	0	0	0	0
B	1	0	0	0	0	0	0	1	1	1
C	1	1	0	1	0	0	1	0	0	0
D	0	1	0	1	0	0	1	1	1	1
E	0	1	0	1	0	1	0	0	0	1

Efficiency $= \dfrac{H}{L} = \frac{5}{10} = 0.5$

(b) $(\bar{p} + p)^{10} = \bar{p}^{10} + 10\bar{p}^9 p + 45\bar{p}^8 p^2 + 120\bar{p}^7 p^3$

$\quad\quad\quad p(0) \quad\quad p(1) \quad\quad\quad p(2) \quad\quad\quad p(3)$

(i) p (parity error) $= p(1) + p(3) + p(5) + \ldots$

$$\approx p(1) = 0.091$$

(ii) p (2 or more errors detected) $= p(2) + p(4) + p(6) + \ldots$

$$\approx p(2)$$

$$= 4.1 \times 10^{-3}$$

(iii) p (symbol error) $= p(3) + p(5) + p(7) + p(9)$

$$\approx p(3)$$

$$= 1.1 \times 10^{-4}$$

Note: If multiple errors occur it is likely that after attempting to correct the received code word it will be found not to be in the list of allowed code words, so that it will be *detected* as being in error. Conversely, a large number of even errors could convert one code word into another, so the error would not be detected. The figures above ignore these possibilities, which are difficult to take into account theoretically.

14.6 Solutions to Exercises on Chapter 6

6.5.1. (i) From $t = 0$ to $t = \theta$ the waveform is given by $f(t) = \dfrac{A}{\theta} t$. Therefore

$$\text{Area} = \int_{-\infty}^{+\infty} f(t)\, \mathrm{d}t = 2 \int_{0}^{\theta} \frac{A}{\theta} t \, \mathrm{d}t = A\theta$$

$$\text{Energy} = \int_{-\infty}^{+\infty} f^2(t)\, \mathrm{d}t = 2 \int_{0}^{\theta} \left(\frac{At}{\theta}\right)^2 \mathrm{d}t = \frac{2}{3} A^2 \theta$$

(ii) Similarly, $\overline{f} = \dfrac{1}{T_0} \displaystyle\int_{-T_0/2}^{T_0/2} f(t)\, \mathrm{d}t = \dfrac{1}{T_0} \int_{0}^{\theta} f(t)\, \mathrm{d}t = \dfrac{A\theta}{T_0}$

$$\overline{f^2} = \frac{2}{3} \frac{A^2 \theta}{T_0}$$

$$\sigma^2 = \overline{f^2} - (\overline{f})^2 = \frac{A^2 \theta}{T_0} \left(\frac{2}{3} - \frac{\theta}{T_0} \right)$$

6.5.2. The mean value can be seen to be close to zero. For a very long sequence the mean would always tend to zero in any case. The mean square value is A^2, and is the same as the variance since $\overline{f} = 0$.

   Since the waveform is repetitive its power spectrum must contain lines spaced at $1/T_0$. However, the sequence is random, so the power spectrum will tend to be constant (having no dominant frequencies) up to frequencies of the order $1/\theta$; the actual form can be shown to be as in figure 14.2. Such sequences are very important, being used in system testing and identification, and in digital noise generators.

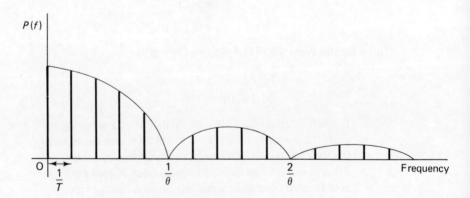

Figure 14.2 Power spectrum of pseudo-random sequence

14.7 Solutions to Exercises on Chapter 7

7.5.1. (i) From the Principle of Equipartition, the energy of the electrons (and their mean square velocity) is directly proportional to absolute temperature, so the total noise is proportionally increased. There would be no noise at absolute zero.

(ii) Johnson noise is caused by current pulses due to collisions of electrons with the lattice. A direct current would have no effect (unless the resistor was significantly heated). Johnson noise does occur in transistors, owing to their ohmic base resistance.

(iii) Shot noise depends essentially on current. It depends on temperature only in so far as temperature may change the current. It does not occur in a resistor carrying a direct current, since there is no potential barrier determining the current.

7.5.2. (i) A probability density distribution $p(x)$ has the property that $\int_{-\infty}^{+\infty} p(x)\, dx = 1$. Therefore $\int_{-\infty}^{+\infty} a \exp(-|x|/b)\, dx = 2ab = 1$ so $a = 1/2b$.

$\bar{x} = 0$ since $x\, p(x)$ is odd and the integral must be zero

$$\overline{x^2} = \sigma^2 = \int_{-\infty}^{+\infty} x^2\, p(x)\, dx = 2 \int_{0}^{\infty} \frac{x^2}{2b} \exp(-|x|/b)\, dx,$$

since $x^2\, p(x)$ is even

$= 2b^2$ (by parts).

(ii) Proceeding as before,

$$p\,(\text{error}) = \int_{v}^{\infty} p(x)\, dx = \frac{1}{2b} \int_{v}^{\infty} \exp\left(-\frac{x}{b}\right) dx$$

$$= \tfrac{1}{2} \exp\left(-\frac{|v|}{b}\right)$$

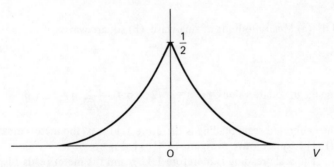

Figure 14.3   Error probability for exercise 7.5.2

Note that p (error) = $\frac{1}{2}$ for zero signal, as may be expected.

Note: Noise normally has a gaussian distribution, of course, but an exponential one is used here since it can be integrated. If one wants to set a question using a gaussian one has to include the appropriate tables of $\int \exp(-t^2/2)\, dt$ etc., which is a considerable nuisance. The writer considers this to be yet another example of the inherently unfair nature of the world.

7.5.3. The mean modulus η of the sine wave of figure 14.4(a) is

$$\eta = \frac{1}{T/2} \int_0^{T/2} a \sin \omega t \; dt = \frac{2a}{\pi}$$

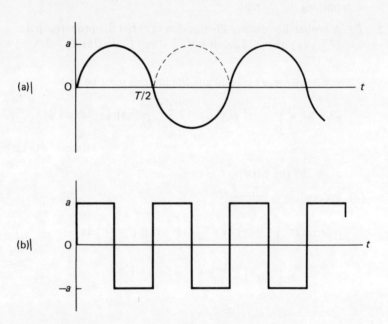

Figure 14.4   (a) Mean modulus of sine wave, (b) square wave

The mean square value ($= \sigma^2$) $= a^2/2$ so $\sigma = \dfrac{\pi}{2\sqrt{2}}\, \eta = 1.11\, \eta.$

The calibrated scale reading is therefore $1.11 \times \eta$ (the meter 'measures' η).

(i) The square wave of figure 14.4(b) has $\eta = a = \sigma.$

The scale reading is therefore $1.11\, \eta$ and the meter reads 11 per cent high.

(ii) The mean modulus of gaussian noise is

$$\eta = 2 \int_0^\infty x \, p(x) \, dx = \frac{2}{\sigma\sqrt{2\pi}} \int_0^\infty x \exp\left(-x^2/2\sigma^2\right) dx$$

This can be integrated easily, giving $\eta = \dfrac{\sigma}{\sqrt{\pi/2}}.$

The scale reading is therefore $1.11 \, \eta = \dfrac{1.11}{\sqrt{\pi/2}} \, \sigma = 0.89\sigma.$

It therefore reads 11 per cent low.

7.5.4. (a) The probability density can be deduced intuitively for a square wave; there must be indefinitely narrow spikes (impulses) at the two possible amplitude values, and each spike must have 'area' 0.5 units. Similarly, a triangle wave has a uniform distribution. For a sine wave $x = a \sin \omega_0 t$

$$p(x) = \frac{1}{\text{period}} \cdot \frac{1}{\text{slope}} = \frac{1}{a \, \pi \cos \omega_0 t} = \frac{1}{\pi \, (a^2 - x^2)^{\frac{1}{2}}}$$

The functions and corresponding probability densities are shown in figure 14.5.

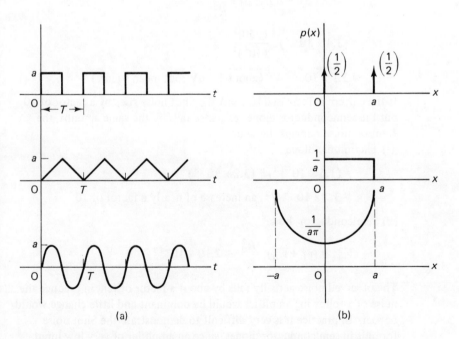

(a)   (b)

Figure 14.5 Various waveforms (a) and their probability densities (b)

(b) (i) Ensemble averages $\int x^2 \, p(x) \, dx$

Square wave: $(x^2)_a \, p(a) = a^2/2$

Triangle wave: $a^2/3$

Sine wave: $\int_{-a}^{a} \dfrac{x^2}{\pi \, (a^2 - x^2)^{\frac{1}{2}}} \to \dfrac{2a^2}{\pi} \int_{0}^{\pi/2} \sin^2\theta \, d\theta = \dfrac{a^2}{2}$

(ii) Time averages $\dfrac{1}{T_0} \int_{-T_0/2}^{T_0/2} x^2(t) \, dt$

Square wave: $a^2/2$

Triangle wave: $\dfrac{2}{T} \int_{0}^{T/2} \left(\dfrac{a}{(T/2)} t \right)^2 dt = \dfrac{a^2}{3}$

Sine wave: $a^2/2$

7.5.5. Referring to figure 7.14 again, the effective resistance of the diode is only 250 Ω, so only a fraction $(R_d/(R_d + R))^2 \approx R_d^2/R^2$ of the previous voltage is measured at the output. That is

$$\overline{v}_{out}^2 = (4RkT\Delta f + 2eIR^2 \Delta f) \, \dfrac{R_d^2}{R^2}$$

$$= (3.4 \times 10^{-9}). \, \dfrac{(250)^2}{(10^4)^2}$$

$$\approx 2.1 \times 10^{-12} \text{ V}^2 \text{ (about 1.4 } \mu\text{V root mean square).}$$

If the current is increased to 1 mA the Shot noise rises by a factor of 10 but the semiconductor diode resistance falls by the same amount, the Johnson noise remains the same.

(i) Thermionic diode

$$= (1.6 \times 10^{-10}) + (3.2 \times 10^{-8})$$

$$= 3.2 \times 10^{-8} \text{ V}^2 \text{, an increase of nearly a factor of 10.}$$

(ii) Semiconductor diode

$$\overline{v}_{out}^2 = (v_J^2 + \overline{v}_S^2). \, \dfrac{R_d^2}{R^2} \approx 2.10 \times 10^{-13}.$$

The observed noise actually falls by about a factor of ten; in practice the noise of a following amplifier would be dominant and little change would be seen. In practice it is very difficult to demonstrate the Shot noise formula in semiconductor diodes, since an amplifier of very low input impedance and very low noise is required, whereas it can be demonstrated very easily with thermionic diodes. However, one usually produces noise either by a pseudo-random sequence or by using a zener diode in the breakdown region these days.

14.8 Solutions to Exercises on Chapter 8

8.6.1.   (i) $f_1 \maltese f_1$ is always even, but not necessarily positive (for example if f_1 has both positive and negative sections).

(ii) $f_1 \maltese f_2$ and $f_2 \maltese f_1$ are mirror images.

(iii) $f_1 * f_2$ and $f_2 * f_1$ are identical.

(iv) In general $f_1 \maltese f_1$ and $f_1 * f_1$ are not the same. They have similar shape if one or both of the functions are even and are identical if both functions are even.

8.6.2.

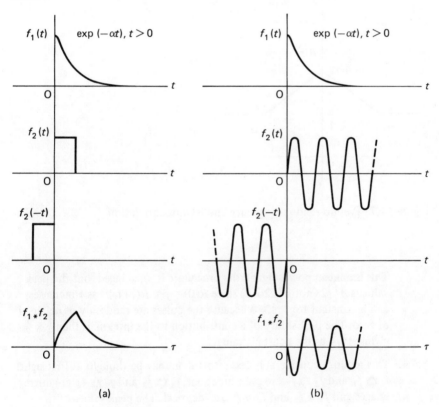

(a)   (b)

Figure 14.6 (a) Convolution of exponential decay with rectangular pulse, (b) convolution of exponential decay with a burst of sine waves

These results represent the response of a first-order system to a rectangular pulse or burst of sine waves. If the pulse is very long, the response becomes a step response (exponential rise). The response to a burst of sine waves is a sine wave of the same frequency, but with an initial transient and phase shift. Continuous sine waves would produce a steady amplitude with a constant phase shift.

8.6.3.

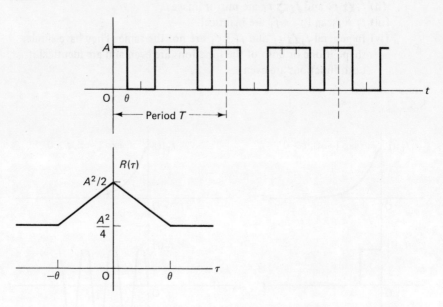

Figure 14.7   Pseudo-random sequence and its autocorrelation

This is a mean power signal; the procedure is unchanged, but the peak value is $A^2/2$ (not $A^2/2 \times \theta$) since $R(0) = \bar{f}^2$. $R(\tau)$ falls as τ increases, and is constant for $|\tau| > \theta$ because the pulses are randomly of height A or zero. The probability of a contribution to the integral is then $\frac{1}{2} \times \frac{1}{2}$ giving $A^2/4$ as the constant value.

8.6.4.   This requires considerably less effort than may be thought at first sight. $f_1 \mbox{✡} f_1$ and $f_2 \mbox{✡} f_2$ are even functions, $f_1 \mbox{✡} f_2$ and $f_2 \mbox{✡} f_1$ are mirror images and $f_1 * f_2$ and $f_2 * f_1$ are identical. The peak values of the functions are important and should be evaluated. Note that although the 'self-convolutions' $f_1 * f_1$ and $f_2 * f_2$ are fairly easy to evaluate they have little practical significance.

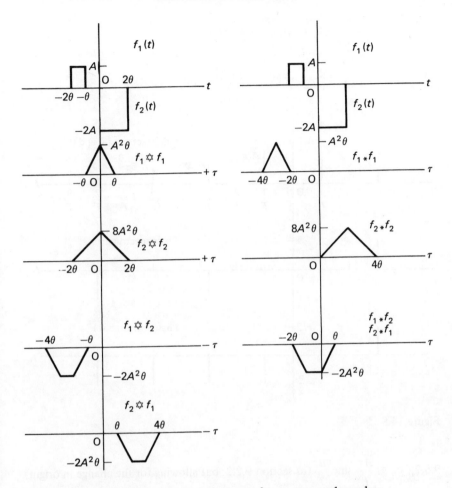

Figure 14.8   Correlations and convolutions of two rectangular pulses

14.9   Solutions to Exercises on Chapter 9

9.5.1.

(a) $c_n = \dfrac{1}{T} \displaystyle\int_{-T/4}^{T/4} A \exp\left(-jn\omega_0 t\right)\, \mathrm{d}t$

$\quad\quad = \dfrac{A}{n\pi} \sin \dfrac{n\pi}{2}$

$\quad\quad = \dfrac{A}{2} \operatorname{sinc} \dfrac{n}{2}$

(b) $c_n = \dfrac{1}{T} \displaystyle\int_{0}^{T/2} A \exp\left(-jn\omega_0 t\right)\, \mathrm{d}t$

$$= \frac{A}{n\pi} \exp\left(-jn\pi/2\right) \sin n\pi/2$$

$$= \frac{A}{2} \operatorname{sinc} \frac{n}{2} \cdot \exp\left(-jn\pi/2\right)$$

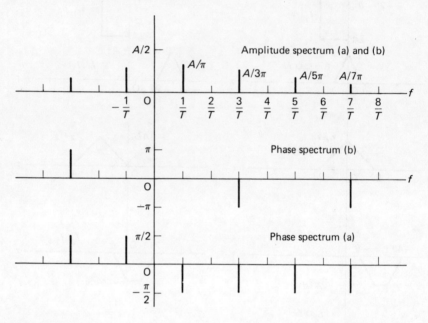

Figure 14.9

9.5.2. $c_n = \dfrac{A\tau}{T} \operatorname{sinc} \dfrac{n\tau}{T}$ (as section 9.2.2, but allowing for the change in origin).

The amplitude spectra are the same, except for an extra line of height A for $f_2(t)$, and are shown in figure 14.10.

9.5.3. (i) The zeroth harmonic gives the mean (d.c.) level.
(ii) Yes. In a perfect square wave they are *exactly* zero.
(iii) No, for example, the repetitive pulse of section 9.2.2.
(iv) The phases of the harmonics of an even function are all zero or $\pm\pi$ (because they refer to cosine waves). Similarly those of an odd function are all $\pm\pi/2$ (they refer to sine waves).
(v) The phases are changed by $\pm\pi$ (that is, the harmonics are inverted).
(vi) A phase term $\exp\left(-jn\omega_0\tau\right)$ is produced for a shift of τ. This moves the origin of the first harmonic by τ, but higher harmonics have to be shifted by greater amounts to keep in step.
(vii) The phases have to be reversed.
(viii) The sixth (120/20), and it does not depend on the origin.

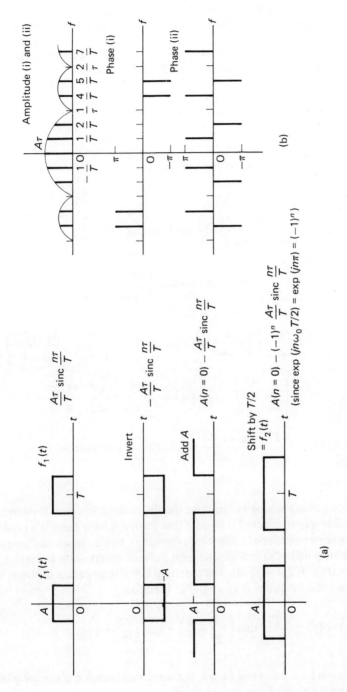

Figure 14.10

(ix) A set of impulses is produced.

(x) Add all the harmonics with the same amplitude but random phases.

9.5.4. One could use the cosine transform here, since it is easier to integrate cos.cos than cos.exp. However, we will use the full transform.

$$F(f) = \int_{-T/4}^{T/4} A \cos \omega_0 t \exp\left(-j\omega t\right) dt$$

$$\frac{F(f)}{A} = \left[\frac{1}{\omega_0} \exp\left(-j\omega t\right) \sin \omega_0 t\right]_{-T/4}^{T/4}$$

$$+ \frac{j\omega}{\omega_0} \int_{-T/4}^{T/4} \exp\left(-j\omega t\right) \sin \omega_0 t \, dt$$

$$= \left[\frac{1}{\omega_0} \exp\left(-j\omega t\right) \sin \omega_0 t\right]_{-T/4}^{T/4}$$

$$+ \frac{j\omega}{\omega_0} \left(\left[-\frac{1}{\omega_0} \exp\left(-j\omega t\right) \cos \omega_0 t\right]_{-T/4}^{T/4} - \frac{j\omega}{\omega_0} \frac{F(f)}{A}\right)$$

$$= \left[\frac{1}{\omega_0} \exp\left(-j\omega t\right) \sin \omega_0 t\right]_{-T/4}^{T/4} + \frac{\omega^2}{\omega_0^2} \frac{F(f)}{A}$$

Thus $F(f) = \dfrac{AT}{\pi} \dfrac{\cos \omega T/4}{1 - \dfrac{\omega^2}{\omega_0^2}}$ (after some manipulation)

It takes about as long as this if we use the cosine transform. However, the sensible way to proceed is to note that the half-cosine pulse is a product between a continuous cosine wave (spectrum two impulses of strength $A/2$ at f_0 and $-f_0$) and a rectangular pulse of height unity and width $T/2$ (spectrum $T/2$ sinc $fT/2$). The spectrum is the convolution of these, which is two sinc functions at f_0 and $-f_0$. Therefore

$$F(f) = \frac{AT}{4} \left[\text{sinc}\left(\frac{fT}{2} - \tfrac{1}{2}\right) + \text{sinc}\left(\frac{fT}{2} + \tfrac{1}{2}\right)\right]$$

This can be done in one's head, but some manipulation is then required to get it into the form quoted above.

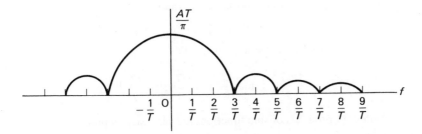

Figure 14.11   Amplitude spectrum of half-cosine pulse

9.5.5. Using the addition and shift rules,

$$F(f) = A\tau \text{ sinc } f\tau \left[\exp(j\omega\tau) - \exp(-j\omega\tau) \right]$$

$$= j4A\tau\pi fT \text{ sinc } f\tau \text{ sinc } 2fT$$

(a) $F(f) = j8A\tau^2 \pi f \text{ sinc } f\tau \text{ sinc } 4f\tau$

(b) $F(f) = j2A\tau^2 \pi f \text{ sinc}^2 f\tau$

Note that (b) is the case where the two pulses just touch.

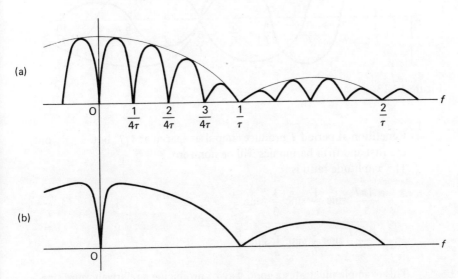

Figure 14.12

9.5.6. (i) The spectrum can be found using the differentiation and shift rules. However, it is easier to note that the pulse is the convolution between two rectangular pulses of widths $T/6$ and $T/3$ (the base of the pulse is the sum of the widths, and the sloping side is the width of the narrower pulse). The pulse has area $AT/3$, so $F(f) = AT/3$ sinc $fT/6$ sinc $fT/3 = K$ say. Combining two such pulses, at $T/4$ and $-T/4$

$$F(f) = K\,[\exp(-j\omega T/4) - \exp(+j\omega T/4)]$$

$$= K.2j\,\sin \omega T/4$$

Thus $|F(f)| = \dfrac{A\pi f T^2}{3}\ |\,\text{sinc}\ \dfrac{fT}{6}\ \text{sinc}\ \dfrac{fT}{3}\ \text{sinc}\ \dfrac{fT}{2}\ |$

Note that products of sinc functions are very easy to plot.

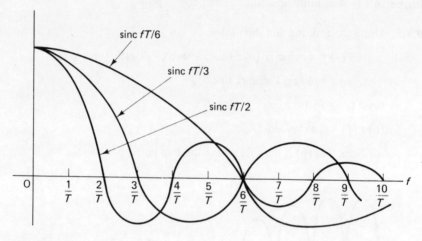

Figure 14.13

Repetition at period T produces impulses spaced at $1/T$, but clearly only the first and fifth harmonics will be non-zero.
The amplitude ratio is

$$\frac{\dfrac{A\pi T}{3}\ \text{sinc}\ \dfrac{1}{6}\ \text{sinc}\ \dfrac{1}{3}\ \text{sinc}\ \dfrac{1}{2}}{\dfrac{A\pi 5T}{3}\ \text{sinc}\ \dfrac{5}{6}\ \text{sinc}\ \dfrac{5}{3}\ \text{sinc}\ \dfrac{5}{2}} = 25$$

This example illustrates a good way of producing a relatively pure sine wave by digital means. The choice of pulse shape makes the 2nd, 3rd, 4th, 6th etc., harmonics disappear, so the total harmonic distortion is only about 5 per cent.

9.5.7. The triangle pulse has a spectrum $A\theta\ \text{sinc}^2 f\theta$, and its repetition produces lines spaced at $1/T$, as in figure 14.14.

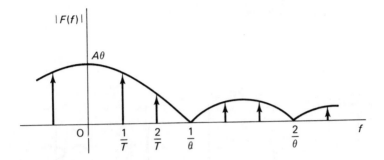

Figure 14.14 Amplitude spectrum for $T = 3\theta$

Clarinet: The even harmonics are zero so $\theta = T/2$.
   $\text{sinc}^2 fT/2$ gives lines $\text{sinc}^2\ 1/2$, $\text{sinc}^2\ 3/2$ etc., with ratios
   $10 : 1.1 : 0.4$ etc.

Trumpet: The fourth harmonic is zero so $\theta = T/4$.
   $\text{sinc}^2\ fT/4$ gives lines of $\text{sinc}^2 1/4$, $\text{sinc}^2\ 1/2$, $\text{sinc}^2\ 3/4$ etc.,
   with ratios $10 : 5 : 1.1$ etc.

Flute: The second line has to be just below $1/\theta$ to give two lines in
   the second lobe so $\theta \approx 0.4\ T$.
   $\text{sinc}^2\ 0.4fT$ gives lines $\text{sinc}^2\ 0.4$, $\text{sinc}^2\ 0.8$ etc., with ratios
   $10 : 0.9 : 0.4 : 0.6$ etc.

9.5.8. Note that it is not correct to convolve the small triangle with a set of
impulses, and then to multiply by the large triangle, as this gives a
different waveform of distorted triangles. See figure 14.15.

$$f(t) = (a(t) \times b(t)) * d(t) \quad F(f) = (A(f) * B(f)) \times D(f)$$

$A(f)$: Impulses of strength $1/a$ at spacing $1/a$

$B(f)$: $4Aa\ \text{sinc}^2\ 4fa$

$D(f)$: $\dfrac{2a}{3}\ \text{sinc}^2\ af/3$

9.5.9.

$$R_1(\tau) = \int_{-\infty}^{+\infty} f(t) f(t + \tau) = \frac{A^2}{2\alpha}\ \exp\left(-\alpha|\tau|\right)$$

$$E(f) = \int_{-\infty}^{+\infty} R_1(\tau) \exp\left(-j\omega\tau\right)\ \mathrm{d}\tau = \int_{-\infty}^{+\infty} \frac{A^2}{2\alpha}\ \exp\left(-\alpha|\tau|\right) \cos \omega\tau\ \mathrm{d}\tau$$

$$= \frac{A^2}{\alpha^2 + \omega^2}\ \text{(by parts)}$$

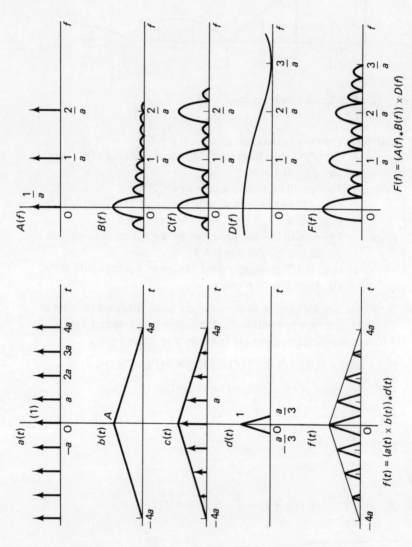

Figure 14.15

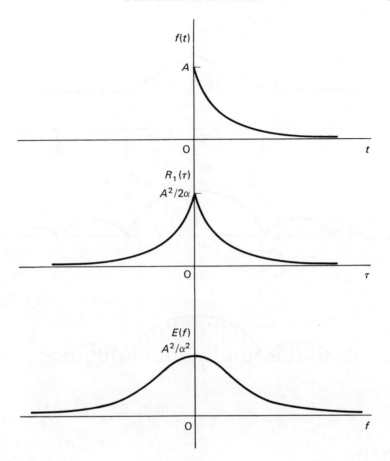

Figure 14.16

$$F(f) = \int_{-\infty}^{+\infty} f(t) \exp\left(-j\omega t\right) \mathrm{d}t = A/(\alpha + j\omega)$$

$$E(f) = |F(f)|^2 = A^2/(\alpha^2 + \omega^2)$$

$$E = \int_{-\infty}^{+\infty} f^2(t)\, \mathrm{d}t = \int_0^{\infty} A^2 \exp\left(-2\alpha t\right) \mathrm{d}t = A^2/2\alpha$$

$$= \int_{-\infty}^{+\infty} E(f)\, \mathrm{d}f = \int_{-\infty}^{+\infty} \frac{A^2}{\alpha^2 + \omega^2}\, \mathrm{d}f = \frac{A^2}{2\alpha} \quad (\tan^{-1} \text{ form}).$$

9.5.10. We have previously found $R_1(\tau)$ for this waveform (exercise 8.6.3). The energy spectrum $E(f) = (A^2\theta/4)\,\mathrm{sinc}^2\,f\theta + (A^2/4)\,\delta(0)$ (as a result of the

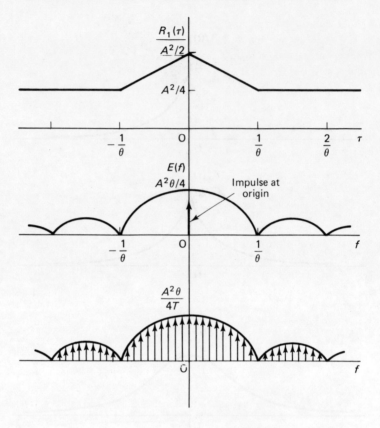

Figure 14.17

d.c. level). The power spectrum $P(f)$ consists of impulses spaced at $1/T$. Ignoring the d.c. component, the power from zero to 1 kHz is $(A^2\theta/4T) \cdot 2.10^3 \approx 0.16$ V root mean square.

Pseudo-random sequences are often used for generating 'random' noise. A long (maximal length) sequence can be produced by feedback around a shift register, and with a 20-bit register and 1 MHz clock noise essentially white up to say 100 kHz is easily produced. In this case the line separation is about 1 Hz so the spectrum is essentially continuous. The method has the advantage that noise of relatively high power is produced with no amplification (and therefore no mains pick up).

14.10 Solutions to Exercises on Chapter 10

10.5.1. $f(t) = +\frac{1}{2}\cos 3\omega_0 t - \cos \omega_0 t$

$\omega_0 t$	$\cos 3\omega_0 t$	$\cos \omega_0 t$	$f(t)$
0	1	1	$-\frac{1}{2}$
60°	-1	$\frac{1}{2}$	-1
120°	1	$-\frac{1}{2}$	$+1$
180°	-1	-1	$+\frac{1}{2}$
240°	1	$-\frac{1}{2}$	$+1$
300°	-1	$+\frac{1}{2}$	-1
360°	1	1	$-\frac{1}{2}$

Reconstruction at the ends of the waveform is not complete because the contributions from samples before or after the range chosen is omitted. An infinite number of samples is needed for perfect reconstruction. See figure 14.18.

10.5.2. $f_s(t) = f(t) \times s(t)$ $\qquad$ $F_s(f) = F(f) * S(f)$ $\qquad$ See figure 14.19.

$f_{sh}(t) = f_s(t) * h(t)$ $\qquad$ $F_{sh}(f) = F_s(f) \times H(f)$

(i) Can be recovered by a simple low-pass filter.

(ii) The distortion due to the hold can be removed by a filter with the inverse characteristic of $H(f)$, that is, $(\text{sinc } f\theta)^{-1}$.

(iii) (a) Recovery is not possible since the sampling rate $< 2W/\text{s}$.

(b) The hold now has relatively little effect, so recovery is easier.

14.11 Solutions to Exercises on Chapter 11

11.5.1. The probability density distribution is shown in figure 14.20. It consists of an impulse of strength one-half at the origin plus the usual uniform distribution

$$H_r(v) = -\int_{-\infty}^{+\infty} p(v) \log p(v) \, dv$$

$$= -\frac{1}{2} \log \frac{1}{2} + \frac{1}{2} \log 2a$$

In this case the mean value is $a/4$ and the mean square $a^2/6$.

$H_r(v) = \frac{1}{2} + \frac{1}{2} \log(24 \overline{v^2})^{\frac{1}{2}} = 1.65$ bits $(\overline{v^2} = 1)$ compared with $\sqrt{2\pi e}$ bits or 2.05 for the gaussian.

11.5.2. The error rate for binary pulses will be very small with this value of P/N ratio (compare with example 7.4), so the information transfer expression will give unity and the information rate is simply given by $2W = 6000$ bits/s. The ideal theorem gives $3000 \log(101) \approx 19,975$ bits/s.

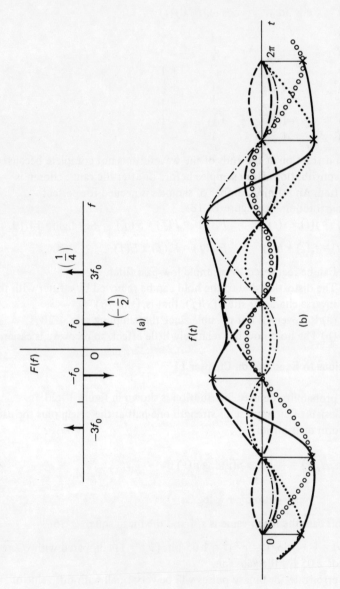

Figure 14.18   Recovery of a signal from its samples: (a) spectra, (b) recovered signal

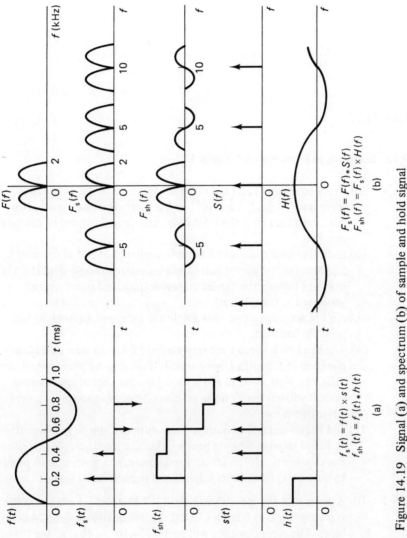

Figure 14.19 Signal (a) and spectrum (b) of sample and hold signal

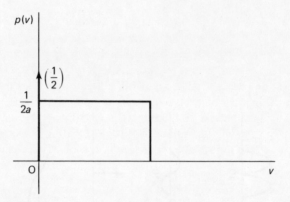

Figure 14.20

14.12   Solutions to Exercises on Chapter 12

12.5.1. (i) From equation (12.1) the mean square value of the modulated
wave is $\overline{v_m}^2 = \frac{1}{2}a_c^2 + \frac{1}{4}m^2 a_c^2$, so the power increases as m^2. However, even for $m = 1$ the sidebands carry only one-third of the total
power.

(ii) Each sideband contains all the information, but AM as opposed to
SSAM is normally used as it is much simpler to implement (SSAM
does not include the carrier in its spectrum, and one must be
generated at the receiver).

(iii) An FM wave has a constant amplitude independent of D, so the
power is constant.

(iv) The amplitude spectra are very similar (as can be seen by expanding
equation (12.2) with D very small). However, the phase spectra are
different. Narrow band FM is used for some special applications,
since it still has better noise tolerance than AM though its power
advantage is lost.

(v) AM has advantages of narrow bandwidth and simple implementation. FM requires a larger bandwidth and a more complex receiver,
but requires much less transmitted power for a given output power-
to-noise ratio (that is, its tolerance of noise is much better).

12.5.2. (i) Assume that the speech bandwidth is 3 kHz and sample at 8000/s.
If we digitise into 8 levels (3 bits) the information will be 24,000
bits/s. The recording time will be $10^6/24.10^3 \approx 40$ s, so the
system would be rather limited in its application. With only 8 levels
the quantisation noise will be high, with $(P/N)_0 \approx 64$.

(ii) The outer track has length $\approx 2\pi \times 50$ mm and carries
$(2\pi.50.10^{-3})/(2.10^{-6}) \approx 16 \times 10^4$ bits, so the 'mean' track will

carry about 8×10^4 bits. There will be about $(50 \times 10^{-3})/$ (10.10^{-6}) = 5000 tracks, so the total number of bits $\approx 8 \times 10^8$.

For high-quality music we need a bandwidth of at least 15 kHz, so the sampling rate $\approx$ 30,000/s. A high root mean square signal-to-noise ratio is needed, say 60 dB at least, equivalent to $(P/N) \approx 10^6$, so the number of levels required is $M = 10^3$. Ten bits are therefore needed per sample, so the bit rate is 3×10^5/s.

The playing time will be $(8 \times 10^8)/(3 \times 10^5) \approx 3000$ s or 50 minutes, so the system is clearly very feasible. The speed of rotation of the disc can be deduced, since there are 5000 tracks, and is 5/3 rev./s or 100 rev./min.

12.5.3. (i) There are 8 tones and one rest, so the information is log 9 = 3.2 bits per tone. The average length per tone is $\frac{3}{4}$ s giving $3.2/\frac{3}{4}$ = 4.27 bits/s or 21.1 bits in 5 s. If the number of 'tunes' is N, then assuming they are equiprobable log N = 21.1 so $N = 2^{21.1} \approx 2.2 \times 10^6$. Quite a lot of 'tunes', but many of them would not be very interesting!

(ii) The spectrum of a given tone lasting a given time is a sinc function (an impulse for a continuous tone convolved with a sinc function for the duration) but since the shortest duration is 0.2 s ($\approx$ 5 Hz) this spreading effect is small, and the bandwidth can be taken as $512 - 256$ = 256 Hz.

   (a) Double sideband AM can easily be used, since the channel bandwidth will be about 500 Hz, so a carrier at about 1.5 kHz could be chosen.

   (b) With $D = 5$, $W_c \approx 2(D + 1) \times 256 \approx 3$ kHz, so FM is just possible.

   (c) With PCM we could sample at say 3×256/s and with 256 levels we have $m = 8$ so the channel bandwidth will be $\frac{3}{2} \times 8 \times 256 \approx$ 3 kHz. This would give a good power-to-noise ratio.

   (d) Each tone requires log 9 = 3.2 bits (4 needed in practice) for pitch plus log 4 = 2 bits for tone. Adding one bit for synchronisation the maximum rate is 7 bits in 0.2 s $\approx$ 35 bits/s. This requires a bandwidth of only about 20 Hz. The system complexity is higher, of course, since the tones have to be regenerated from the code received.

14.13   Solutions to Exercises on Chapter 13

13.5.1. Suppose the pad measures 10 cm $\times$ 10 cm. Using an 8-bit ADC gives a resolution of 100 mm/256 $\approx$ 0.5 mm, probably enough for most applications. In general, for a square of side L an n-bit ADC will give resolution of $L/2^n$, producing $2n$ bits/sample. With a 3 kHz channel we have number of samples/s = 3000/$2n$ and the time to traverse the page is 2^n/samples/s = $2^n \times n/1500$

n	Resolution	Time/line (s)
4	6.25	0.04
6	1.56	0.26
8	0.39	1.37
10	0.10	6.83
12	0.02	32.8

8-bits is clearly a reasonable compromise.

The particular advantage over a facsimile system is that only lines drawn are 'scanned', rather than every possible line (many of which are blank). The proposed system is clearly good for sketches, circuit diagrams, signatures etc., but its advantages fall as the complexity of the sketch etc., increases.

13.5.2. (i) There are $400 \times 600 = 24 \times 10^4$ 'pixels' per page, and the maximum bit rate is 3000/s (using AM with 1.5 kHz per sideband). The time taken to transmit a page is $24 \times 10^4/3000 \approx 80$ s. Slow, but can handle documents, pictures etc.

(ii) Assuming five letters per word on average, number of bits/page = $300 \times 5 \times 5$. The time taken is $300 \times 5 \times 5/3000 \approx 2.5$ s. Fast, but expensive hardware.

(iii) Speaking at 2 words/s takes about 150 s. Rather a waste of time and money, unless speaking to one's girlfriend.
Ideally $C = W \log(1 + P/N) \approx 3 \times 10^4$ bits/s, or about ten times faster.

13.5.3. This is really an essay-type question, but the main quantitative points are as follows.

TV picture: $625 \times 625 \times \log 32 \approx 2 \times 10^6$ bits
newspaper picture: assume 10 cm $\times$ 10 cm with two dots/mm and 16 shades, information $\approx 200 \times 200 \times \log 16 \approx 10^5$ bits
text: 1 bit/letter on average (much more in this book)

Most attempts at this question conclude that a picture is usually worth considerably more than a thousand words.

13.5.4. As above, the information per frame $\approx 2 \times 10^6$ bits.
Assuming outer track diameter 15 cm, inner track diameter 7.5 cm, the minimum track length is about 0.5 m and the minimum spacing about 0.25 μm. The total number of frames is $7.5 \times 10^{-2}/0.25 \times 10^{-6} \approx 3 \times 10^5$ so the playing time (25 frames/s) is about 200 minutes. (This is rather longer than practically likely, because the radial spacing would usually have to be larger than that along one track.)

The digital information primarily produces the brightness. If it was arranged in 8-bit bytes then 5 bits could be used for brightness, say, plus three for colour and parity. The baud rate will be very high ($2 \times 10^6 \times 25 \approx 5 \times 10^7$), requiring a bandwidth of 25 MHz. This is because the system is entirely digital. However, if the brightness information was contained in say the lengths of the depressions, the rate would be reduced to 10^7 baud, equivalent to a bandwidth of 5 MHz (as for the usual TV picture), and the minimum spacing would be eased. Sound information is required only occasionally (30,000 samples/s for bandwidth 15 kHz) so occasional 'sound bytes' could be used.

13.5.5. Assuming a page of 300 words with 5 letters per word, a 5-bit code would lead to $300 \times 5 \times 5 = 7500$ bits. At a transmission rate of 6000 baud this would take only about $1\frac{1}{4}$ s, so about 12 pages could be sent in 15 s at a cost of 3p, comparing favourably with the cost of a First Class letter. Such a rate is very optimistic and a lower one would be necessary in practice.

Note: This question was first set in 1976, as may be guessed from the costs quoted. In fact the minimum phone cost now (5p) makes the comparison less favourable. Also, at that time home computers were not available whereas now one could use the ASCII codes obtained via the keyboard. The data in cassette-loaded systems are in the form of two tones (typically 2400 Hz and 1200 Hz), equivalent to FSK, and could therefore be used directly, though speed-up on replay would not be possible. Typical data rates are 300 (Kansas City standard) or 1200 baud, higher rates being used only exceptionally.

13.5.6. Most of this question is answerable directly from the discussion in this chapter. There are 8000 samples/s giving 8×10^4 bytes in 10 s.

(a) Vocoder systems divide the spectrum into fixed ranges and attempt to reduce the bandwidth in each range. A factor of reduction of about 10 is feasible.

(b) By exploiting the particular characteristic of speech in the time domain (via phase adjustment, half period zeroing and delta modulation) a factor of reduction of about 30 is possible.

(c) Vocal-tract models are similar to vocoders, but the spectral ranges chosen correspond to known resonances in the vocal tract, and may be entirely synthetic as in phoneme systems. Factors of reduction of 100 or more are possible.

The distinction between the systems tends to diminish on closer inspection. (a) and (c) are clearly very similar, but (b) is essentially a time-domain approach. However, from Fourier Theory it is known that time and frequency representations are equivalent, and in this sense (b) is another way of looking at the processes of (a) and (c).

References and Bibliography

The literature of Information Theory is very extensive. However, the vast numbers of references which many authors delight in are often somewhat overwhelming and relatively unhelpful in getting into a new subject and the references quoted here have been kept to a minimum. A short Bibliography is also included of books providing valuable background information or more detail as explained below.

References

Abramson, N. (1963). *Information Theory and Coding*, McGraw-Hill, London and New York.

Bell, D. A. (1953). *Information Theory*, Pitman, London and New York.

Bose, R., Chandhuri, D. and Hocquenghem, A. (1960). *Int. J. Information Control*, Vol. 3, p. 68.

Dudley, H. (1936). 'Synthesising Speech', *Bell Laboratories Record*, Vol. 15, p. 98.

Fano, R. M. (1961). *Transmission of Information*, MIT Press, Cambridge, Massachusetts.

Fano, R. M. (1963). *IEEE Trans. Information Theory*, Vol. IT9, p. 64.

Fire, P. (1959). *Stanford Electronics Laboratory Report no. 55*, Stanford, California.

Hagelberger, D. W. (1959). *Bell System Technical Journal*, Vol. 38, p. 969.

Hamming, R. W. (1950). *Bell System Technical Journal*, Vol. 29, p. 147.

Hartley, R. (1928). *Bell System Technical Journal*, Vol. 7, p. 535.

Howatson, A. M., Lund, P. G. and Todd, J. D. (1972). *Engineering Tables and Data*, Chapman and Hall, London.

Huffman, D. A. (1952). *Proc. IRE*, Vol. 40, p. 1098.

Johnson, J. B. (1928). *Phys. Rev.*, Vol. 32, p. 97.

Nyquist, H. (1924). *Bell System Technical Journal*, Vol. 3, p. 324.

Nyquist, H. (1928). *Phys. Rev.*, Vol. 32, p. 110.

Rice, S. O. (1950). *Bell System Technical Journal*, Vol. 29, p. 60.

Rosie, A. M. (1973). *Information and Communication Theory*, 2nd edn, Van Nostrand Reinhold, New York.

Schwartz, M. (1970). *Information Transmission, Modulation and Noise*, McGraw-Hill, London and New York.

Shannon, C. E. and Weaver, W. (1949). *A Mathematical Theory of Communication*, Univ. of Illinois Press, Champaign, Illinois.

Stuart, R. D. (1966). *An Introduction to Fourier Analysis*, Science Paperbacks, Methuen, London.

Wozencroft, J. M. and Jacobs, I. M. (1965). *Communication Engineering*, Wiley, New York.

Bibliography

N. Abramson, *Information Theory and Coding*, McGraw-Hill, London and New York, 1963. Comprehensive treatment of principles of coding in discrete systems.

J. Brown and E. V. Glazier, *Telecommunications*, 2nd edn, Science Paperbacks, Halsted Press, New York, 1974. Deals primarily with telecommunications but provides some useful information on information theory.

J. P. Cater, *Computer Speech Generation*, Howards Sams, Indianapolis, Indiana, 1983. Primarily for laymen but gives useful details on available systems.

F. R. Connor, *Signals*, Edward Arnold, London, 1972. Useful introduction to signal analysis, coding and information theory.

M. A. Jack (editor), *The Impact of Microelectronics Technology*, Edinburgh University Press, Edinburgh, 1982. Deals with applications of Information Technology, including Teletext and Viewdata.

A. M. Rosie, *Information and Communication Theory*, 2nd edn, Van Nostrand Reinhold, New York, 1973. Comprehensive coverage of many aspects of information and communication theory.

M. Schwartz, *Information Transmission, Modulation and Noise*, McGraw-Hill, London and New York, 1970. Very thorough treatment of communication aspects of signal theory.

R. D. Stuart, *An Introduction to Fourier Analysis*, Science Paperbacks, Methuen, London, 1966. Relatively readable, though mathematical, introduction to Fourier Series and Transforms.

P. Woodward, *Probability and Information Theory with Applications to Radar,* 2nd edn, Pergamon, New York, 1964. Compact and elegant approach to signal and information theory, but requires some prior knowledge.

Index